CHILDREN'S SOCIAL VALUES

AN ACTION RESEARCH STUDY

CHILDREN'S
SOCIAL VALUES

AN ACTION RESEARCH STUDY

By Arthur W. Foshay

Director, Bureau of Educational Research
The Ohio State University

Kenneth D. Wann

Associate Professor of Education,
Teachers College, Columbia University

and Associates

40288

A PUBLICATION OF THE
HORACE MANN—LINCOLN INSTITUTE OF SCHOOL EXPERIMENTATION,
TEACHERS COLLEGE, COLUMBIA UNIVERSITY

BUREAU OF PUBLICATIONS
TEACHERS COLLEGE, COLUMBIA UNIVERSITY
NEW YORK—1954

Foreword

Fᴏʀ a large group of teachers representing a number of school buildings to work cooperatively for a period of years to improve an aspect of their teaching is no longer unusual. The teachers of Springfield, Missouri, who wrote this book in collaboration with three consultants from the Horace Mann-Lincoln Institute of School Experimentation, did more than just work together. To do that is indeed hard enough; but they went further. They attempted to improve their understanding of their pupils' social values and of how to teach social values in a relatively systematic way. They wanted to base their changes in practice on evidence they sought, found, and tested in their own teaching situations. "Action research," they called it. Their report not only describes what they learned about the social attitudes and values of the children they were teaching; it also—and this is equally important—describes the way they went about learning what they learned.

Both of these descriptions are significant. Although Springfield is a reasonably typical American city, the authors do not contend that children growing up there will learn the same social values as children growing up in St. Louis or

New York City or Seattle. The Springfield teachers did realize, however, that they must learn about their own children
if they were to understand and influence them most effectively. Teachers in any school system must do the same
thing. One of the advantages of action research is that it is
conducted by practitioners in the situation in which they
work.

The kind of research that the teachers who helped write
Children's Social Values engaged in deserves special comment. Their method of trying to cope with practical instructional problems seems to be appropriate and promising no
matter what type of community the problems arise in. Action
research puts a premium upon the initiative and resourceful-
ness and creativity of teachers, individually and collectively.
It represents a way of tackling practical instructional problems that is more objective and scientific than the method
most of us employ when we try to improve on the job. Action
research requires careful problem definition, a thorough and
critical search for promising solutions, discriminating and
thoughtful introduction of change, and painstaking accumu-
lation of evidence throughout the entire research process.

To improve instruction by engaging in action research is
not easy. New attitudes and understandings and skills must
be learned. Anyone who reads the reports of studies undertaken by the several groups in Springfield as they are described in Part II of this book will realize how much progress
these teachers made in the direction of better methods of
inquiry and better methods of practical problem solving.
Judging what they did against ideal standards of research
procedure is an interesting activity but it misses the main
point. The main point is that the teachers learned better
and better methods of investigating practical problems and
testing promising hypotheses in respect to them.

Before action research can become a commonly accepted
problem solving method, administrators and supervisors

must take especial pains to do what they can to create the kind of general psychological atmosphere that encourages teachers to experiment. Teachers are helped, too, if the consultative services of persons experienced in the scientific method of problem solving are available to them. These conditions that facilitate action research are discussed by the authors in Part III, where they report their evaluation of the action research studies in which they engaged.

The authors of *Children's Social Values* do not contend that teachers generally should accept the findings that resulted from the Springfield studies and act upon them. They urge instead that other school people engage in similar investigations with their own pupils in their own communities. This, it seems to me, is the central theme of the book; and it is a valid theme. The research done by people elsewhere is often a rich source for hypotheses regarding what should be done in one's own situation. This situation is always unique, however, and its very uniqueness precludes any automatic application of results from research conducted by someone else. The worth of these results must be tested in a specific situation by the people who will act in this situation.

STEPHEN M. COREY
Horace Mann-Lincoln Institute
of School Experimentation

The Associates

STAFFS OF six elementary schools, a group of teachers from the high school, members of the central office staff of the Springfield, Missouri, Schools, and three consultants from the Horace Mann–Lincoln Institute of School Experimentation of Teachers College, Columbia University, were associated in the development of this study. D. C. Rucker as curriculum director assumed local responsibility for directing the cooperative study. Alice Pittman, director of elementary supervision, was associated with him. H. P. Study was superintendent of schools. Ruth Cunningham, professor of education at Teachers College, Columbia University, served with the authors as a member of the consultant group. The following teachers were members of the staffs of the participating schools:

Virginia Askins	Elenora Boyd	Maude Cloud
Georgia Aton	Margaret Brown	Helen F. Coffman
Stella Babb	Esther Bustrin	Belle Copsey
Opal Baker	Elsie Butler	Marcella Cotter
Mary Barnett	Elizabeth Cadle	Bertha May Crain
Anne George Billings	Juanita Cannon	Elsie Davis
Shirley Lovell Blair	Mary Challes	Mary Dillard
Beatrice Bolin	Eleanor Chapman	Florence Dollison
Nellie A. Bowler	Meldetta Chapman	Edna Dugan

Mildred Eaton
Jessie Elliff
Dorothy Engelking
Naomi Hall
Gladise Hallam
Eliza Hayes
Ruth Hayward
Nelle Hofer
Mildred Hoffman
Helen P. Howe
Wenonah Hutchens
Doris Johnson
Gwendolyn Jones
Mildred Jones
Homer R. Kesterson
Margaret Langsford
Maxine Lunsford
Edith Lynn

Ruth McClain
Lillian McDonald
Gloria McIntosh
Pauline McKenzie
Anna McMillen
Henrietta Miller
Edith Moore
Cassie Moorman
Ruth Neil
Florence Norcross
Allie Powell
Wanda Rosenbaum Rimer
Alice Roop
Billie Ann Schaller
Hazel Seddon
Nell Sewell
Roy Sharum
Pearl Shook

Virginia Shouse
Nelle Smith
Edith Snyder
Ruby Stecker
Lois Stewart
Harry Suttle
Charles R. Swan
Margaret Tippin
Sarah Townsend
Grace Waddell
Margaret E. Waesp
Florence Weaver
Alma West
Marie J. White
Nola Winkle
Edna Wood

Contents

PART III

What We Think About Action Research

APPENDICES

PART I
WE STUDY CHILDREN'S VALUES

Introduction

Y<small>OU LOOK</small> at the children. The way they come into the room, the way they sit, the way they look at you, all suggest the attitudes they have: toward you, toward school, toward one another, toward themselves. More than anything else you want to have a constructive effect on their attitudes while they're in your care. But what attitudes they have, where these came from, how you really influence them are exasperatingly intangible matters.

You have lots of company. There are about a million American public school teachers, and most of them feel just as you do. This is the report of the work of some fellow teachers in Springfield, Missouri, who spent two years trying to clarify their thinking about these intangibles and to find answers to some of their questions about them. We * real-

* "We" were the teachers in six elementary schools and a group of teachers in the high school in Springfield, the elementary supervisor and the curriculum director of the Springfield schools, and three members of the staff of the Horace Mann–Lincoln Institute of School Experimentation who served as research consultants. Some of this book is written as if by our collective hand, some as if by those of us working at one of the specific researches reported in the chapters of Part II, and some as a study *of* the teachers *by* the consultants. It all amounts to the same thing, however: the report as a whole is both by and about all of us.

Two of the consultants assumed the responsibility for preparing the manuscript. Arthur Foshay wrote Chapters 1, 2, 4, 5, 6, 7, and 8, and Kenneth Wann Chapters 3, 9, 10, 11, 12, and 13.

3

ized that final answers to questions about the nature and development of attitudes are not to be found in our present state of knowledge, but it was good, and exciting, to be thinking critically—doing research—in the course of the day's work.

This book reports and analyzes not only what we learned about children's social behavior but also what we found out about the values, difficulties, and satisfactions of cooperative action research. Here in Part I is the over-all perspective: Chapter 1 describes the setting of the study and the background of beliefs and questions that motivated us; Chapter 2 traces the development into a rationale of our intuitions and ideas about attitudes and social behavior; and Chapter 3 summarizes the action research procedures used and our view of them as compared with other approaches to educational problems. In Part II, each chapter reports in detail the study undertaken in one of the schools, about one "intangible," and the conclusions drawn from it. Finally, in the five chapters of Part III, our experiences with action research as method are discussed and their implications for education explored.

We think that a preview of some of the general conclusions we reached—both about our way of working and about the children we taught—will provide the best possible background for your reading of the report. This, accordingly, follows.

These are some of the most definite and important things we decided about our mode of work:

1. *Teachers can adapt many research methods to classroom use.* There is a fundamental difference between the usual approach to classroom problems, and the approach we describe here. Usually, we simply plug away at a problem, feeling gratified if things seem to improve, but making little effort to see why our trials succeed or fail. We have found

that we can adopt a research approach to our problems that helps us to learn much more from our own activity than we usually have. By "research approach," we mean simply making our hunches explicit, getting better evidence as to what our problems are, keeping track of what happens when we act on these explicit hunches, making our learnings from these happenings explicit, too. This is an informal (but for us a descriptive) way of saying that we formulate hypotheses, gather data to test them, and draw conclusions.

2. *A research approach gives direction to our teaching.* We've all heard of the teacher who has had only one year's experience, which she has repeated for thirty years! That's pretty hard on teachers, but it reflects a state of mind that some people are willing to ascribe to others, though seldom to themselves. We are convinced that the action research approach to teaching offers a means of escape from this state of mind. A teaching process that constantly makes the purpose of teaching activity explicit, and leads one constantly to test the adequacy of one's hunches against the facts, has the effect of making one's teaching get somewhere. It gives direction to teaching; it leads to constructive change.

3. *This kind of classroom research is best done by groups of teachers.* When you try to discover something new, you are apt to find yourself in a morass of unknown method, doubts concerning your ability to do the new job, even a good deal of discouragement. Such misery needs company. We needed the mutual support that we obtained from each other as we attacked these problems in groups. Of course, we weren't all equally interested in doing this work, and some of us remained skeptical about its value to the end. But we liked it more and more as we did it. Almost all of us are very enthusiastic about it, having tried it. And those of us who worked most closely with our fellow teachers are the most enthusiastic of all.

4. *This kind of work requires leadership to start it and to sustain it until it is steadily under way; but ultimately it can sustain itself.* The leadership, in our case, came from our Institute consultants, who were with our individual school staffs six half-days per year, and our local elementary supervisor and our curriculum director, who were doing a great many other things at the same time. We found much of the work puzzling for a while. But we caught on to the pattern of hunch–test–conclude, and by the end of our two years' association, a number of us were gathering data and testing ideas on our own. Several of us have published reports of our work in national professional magazines.

5. *Teachers who attempt research become better "consumers" of research.* We have found ourselves paying much more attention than we used to, to reports of research from others. Having attempted some ourselves, we can appreciate what it means to bring a piece of research to the point at which it has significance for others. We read descriptions of experiments both for findings and for method, for we can use both.

We also arrived at some very interesting generalizations about children's social attitudes—the attitudes that govern their social behavior:

1. *Attitudes are learned, not "caught."* The more we studied the matter, the less confidence we had in the maxim, "Attitudes are caught, not taught." Everything we have done and thought suggests that they *can* be taught, and not only unwittingly—that the teaching of attitudes can be structured so as to produce one learning rather than another. Children learn many of their attitudes toward other children from the child-society they live in. Their social behavior results from their attempts to deal with the stresses and reward systems of this society, as these things appear to them as individuals.

We discovered a few things about the way this society appears to the children, chiefly through our analyses of their responses to open-ended questions and unfinished stories. Some of the children's perceptions are disturbing to us. We don't like to think of their world as the jungle-like place that many of their responses seem to indicate. We wish it weren't so strongly suggested that much of their social behavior rests on the "eye for an eye" principle. Also, we didn't know that we teachers occupied such a prominent place in the child's system of self-evaluation.

Having found out these things about our children, however, we believe that much of the mystery of children's social attitudes can be removed by such study as we have carried on. While we probably never will "teach" responsibility as precisely as we teach reading, we certainly need not therefore throw up our hands, call it "intangible," and leave it to be "caught," somehow.

2. *Children's social attitudes in school are largely determined by the forces of school society as the children see them.* Children's social behavior in school, that is, their behavior toward other people, is an attempt on their part to keep certain forces in balance. We had a look at some of these forces: the teacher's opinion; "keeping even"; status among classmates. We assume that what we have seen is only a small part of a much larger whole. Furthermore, we assume that what we have found explains some of the school behavior of our children, but that it does not necessarily explain the behavior of these same children in other social situations—at home, in church, on the street, at the movies, or at another child's home. Psychologists point out that behavior is specific to situations.

3. *The code of children's social behavior at school is largely the product of their attempts to keep these school social forces in balance.* Our children do in school what they think they have to do to keep a good opinion of themselves, and to win the approval of their classmates and their teachers. The code they act on is best viewed as largely expedient.

This implies that, if we teachers are to have a consciously constructive effect on children's social attitudes, we must try to influence the actual forces that operate in the child's school world, and, at the same time, try to teach children how to act on worthy principles in their interpersonal relationships. We do the first of these when we attempt to help a child to achieve higher status with his classmates—when we help him "put his best foot forward." We do the second when we direct children's attention to the bases on which friendships may be developed. Studies of children's friendships, and our own data on the factors our children use in self-evaluation, suggest that children often choose their friends on rather superficial bases. We should help them to see the other possibilities. If we can help them choose their friends on more fundamental and enduring bases, we can also expect their behavior toward one another to be governed more by good principles and less by expediency alone.

In a way, what we are implying here is that teachers should help children to develop a more effective conscience with respect to their interpersonal relationships. How we can do this better than we do, without merely producing unhealthy anxiety among the children, is an old problem that remains before us. But we have found some "leads," in our study, toward a better understanding of the forces that cause children to act toward one another as they do. We can do something of value in the short range if we exert a beneficial influence on these forces. We will be able to do something of value in the long range when we know more about how to help children to learn what it means to act on high principles.

4. *Teachers have a powerful effect on children's social attitudes and values in school.* Our children told us in every way they could that what they saw as our appraisals of them, and our activities on their behalf, have a real effect on their social behavior in school. Probably we also have an

effect on their behavior out of school, too, but we did not seek evidence on this during the present study.

To us, this means that we have reason to be hopeful about the future. While we teachers are far from being the main force in the development of children's social attitudes (other children, parents, the clergy, and other adults in positions of authority certainly are major forces) we nevertheless are one of several powerful influences on them. The more we know, therefore, about how we may make our influence beneficial in a fundamental sense, the more we may expect the social attitudes of our children actually to improve. We think we have reason, on the basis of the activity reported in this book, to expect to change more of our hoping into knowing and doing.

CHAPTER 1

The Setting and the People

THIS STUDY was undertaken at a specific time, in a particular place, by a certain group of people. You should know something about Springfield and the people who live there.

Where We Work

Springfield, Missouri, is a city of approximately 65,000 people, in the Ozark Mountains. The nearest large population center is St. Louis, about two hundred miles northeast. Between St. Louis and Springfield, Highway 66 winds through flat, fertile farm land for a while, then rises and falls as the Ozarks begin.

Highway 66 plays a large part in Springfield's life; it is the main trucking route from the Great Lakes area to the Southwest and Southern California. Springfield is an easy day's drive from St. Louis, and a number of large trucking concerns have Springfield headquarters.

Similarly, the Frisco Railroad (the St. Louis and San Francisco, which runs from Illinois to Texas) is a major local industry. The company maintains its yards and repair shops in Springfield, and recently both have been substantially enlarged. Wherever one is in Springfield, one can hear the

11

horn on the Diesel engine pulling the crack Texas Special, as it whistles at the crossings in town every night about 10:30, heading South.

Transportation, then, is a major Springfield industry.

Dairying is another. For many miles around Springfield there are dairy farms. They stretch up into the Ozarks, and occupy the flat land of the valley. The Missouri Farm Association (M.F.A.) is one of the largest corporations in town. Go to the weekly meeting of the Springfield Chamber of Commerce. Whether the topic discussed is roads (Let's Get Missouri Out of the Mud!), public power (What about the Dam?), or the coming school board election, the opinion of the M.F.A. carries great weight.

One other sizeable activity should be mentioned—the publishing of religious literature. The Assembly of God maintains a huge publishing plant in Springfield, which is the world headquarters for this sect. Assembly of God literature accounts for a third of all the outgoing mail in the Springfield Post Office. Many of the children in the schools come from families employed by this large religious organization.

Most of the teachers in the Springfield schools come from the city or its neighborhood. Many of them went to college either at Southwestern Missouri State College (S.M.S.) or at Drurie College, a liberal arts college, both in Springfield. The teachers love their city, its children, and its schools. They are proud of the fact that, since the war, many a veteran who spent some time at O'Reilly General Hospital has chosen to make Springfield his home.

Almost all the teachers are active members of some church. In this they are like most Springfieldians. They will tell you that Springfield is in the "Bible Belt"—and to them the phrase doesn't mean at all what it meant a generation ago, to Mencken. The many churches of all faiths are important centers of community life, and in Springfield worship is a normal aspect of everyday living.

At the time this study was carried on, there were twenty-three schools in Springfield, including three junior high schools, a high school, and a small twelve-grade school for Negroes. The teachers in these schools do not differ in training from teachers in other Midwestern communities of similar size; the level of financial support of the Springfield schools is somewhat lower than in comparable Midwestern cities.

For more than twenty years, however, it has been school policy to maintain close contact with the most prominent leaders in American education. During this period, there has been a steady procession of conferences and workshops at which outstanding educators have appeared.

The contact of Springfield and the Horace Mann-Lincoln Institute of School Experimentation grew out of this tradition. When the Institute was formed, in 1943, Springfield was one of the school systems invited to participate as an Associated School System. For five years before the present study was begun in 1948, the teachers in Springfield had been working with Institute research associates. Two Institute publications were based in large measure on research carried out with Springfield teachers.[1] Following the usual procedure for Institute field projects, Springfield paid its expenses (including sending representatives to Teachers College for summer work on the projects, purchase of equipment, and employing substitute teachers) and the Institute paid its expenses (chiefly consultants' travel expenses and salaries, and clerical work).

The present study grew out of a series of exploratory conversations between Institute and Springfield representatives,

---

[1] Florence B. Stratemeyer, Hamden L. Forkner, and Margaret G. McKim, *Developing a Curriculum for Modern Living.* New York: Bureau of Publications, Teachers College, Columbia University, 1947. Arthur T. Jersild and Ruth J. Tasch: *Childrens' Interests and What They Suggest for Education.* New York: Bureau of Publications, Teachers College, Columbia University, 1949.

in the winter of 1948. At this time, a "problem area" was named: the "intangibles" of the school curriculum. The matter was discussed further at two meetings of the Springfield school principals, the principals having consulted with their building staffs before the second meeting.

Seventeen of the twenty-three school staffs expressed a desire to undertake such a study. This was too many, so at a later meeting representatives of the seventeen schools developed criteria which they used to select six elementary schools and the senior high school as participants. The criteria finally employed were these:

1. Only six schools can participate: more would be unwieldy.

2. The schools should be representative of the range of each of the following factors, as they are in Springfield:

   a. School level.

   b. School size.

   c. Type of neighborhood.

   d. Staff had not participated in previous Institute project.

Once the schools were selected, the Institute consultants and the school staffs began the meetings and the work reported in the remainder of this book.

What We Believe

In a report such as this, it helps to know something of the point of view the participants had as they began. These teachers were experienced, and they shared some beliefs about the way children should be taught. These beliefs had grown through many years, along with the Springfield tradition of excellent local leadership, with the teachers' training in colleges and universities, and with their opportunities to hear and work with outstanding educators. There were many such opportunities during the twenty-eight years of H. P.

Study's superintendency. Knowledge thus acquired was important to the teachers. More important, though, was the fact that their personal experiences with children had long since verified its essential soundness. These ideas were part of them; they no longer required much discussion. It helps in this sort of study, however, to remember these shared beliefs. Here are some of them:

TEACHING SHOULD BE CONSISTENT WITH
CHILD DEVELOPMENT

Everyone involved had carried on enough child study to feel familiar with its most striking generalizations. They took every opportunity they found to learn more about children. They had long since modified their ways of teaching reading, for example, to match the findings of research; they knew quite a lot about reading readiness, and about the stages in the development of reading skill. What they had done with reading they had done, also, with the other R's; and in addition they had learned the value of study of their own community and the necessity of much firsthand experience for the children. They had learned, too, as they worked with children, the importance of gentleness and understanding.

Not that they thought they knew all about these things—far from it. They knew enough to be aware that there was much more to know. But this they were certain of: the experiences children had in school should be "developmentally oriented." Translated from the Pedagese, this means that what the staff had learned about child development, they tried to apply to teaching.

THE SCHOOL SHOULD EXEMPLIFY
AMERICAN DEMOCRACY

This sounds a little pretentious, but these people believed it deeply. Some of them, working with members of the Horace Mann-Lincoln Institute, had at one time helped in

the development of a detailed statement of this belief, called
Basic Tenets of Democracy,[2] which went beyond mere plati-
tudes and offered in detail some of the tough principles that
underlay their patriotism. When they tried to apply these
principles, however, they sometimes had difficulty because
our democratic beliefs imply child behavior that is hard to
bring about even when the means are known. These beliefs
are both implicitly and explicitly recognized in the Springfield schools. In a democracy everyone has equal rights; in
school, too, everyone has equal rights. In a democracy, the
integrity of the individual is paramount; in a school, therefore, the individuality of children is to be recognized and
respected.

Working to make their beliefs function in the classroom
was not new to Springfield teachers. Cooperative planning
in the classroom had appealed to them as a way of putting
their democratic beliefs to work. Some Springfield teachers
had taken part in the development of a study of cooperative
planning in association with the Horace Mann-Lincoln Institute.[3] This mode of teaching promised a way of demonstrat-
ing to the children the meaning and consequences of democratic processes. If the children were directly involved in
planning their own work, it was supposed, they would
understand its purpose better, and would take part in their
own education with more enthusiasm. More important, the
children would have personal experience with some of the
basic skills needed for a democratic society, in which the

---

[2] "An Analysis of Basic Tenets of Democracy with Some Implications for
Public Education in Grades 1 through 12." Mimeographed: Springfield
Public Schools in cooperation with the Horace Mann–Lincoln Institute of
School Experimentation, 1946. This report is an analysis of *Education and
the Promise of America* (New York: The Macmillan Company, 1945) by
Professor George S. Counts of Teachers College (then a member of the
Institute staff). Professor Counts has since written another book dealing
with these ideas: *Education and American Civilization* (New York: Bureau
of Publications, Teachers College, Columbia University, 1952).

[3] Alice Miel and Associates. *Cooperative Procedures in Learning.* New
York: Bureau of Publications, Teachers College, Columbia University, 1952.

ability to work effectively with other people is of fundamental importance.

Belief in democratic procedures led the Springfield staff to intensify their efforts in using other practices, too. Student councils flourished, especially in the elementary schools, where they had not been common. In the high school, the students were encouraged to take a greater interest in local government and other municipal affairs.

Here, too, though, as in the case of their child development study, the teachers wished they knew much more about how to apply their beliefs. (And so did their consultants!) They wanted to be practical idealists, but in some ways they thought they simply didn't know how.

THE SCHOOL SHOULD TEACH MORE THAN THE THREE R'S

The tradition within which teachers work had to be recognized. The elementary school is an old social institution with tremendous potentiality for good and a superb record of certain kinds of achievement. But the tradition is limited in its application when the school is thought of as "the breeding ground of democracy." American democracy had flourished during the hundred years of the common school after 1850, but not primarily *because* of the school. The curriculum of this school had been the three R's and little more. Anyone might learn these skills—and that was good. Attempts had been made in many schools to teach children that these skills were to be used for the common good; but the chief emphasis of the school remained on the skills themselves, not on the wise use of them. Many a student grew up to be a wise man, but not chiefly because of his schooling. In schools, he learned skills. Wisdom was usually learned elsewhere. There was a sharp distinction drawn, traditionally, between learning and thinking—and the elementary school was concerned chiefly with learning.

Most of the parents of the teachers who carried on this

study had attended one of these three R's schools, as had many of the teachers and consultants. The study group was aware of the limitations of such a school—its lack of significant direction and the barbarism that often flourished, checked only by a hickory stick or its verbal equivalent. But the study group was aware, too, of the fact that many laymen see no need for more than a three R school. In order to be allowed to broaden their own purposes, the teachers had to be able to prove that teaching of the three R's was going on as well as ever.[4]

The three R's are necessary, but not sufficient. What is needed is a school in which the whole school program is more clearly relevant to the whole range of problems of growing children. That the traditional school was too limited was plain enough to the teachers. Attempts to make it more than that had long since led the Springfield teachers to give more attention to the social studies. The elementary school curriculum also included experience in art and music; and in many of the elementary schools such activities as physical education and a hot lunch program were viewed as fruitful sources of learning. In recent years, there had been an increase in the attention paid to developing a science program in the elementary schools. In the high school there was a concerted effort to incorporate the emphases of the Life Adjustment Commission. The high school principal was an active member of the national group concerned with this program. And, as has been mentioned, an attempt had been made to examine the educational implications of fundamental democratic beliefs.

These, then, were some of the convictions of the Springfield teachers, based on experience and study: teaching

---

[4] Accordingly, they were pleased to have the evidence presented through a University of Illinois survey that children in the Springfield schools in 1948 were able to do a bit better on a 1930 reading test than their parents had in 1930. Illini Survey Associates: *A Look at the Springfield Schools.* Urbana, Illinois: The University, 1948.

should be consistent with child development; the school should exemplify American democracy; the school curriculum should be broadened beyond the three R's. There was nothing new about these convictions. They had been expressed again and again, in various ways, by educators, philosophers, politicians, and business men, since the foundation of the Republic.

What We Wanted to Know

When the teachers had attempted to apply their beliefs, however, they had found themselves asking questions that could not be answered easily. We shall mention here three of these questions, arising from the three beliefs described above, which arose again and again both in planning and in carrying out this study.

WHAT SOCIAL MATURITY SHOULD WE EXPECT OF CHILDREN?

The school staff's concern with social maturity was one of those which arose from their conviction that teaching should be consistent with what is known about child development. The term "social maturity" has been used in the schools for a long time to refer to characteristic ways that children of varying ages have of dealing with one another and with their elders. For some time, children have been grouped in elementary school according to their chronological age, because it was assumed that chronological age was an objective factor more closely associated with social maturity than were such purely academic factors as achievement in the three R's. Chronological age grouping, it was assumed, would reduce the spread of social maturity in a class. Since classes were thought of as working groups, such a reduction was thought desirable.

This policy implies recognizable levels of social maturity

as a factor influencing learning. However, when they came right down to it, the school staff found little to help them identify such levels of maturity. There was considerable information concerning the effect of emotional disturbance on the social behavior of children, but relatively little that would allow the school staff to be as specific about levels of maturity as it is possible to be, for example, about levels of achievement in reading or arithmetic.

To put it briefly, the problem is this: how is the curriculum to be made consistent with what is known about the social development of children? The difficulty arises from the fact that there is entirely too little evidence on children's social development. It was difficult, therefore, to know what the curriculum should offer by way of social learning.

IN WHAT WAYS SHOULD THE SCHOOL CURRICULUM BE RELATED TO THE BROAD PROBLEMS OF HUMAN SOCIETY?

If the elementary school should exemplify American democracy, it follows that the elementary school should devote specific attention to the development of ideas about our society, and of understandings that would have a discernible effect on the way the children accept the rights and duties of citizenship. A school which builds a feeling of loyalty to the United States, as well as a personal commitment to our institutions and our ideals, must bear a constructive relationship to our society both as it really is and as it might become.

Faced with this problem, the elementary school teachers were compelled to cope not only with the varying notions of society that are expressed by the public, but also with the problem of attempting to see society through the eyes of children so that the development of the children's conception of society would at least be comprehensible to the teacher. Obviously, before a teacher could exercise intelligent guidance concerning what aspects of society children should study, it was necessary to know what the children thought society was. Such knowledge would help the teacher to start with the children's present understanding and broaden it. To gain such information, means had to be found for seeing the matter as the children did, so that what was studied would include what the children thought significant, and so that children's distorted or inadequate ideas could be corrected. The participants in this study wanted to know a great deal more about how this could be done.

WHAT IS IT THAT LIES BEYOND THE THREE R'S?

The staff had often said, "We teach the three R's, *plus*." Exactly what the "plus" referred to was not clear. It was variously described as "social values," "the good life," "getting along with others," "education for modern living," and so on. Many things were done in school to offer these "plus" values. The teachers gave a great deal of attention to good human relationships between themselves and the children. They encouraged the children to work with one another as much as possible, on the assumption that this would help them to learn the value of cooperation. Problem situations were treated as they arose on the assumption that such treatment offered fruitful sources of learnings about problem-solving.

It was when the teachers attempted to be specific about what they were trying to teach in addition to the three R's that they ran into difficulty. In the course of twenty years, a number of revisions of the school report cards had been made. Each revision represented an attempt to report to parents certain things that lay beyond the three R's. The teachers and many of the parents were not satisfied, and the school survey of 1948 [5] showed that many employers evinced

[5] Illini Survey Associates, *op. cit.*

more interest in qualities of character than they did in academic achievement. When graduates of the high school sought employment in large corporations, several years after high school graduation, the personnel offices of these corporations required the completion of forms which often asked only for a brief summary of academic achievement, providing considerably more space for "evidence of responsibility, leadership, dependability, honesty" and other personal traits. But when the high school teachers and administrators attempted to fill out these forms they found that they were forced to rely too heavily on their personal memory of students. School records did not furnish adequate evidence. Teachers checked such traits as these on a rating sheet made out for each senior student, and offered whatever evidence they could remember to support the ratings they had made; but they conscientiously felt that this was too subjective and that there was entirely too great a chance that a negative rating was unfair. However, these ratings were the best way they had found so far for offering any evidence at all with respect to a student's character. (There was, of course, a place for activities to be recorded so that a student who had held student office, taken part in athletic affairs, been active in dramatics or music, and the like, had evidence of such activity. However, the information thus made available was meagre at best—at least, it was so viewed by the high school staff.)

An attempt has been made here to state plainly what it was that bothered the people who undertook this study. The questions and the problems have been described in the terms that the participating staff members were using at the time the study was begun.

To recapitulate:

The school staff held the following convictions, among others:

1. The curriculum of the school should be consistent with what is known about child development.

2. The elementary school should exemplify American democracy.

3. The elementary school curriculum must be expanded to include more than the three R's.

Out of these convictions grew a number of questions and practical problems of which the following are illustrative:

1. What is known about the social development of children, and how can we apply it to the school curriculum?

2. What should the relationship be between school experience and human society as it is and as it might become?

3. How shall we specify the content of the school curriculum that lies beyond the three R's?

It was questions like these, then, that the teachers hoped to clarify by their inquiry into specific "intangibles" of social learning.

Our Ideas About Social Attitudes

OUR WORK TOGETHER began with a consideration of practical questions like these: *How can we report social maturity to parents? What do we mean by these "intangibles"—"initiative," "democratic behavior," "sharing," "considerateness"? Some of the children don't follow through on plans even when the plans are made cooperatively with them. Why?*

As the work progressed, and data accumulated, we came to feel the need for a rationale that would help us explain what we were observing. After the period of data-gathering, we continued our attempts to develop a theoretical basis for the explanations, feelings, and hunches concerning what we had found. We borrowed ideas freely and developed a few of our own.

We shall present here a sort of running record of our progress with these ideas, pausing here and there for elaboration of the basic concepts involved. These fall into two main categories: (1) our conception of the nature of social attitudes—how they may be thought of, how they develop, and (2) our conception of how social attitudes of children are influenced by their culture.

24

What Is an Attitude? [1]

The social maturity of children, the development of appropriate attitudes toward our country and its institutions, and the development of such qualities as responsibility, considerateness, and honesty—all these problems fell within a field of inquiry that could be identified as the study of children's social attitudes. Since we were going to try to find out more about the social development of children, it was important that we develop some rational structure within which to work.

ATTITUDES AND REFERENTS

Let us begin with the widely accepted definition of an attitude as a predisposition to react favorably or unfavorably toward something, under certain conditions. An attitude is a sort of psychological set or stance—an inclination toward or away from something.

Basic to understanding the term "attitude" is an understanding of the term "referent." The referent of an attitude is the something toward which the attitude is directed, be it an idea, an object, a person, or a course of action. The first question to ask about an attitude is: Toward what is the attitude directed? What is its referent?

Our attitudes are always in reference to something of which we are more or less aware. A referent may be quite general, as a class of objects: "teachers." It may be quite specific: "Miss Smith, my teacher."

We have attitudes toward such referents as physical objects: snake, bicycle, diamond. We also have attitudes toward referents that are abstract ideas: communism, monarchy, monopoly, American democracy, and the free enterprise system. Children, too, have attitudes toward these ref-

[1] We are indebted to a colleague in the Horace Mann–Lincoln Institute of School Experimentation, Stephen M. Corey, for help in the development of these ideas about attitudes, values, and aversions.

erents. They are in the child's world. Figuring more prominently in his world, though, are referents such as mother, school, teacher, reading, baseball, and singing in front of the class.

VALUES AND AVERSIONS

All of us have attitudes toward many different referents. In order to distinguish among our attitudes, it is useful to remember that we consider some things attractive, others repulsive. For purposes of this discussion, we shall call referents that we consider attractive "values." We shall call referents that we consider repulsive "aversions." Thus, for many of us, a high mountain in summertime is a value: moving all our furniture to a new house on a hot summer day is an aversion.

The value or aversion status of a given referent is determined by the situation (as seen by the individual in whom the attitude exists) in which the referent is found. If one is hungry, a slice of bread is a value; if one is not hungry, it may be an aversion. If one is a ten-year-old, going to the circus is probably a value; to a very young child it sometimes is an aversion. A shiny new bicycle is a value to its owner; it is certainly an aversion (though perhaps only momentarily) to a child who is menaced by it.

The situation is what it is perceived to be by the individual who is assigning value or aversion status to a referent in it. In order to understand the attitude of someone else toward any referent, one must look at it through his eyes. A classroom test is an aversion or a value to a child, according to the way he views the test. It does not have value or aversion status of itself.

This line of thinking was helpful. We stopped talking about attitudes in general, and spoke of them as shown in specific situations, toward specific referents. We tended, more often than we had previously, to ask, "What does he like?" "What does she avoid?" The concept, "referent," guided us to more sharply focused inquiry.

We had learned to use the idea of direction, or valence, as applied to attitudes. That is, we recognized that repulsion was as much an attitude as was attraction—that aversions were as real as values.

ATTITUDES DIFFER IN INTENSITY

Another characteristic of attitudes is their intensity, or distance-from-apathy. Things do not have equal value or aversion status to a person. One may like one kind of food more than another, or dislike one kind of food more than another. One may value certain aspects of good human relations more than one values food. Our values and aversions exist along a sort of continuum extending from those values we hold most intensely through referents toward which we are apathetic, to those aversions we hold most intensely. The idea is represented in the diagram which follows:

VALUE— — — — — — — —APATHY— — — — — — — —AVERSION

Life	Respect of others	Steak	Baby chick in one's hand	Salamander in one's hand	Sour milk	Ridicule by others	Death

To read this diagram, consider the base line as representing the continuum of intensity along which referents are arranged in the attitude system of a person, from high value (e.g., life and respect of others) to high aversion (death and ridicule by others). Other referents have less intense value or aversion status; the referent "chick in one's hand" has slight value status, and "salamander in one's hand," slight aversion status. It will help our discussion if we describe attitudes by naming their intensity with respect to specific referents. Thus, one referent which has strong value status to children is the esteem of their fellows. And ridicule by their fellows is an even stronger aversion to most children than is disapproval by the teacher. In both cases, the attitudes are quite intense. Children *care* a lot about these referents. These things "matter."

Now let's pause and review what we've said. We have considered attitudes and their referents. We have seen that attitudes exist only with respect to referents; and that some referents are values, others are aversions. We have noted that values and aversions (i.e., the status of referents) may differ considerably from one person to another, and that the intensity of an individual person's attitudes toward different referents varies along a continuum. Throughout our discussion we have emphasized the point that whether a given referent is a value or an aversion depends on the situation it is in, as the individual sees the situation.

How Are Attitudes Developed?

People are inveterate evaluators. Attitudes toward things, courses of action, people, and all the infinite number of possible referents are constantly developed in individuals as a consequence of their own evaluation of their conscious or unconscious, direct or indirect, experience with these referents. Such evaluation may be unconscious, but it is inevitable. An infant has no attitude toward steak as food, although he may like to touch it. He has, on the other hand, intense attitudes toward his bottle and his mother. He has attitudes, that is, toward those things with which he has had experience. He has no attitudes—he is apathetic—toward those things with which he has had no direct or indirect experience. His fear of being dropped, his fear of loud noises, and his desire to explore new objects are usually considered instinctive.

Many of our attitudes are acquired through the association of a new referent with some class of referents toward which our attitudes already are formed. Thus, a child may learn to like the prospect of learning to read because it is surrounded with values—smiling teacher, approval by parents, identification with older children. Or he may learn to dislike eggs because someone has told him that they feel like something slimy and repulsive.

The child appears in the kitchen with a snake in his hand, and mother screams. The child learns, both by imitation of his mother and by association (mother has given him the same cue for a sharp knife he started to pick up and for a swiftly approaching truck) to treat "snake" as an aversion. Some attitudes are taught deliberately through a calculated association of a referent with an existing value or aversion. Thus, the advertising of a cereal as the "breakfast of champions," and the association of chewing gum with a cowboy hero, makes use of the device of forming a new value by associating the product with an already existing value.

Some of these associations are made unconsciously. Conscious or not, however, the association leads to the formation of an attitude. The new referent becomes a value or an aversion in some degree: it acquires valence and intensity. These associations are part of one's experience with referents. Attitudes are a consequence of such experience.

Attitudes are formed, too, as the result of a course of action. Results of an action are more or less pleasant or unpleasant, desirable or undesirable. The attitudes formed toward the visible referents in the action are accordingly favorable or unfavorable, and the referents become values or aversions. Attitudes of this type are the outgrowth of direct experience. Thus, most children like to be with others near their own age, because they "have fun together," as they will tell you. Over the years of childhood, the referent "school" may become more and more an aversion to a child, as experience accumulates.

Experiencing goes on all the time, of course. Experience

with some referents is more continuous than experience with others. Toward those referents that are often present, attitudes build by accretion; each new experience adds to the sum of feeling. When a child has come to like school in the course of a number of years of experience with school, his attitude toward school is likely to be quite stable.

A single severe, traumatic experience, however, can form an attitude. Most children require only one burned finger to learn that a hot skillet is an aversion. Similarly, one experience with an overbearing adult can leave a child fearful of strangers. One of the children in Springfield apparently needed only one experience (as a part of a church event) distributing Christmas food parcels to acquire a rather mature attitude toward poverty.

Vicarious or indirect experience, as through hearsay, reading, movies, and the like, leads to the formation of a great many of our attitudes. Children often think of the referent "witch" as an aversion, for instance. Their attitude toward witches was handed to them ready-made, so to speak, and subsequent experience with the referent, all of it indirect, reinforces the aversion status of witches.

The development of attitudes, then, must be thought of as learning. Learning is a consequence of experience; attitudes are a consequence of experience. To say that attitudes are learned should not necessarily imply that they are consciously taught, however. Even when they are taught, the teaching may not be intentional. One of the interesting differences between the teaching of attitudes and other teaching lies in the fact that much teaching of attitudes is unintentional. It is in this latter sense that attitudes are "caught, not taught." However, even the present short sketch of the modes by which attitudes are learned indicates that it is not necessary to cloak attitude formation in mystery—leave it all to be "caught." We teachers can have a deliberate effect on at least some of our children's social attitudes.

How Do Attitudes Change?

The change in meaning, or value–aversion status, of some referents is determined in part by organic changes. This is the case when the referent "girl" changes from aversion to value as a boy reaches adolescence. The same is true of such referents as food with strong flavors, certain kinds of wheeled vehicles, and so on. Young children commonly dislike strongly flavored food, but their tastes change as they grow older. Young children like tricycles; later, when their legs are longer, they will prefer bicycles.

However, it is likely that most social attitudes rest on factors other than organic change. Let us consider for a moment how some social attitudes shown in school can develop and change.

Many little children coming to school for the first time behave toward their teachers in much the same way as they behave toward their mothers. This is especially true if the teacher behaves in a "motherly" way toward the children. Kindergarten children frequently climb onto the teacher's lap, cling to her, and in other ways require demonstrations of affection. However, as the children grow older and have more experience with teachers they differentiate "teacher" from "mother" more and more sharply. Later they differentiate among teachers themselves, thinking of one as more or less fair, kind, amusing, or helpful than another. As a consequence of their experiences with teachers, children's attitudes toward teachers as a group is less and less changeable. Some children learn from their experience with teachers to treat all teachers as aversions. Others learn to treat most of them as values. Similarly, children learn to attach value or aversion status to school, policemen, and arithmetic.

To children, one crucially important class of referents in school is the other children. The experience each child has with other children, what he hears about them, what he is taught to associate with them—these experiences lead him to form attitudes toward other children. To each child, some other children are values, some are aversions. For each child, his classroom group may acquire value or aversion status as a group.

As a child accumulates experience with other children, his attitudes toward children in general become more and more stable, through they may have fluctuated considerably during his early years. These attitudes begin to form even before he comes to school, and every time he deals with other children his attitudes toward children in general are affected in some degree.

Now, the fact that attitudes toward school, toward teachers, and toward other children are in large measure a consequence of school experience is obvious enough. What concerned us in Springfield was what we could do about these attitudes. It was helpful to be explicit about the continuousness of attitude formation, but we couldn't stop there. As we thought over the ideas summarized in the preceding pages, it appeared to us that there were these five approaches to changing attitudes:

1. Adding new and desirable experience with a referent.
2. Offering appropriate associations with a referent.
3. Offering a ready-made attitude toward a referent.
4. Providing for vicarious experience with the referent.
5. Arranging a very dramatic experience with a referent.

Thus, if standing before the class is an aversion for a child, the teacher might *add* new pleasant experiences with this referent by arranging a success with it. She might *associate* it with a value by placing the child with friends when he does stand before the class. She might offer him a *ready-made attitude* toward standing before the class by talking about the value of the experience. She might influence his attitude through *vicarious experience* by telling a story about a boy who overcame his fear of standing before a class. She might make a *dramatic occasion* out of standing before the class—for example, bringing an important message to the class ("We won the pennant!"). Actually, these approaches would always appear in some combination in school. But naming them helped us to think about how we might deliberately seek to have a constructive effect on the attitudes of the children. It appeared to us that the formation of attitudes in school could be less a matter of chance, and more a matter of deliberate planning, than we had usually thought possible.

The Attitudes and Values of the Culture[2]

Our social attitudes arise for us as individuals largely from our experiences with the human world around us. This human world consists, in major part, of the habits and customs we call our culture. As individuals, we do not determine what the culture shall be in its major aspects; it is up to us to conform with it or be treated as nonconformists. For example, children must learn to abide by a large number of rules that they don't understand very well: to salute the flag, to be clean, to respect private property. A great many values are culturally determined in this sense: the church, education, kindness to others. Even children's attitudes toward certain foods are determined by other people who belong to the culture. They are taught (often by their parents, but also by many others) to consider as values certain meats, vegetables, and fruits; they are taught to treat as aversions certain other meats and vegetables and fruits. (In some cultures meat is forbidden. That is, meat is a culturally determined aversion.)

[2] For a discussion of this matter by an educator, an anthropologist, a child psychologist, a sociologist, and a psychiatrist, see Section II (pp. 84-119), "Cultural Expectations," in *Growing Up in an Anxious Age*, 1952 Yearbook of the Association for Supervision and Curriculum Development of the National Education Association. Washington, D. C., The Association, 1952.

They find that generally speaking, in our Western culture, cruelty between individuals is also to be viewed as an aversion.

Two characteristics of culturally determined values and aversions should be mentioned. First, they fluctuate according to broad social situations, such as war. Second, they do not come singly. Any given social situation contains a combination of referents; the action of an individual must be understood as an attempt to place these referents in a relationship that is as satisfactory as possible to him.

When we are at war, victory is the supreme value. Other values, such as mercy, kindness, and even respect for individual rights, are subordinated to this supreme value. It is possible then for individuals to use weapons which in any other situation would be unthinkable because of their terrifying force.

Value conflict is a persistent part of any given social situation. The knotty moral problems we face grow out of such conflicts. Values don't come singly, either for children or for adults. Here is a child caught between a value and an aversion: he must decide whether to take flowers to the teacher, whom he admires deeply, at the risk of being called a sissy. Here is a child caught between two values: he must decide whether to play baseball with his friends or go swimming with his family. Here is a child caught between two aversions: he must decide whether to fight another boy and risk the teacher's wrath, or to obey the teacher and be called a coward.

It will be helpful, then, to consider the culture as being made up of a number of referents toward which we, as members of the culture, are expected to have certain attitudes, and to remember that these attitudes may conflict. Some of these attitudes are part of the culture in which we Americans live, and not part of other cultures. Some are part of Occidental, but not of Oriental, cultures. Still others that we

Americans have are shared by all cultures; and within our American culture, there are attitudes which are determined by the social class to which we, as individuals, belong. These differ from one class to another.[3]

Consider for a moment the list of values and aversions given below. These referents are categorized as most middle-class Americans would categorize them, but in each case there are other cultures that would reverse their value or aversion status. Thus, the referent "beef" is a value in our American culture; grasshoppers as food are an aversion. But the Plains Indians are said to have valued grasshoppers as food. Modesty is a value to us; boastfulness is an aversion, at least as a matter of individual behavior. But in old Teutonic legend boastfulness was a value, and the "hero's boast" was used as recently as Hitler.

Value	*Aversion*
Beef	Grasshoppers
Modesty	Boastfulness
Kindness to animals	Cruelty to animals
Personal cleanliness	Body odor
White, regular teeth	Stained teeth
Personal independence	Servility
Punctuality	Tardiness

Some of these referents are specific objects, and some are rather generalized courses of action. A value such as "personal independence" must be stated as behavior-in-context in order to be understood; behavior interpreted in one situ-

[3] The influence of social class membership on the attitudes of individuals will not be discussed further here. For illustrations of differences among social classes, the reader is referred to such studies as these: A. G. Hollingshead, *Elmtown's Youth*, Wiley, New York, 1949; Celia B. Stendler, *Children of Brasstown*, Urbana, University of Illinois, 1949; Alfred C. Kinsey *et al.*, *Sexual Behavior in the Human Male*, Saunders, Philadelphia, 1948; the studies of W. Lloyd Warner, Allison Davis, and other studies conducted under the Committee on Human Development of the University of Chicago. Our purpose here is to consider in broad terms the way the culture functions as a determinant of social attitudes.

ation as representing personal independence may not be so interpreted in another. Nevertheless, personal independence is in this culture an important value.[4]

Equally interesting, however, is the list of culturally determined aversions. We don't eat grasshoppers, not because they cannot be eaten but because we have been taught to regard the eating of insects as disgusting. Similarly, some of us have been taught to avoid slimy objects and such creatures as snakes and rodents. That is, we have learned to regard these referents as aversions. As small children, perhaps, we handled slimy objects and rodents, and tasted insects and mud, indiscriminately. We learned our discrimination largely from our parents, and to some extent from other older people —only in part, if at all, from our firsthand experience with the things themselves. Much of the learning experience was traumatic: the object was snatched away; mother was obviously upset; older children ridiculed the baby; stern warnings were issued. Typically, the violation of these cultural aversions was punished—immediately and severely.

The point is that we *are supposed* to treat these things as aversions. The culture demands it. This cultural demand becomes clearer when we consider qualities like boastfulness and cruelty.[5] There are cultures in which boastfulness is a

[4] The times being as they are, it is necessary for the writers to enter a disclaimer at this point. The objectivity with which the values and aversions of the culture are discussed here is necessary, if we are to get on with the argument. This objectivity is not to be confused with the writers' personal convictions concerning the justice of these and other culturally dictated values and aversions. The structure of Western culture is not a matter of chance; the most important of our values—especially our social values—are founded on ethical and religious beliefs that give our culture its magnificent vitality.

[5] From one point of view, the paragraph that follows is an oversimplified version of the cultural requirements. Boastfulness, lying, and cruelty are aversions, when considered as individual behavior in private social situations. But there are social situations in which they are permitted. It is legitimate, for example, to boast through advertising, to be cruel to animals for medical purposes (though under strict controls), and to lie to prevent gross injustice to another (again, under strict controls). If this confuses adults, think of how confusing it is to children!

value; and there have been times in our own culture when it was. However, we are taught from early childhood on that boastfulness is to be avoided. One is supposed to be modest about his personal accomplishments. With respect to cruelty to animals, the cultural dictum is equally clear; but in some cultures a society for the prevention of cruelty to animals would be quite inconceivable. Our attitude toward animals might well be mistaken by members of these other cultures for a basic confusion of the status of man with the status of the beasts. Much the same can be said with respect to body odor, stained teeth (there are, of course, cultures in which stained teeth are a mark of beauty), and servility (we call it "obsequiousness" and are taught to "hold our heads up"). And in school, especially, tardiness is to be avoided (yet in some cultures the clock is supposed to be "a servant, not a master").

Both the values and the aversions of the culture must be learned. In the degree that one's personal values and aversions are consonant with one's culture, one is thought to be acculturated, and is therefore accepted by others. In the degree that one's personal set of values and aversions is not in agreement with the culture, one is considered "strange," "peculiar," perhaps "bohemian." All of us spend a great deal of time seeing to it that we stay within the boundaries set by our peers. This is as true of children as it is of adults.

Violation of this complicated cultural value-aversion system brings with it rather quick punishment by other members of the culture. After all, most of us do not wish to be thought of as "strange," "peculiar," or "bohemian." We would rather be thought of as a "good fellow," as being like other people in most ways, as someone who "knows his way around." Each of us knows full well, however, that these appellations of acceptance must be earned by relatively subtle acts of conformity with the culture. We dress alike, we eat alike, we carry on roughly the same kinds of recreation, we do certain culturally approved things to earn our livelihood, we behave in certain ways with our families, and so on.[6] Our attitudes and thus our behaviors with respect to these aspects of living are determined for us chiefly by the culture.

The Culture's Reward–Punishment System

It has been observed above that violation of the cultural value–aversion system brings punishment. Actually, the cultural value–aversion system is in fact learned by children largely through these punishments, and through the rewards of conformity. But, for children, the punishment is more immediate and visible than is the reward. To be called such names as "strange," "bohemian," and so on is to suffer only a relatively mild kind of displeasure. But consider, for example, our name-calling when the offense involved is cruelty to animals. We call such offenders "sadistic," "inhuman," perhaps "bestial." That is, we accuse the offender of insanity, we deny him membership in the human race, we assign him to another species! Name-calling can scarcely go farther.

The fact is (and each of us knows this from personal experience) that in addition to the imposition of a long series of values and aversions, the culture indicates many of the particular rewards and punishments that are to accompany compliance or violation of the system. This system of rewards and punishments, imposed by the culture, amounts to a system of learning.

[6] Margaret Mead, the cultural anthropologist, points out that becoming "Americanized" is largely a process of learning the cultural customs of the United States. (She was not discussing at this point the political aspects of Americanization.) The immigrant family adopts more and more American customs, and in a fixed order: from the most public aspects of the culture to the more private. Our culture enters the house from the street, so to speak: first the car, then the garden (front), then the living room (Grand Rapids furniture, television set, electric clock), then (but much later) the kitchen. It may never enter the bathroom or the bedroom in the immigrant's lifetime. (From a lecture at the Eastern Arts Association convention, 1949.)

The reward system

The culture rewards us for compliance with its value–aversion system through somewhat complicated means, but the general reward is acceptance by our fellows. Unusually complete compliance with the culturally dictated system may result in special comment of treatment; it is, perhaps, a contributing factor in establishment in some kinds of social position or occupation; but the basic reward for compliance with cultural standards is social acceptance.

Let us consider two examples of this. One referent which is a cultural value is the flag. How are we expected to behave toward it? Some requirements have been codified: we are to salute it, it is to be raised and lowered at certain times, and so on. The code of flag etiquette is detailed and explicit. One is presumed to show one's attitude toward the nation through observing flag etiquette.

Now, this etiquette is enforced by all of us upon one another. When we comply with it, we feel that we are one with our fellows; observance may even produce in us a feeling of unity with the country itself. Some of us choose to make the flag an important part of our daily lives—one frequently sees a flag displayed outside a private home, for example. There is a man in Springfield who observes a daily flag ritual, raising and lowering the flag "in a military manner." People who behave in this way are usually thought by others to be doing an honorable, admirable thing. Such behavior brings about occasional favorable comment.

Our occasional references to such behavior constitute the chief reward we offer one another even for this unusually complete observance of the cultural value. Actually, we say and do little to reward people who thus show their attitude toward the flag. We are likely to believe that such behavior is admirable, but a matter of personal choice: "It's his business."

Generosity with one's possessions is another cultural value. There is a fifth grade child in a Springfield school who is unusually generous. She shares most things she has—her bicycle, her candy, her clothing. If anyone expresses interest in this child's possessions, she is likely to find a way of sharing them. She is not considered "generous to a fault," nor do her parents and teachers believe that her generosity arises from anything but a somewhat unusual warmth toward others. (The possibility of other interpretations of this little girl's behavior is not being examined, because the purpose of this illustration is to indicate the way others treat what they think of as this child's unusually fine compliance with the culturally dictated attitude toward one's possessions. It is the cultural reward we are considering here, not the other possible psychological causes of the little girl's generosity.)

Disregarding the question of the origin of this child's behavior, let us look at its consequences. What rewards are there for this exceptionally well-acculturated child? In school, she receives the teachers' unqualified approval, probably manifested by comments on her report card and occasional references to her model behavior. The children in her class may think of her as rather grown-up and like her a good deal. If a chart of the friendship patterns in the class were made, she might be near its center, associated with the children with the greatest group acceptance. This acceptance by the other children might be shown through invitations to birthday parties, many Valentines, companionship on the playground, and the like.

Now, these "rewards" are very real, and are important to many children; failure to achieve them may lead to anxiety. However, we are talking here about a child who is exceptional with respect to the degree of compliance with one aspect of the culture—attitude system surrounding property. By the very fact that her behavior is exceptional, the rewards we are considering are those above and beyond whatever rewards are attached to normal or typical compliance.

THE PUNISHMENT SYSTEM

Compliance with the culture's chief values and aversions is a minimum requirement for membership in the culture. The reward for meeting this minimum, acceptance by others, is real. The reward for exceeding the minimum, a certain amount of praise, is real too. But the punishment associated with failure to meet the minimum requirement of compliance is very severe indeed.

Let us consider the consequences of violating the cultural value–aversion system. What happens if one desecrates the flag instead of treating it properly? Suppose that instead of displaying the flag and conducting a daily ritual, our Springfield man had sought opportunities to display disrespect and disregard of this symbol. In the first place, there are laws about such conduct. When children belonging to a certain religious sect were instructed by their parents not to salute the flag, the matter became a case for court action. But suppose, instead of their relatively passive behavior, these people went about pulling down the flag wherever they saw it. Suppose they conducted ritualistic flag burnings, or ridiculed those who choose to display the flag at home. Punishment would be swift, sure, and severe. Such malefactors would be subjected to public censure in newspapers and radio; they would be scolded from pulpit and rostrum; undoubtedly, they would be imprisoned and their children ostracized.

The punishment for violating the cultural flag-value would be far more poignant than the reward is even for exceptional compliance with the cultural flag-value.

SPECIFICITY OF SOME PUNISHMENTS

Not only do people in a culture punish, but in many cases they decree exactly what the punishment is to be. For generations, the traditional punishment for using foul language was that the child's mouth be "washed out" with soap. Among children, there are specific punishments for some offenses: a young boy who consorts with girls is called a "sissy" until he fights (and his fighting is also part of the code); the child who "tattles" is to be snubbed.

Furthermore, failure to inflict these punishments in the prescribed manner can lead to trouble; the parent who fails to punish a child for using foul language may be thought to be condoning the language. Much of the present confusion about discipline in the schools arises from the apparent failure of the teacher to punish, when the culture seems to parents to call for punishment. The teacher, having violated the cultural expectation, is himself punished—through name-calling, scoldings, and ridicule.

It is significant that such punishment is not keyed to the person who receives it. The cultural reward–punishment mode of teaching fails to provide for individual differences. The punishment fits the crime, not the criminal.

What Significance Has This for Teachers?

The foregoing brief discussion of attitudes, of values and aversions, of the culturally determined system of values and aversions, and of the reward–punishment system associated with these values and aversions helped us as we tried to comprehend how the social attitudes of children are to be understood and improved. One of the teacher's primary responsibilities is to be an agent for bringing children into the culture. Teachers, more than most other identifiable groups in the population, know the culture and personally accept it and live in accordance with it. They are expected to teach children certain intellectual skills and understandings, to be sure. But fully as important as those intellectual learnings are the learnings about cultural expectations that the teacher, cooperating with home and church, is expected to teach. This point will not be labored further here; it is verifiable in the lives of all of us.

THE LEARNING METHOD PRESCRIBED BY THE CULTURE

Now the culture, as has been observed, consists in a sense of certain values and aversions, and it prescribes in large measure how these are to be taught—through mild reward and severe punishment.

Furthermore, as has been observed above, these cultural values and aversions are learned by each individual as a consequence of his personal experience with the culture, as he interprets it. His attitudes toward its referents (including social referents—other children, school, parents, adults in authority, and so on) are learned chiefly through application of the cultural reward–punishment system.

Now, there are some able psychologists who think that in the last analysis all learning rests on rewards and punishments. We don't dispute the matter. But to most educators (and to these psychologists, too) it is clear that the *popular* meaning of learning through rewards and punishments is a dangerous oversimplification. Such an approach to teaching connotes a simple stimulus–response situation, in which people, like animals, are conditioned to behave in a specific, simple way when given a specific, simple signal of some kind.

Our point here is that the cultural rewards and punishments are not simple. When people think they are, they administer the rewards and punishments in a way that is bound to miss the mark. If one derives one's entire approach to building the cultural values and aversions in a child from a simple reward–punishment analysis of the culture's requirements, children will almost of necessity learn the wrong things about the culture's values and aversions.

The central weakness of such an approach is precisely that

it builds a simple response, and that alone. It cannot be expected to build understanding, though it may build unquestioning compliance. But unquestioning compliance is not what we seek. We seek devotion to the purposes *behind* the rules as our major educational objective. Failure to achieve this objective leaves our children open to the assault of any authoritarian figure who chooses to challenge the rules; it leads directly to the "it's all right if you just get by" attitude.

In the degree that we are correct in concluding that the usual application of cultural sanctions implies a simple reward–punishment approach to building appropriate social attitudes—that is, to learning the culture's values and aversions—we believe we are correct in asserting that the culture employs a poor way of teaching its mores.

This reward–punishment approach arises (as we have already indicated) from the application to each of us of minimum standards for acceptance into the culture. What is expected of us is that we comply with certain basic rules of conduct. If we comply, we are acceptable. If we don't, we are not acceptable. Now, acceptance by others is an exceedingly valuable reward—at least, it is for most of us. By the same token, rejection by others is an exceedingly severe punishment.

But the reward and punishment differ in quality. The acceptance of us by others is usually quiet and undramatic. People don't usually organize celebrations over the fact that one of us has done something acceptable, or even exceptionally acceptable. Celebrations are for heroes. But violation of cultural standards brings swift, severe, and very dramatic punishment. And dramatic punishment is far more common in our society than is dramatic reward.

This mild-reward–severe-punishment situation is confusing to children. It even confuses some adults. For one thing, it obscures the meaning of the values we seek to teach.

When mother washes out Junior's mouth for using foul

language, what is she teaching him about language? Ask
Junior, and he will probably say that she has taught him to
avoid using foul language—at least within earshot of mother.
This is the "simple response" we mentioned earlier. But has
she taught him what good language is? When teacher pun-
ishes Johnny for pilfering, has she taught him what honesty
is? Ask Johnny what honesty is, and he will probably say
that honesty is not stealing—for that is all he has been taught.
If one reads McGuffey to learn what kindness is, too often
one finds that kindness is the avoidance of cruelty. A "kind"
child is one who resists the temptation to ridicule, or otherwise to injure, someone else.

But virtue is not the absence of vice; virtue is a positive
thing-in-itself. Black is not the absence of white, nor is white
adequately defined as non-black. Yet many a parent says to
a visiting school official, "My Billy is a good boy; he stays
out of trouble"—as if "staying out of trouble" were an adequate description of "good boy."

Yet if one were to follow the culturally implied mild-
reward–severe-punishment system of teaching, one would be
implying that virtue is non-vice, and little more. The evidence is all around us that precisely this definition of the
culture's values and aversions—a definition by opposites—is
learned by many children and retained by many adults. It's
too naïve. It won't do.

Not only does the culture suggest strongly a method to be
used for teaching, but it also, in some degree, specifies the
time to be allowed for the learning. One example of this culturally determined learning time is that suggested when one
considers at what age adults become intolerant of children's
"swiping." By and large, we require children to observe in
their behavior the difference between "mine" and "thine" by
the time they are about four. This is enforced within families, and four-year-old children commonly comprehend the
difference, though they may continue to violate it. But by

about the time they are in second grade, we expect children to have applied this distinction well enough that minor "swiping" of other people's property has ceased. Between these approximate times punishments for "swiping" become increasingly severe. At the end of the second grade, children are expected to "know better" than to take the property of anyone else. Later, such behavior is called "theft" and leads to still more severe punishment.

We have, then, two characteristics of the learning method prescribed by the culture: values and aversions are to be acquired through learning to avoid their violations; and some of these values and aversions are to be learned by set times regardless of individual differences.

COMPLICATED CULTURAL STANDARDS

Not only is the learning method suggested by the culture somewhat paradoxical, but the stuff of the learning itself is quite complicated. This complication arises primarily from the fact the values and aversions of the culture are frequently in conflict with one another in real life situations. We have discussed property rights above, so let us continue thinking of this aspect of the value–aversion system.

Property rights are to be respected. That is clear enough. What is mine is not thine, what is thine is not mine; I may not take to myself anything that is not already mine, except under rigidly defined conditions. This is a relatively simple idea and children ordinarily can grasp it fairly early in life. But there is a serious complication in the culture: From the child's point of view, the value called ownership is sometimes in conflict with a value called generosity.

Children must learn to make a clear distinction between what is their own and what is someone else's; but with respect to those things which they own, they are expected to be generous. They must share their possessions. They are taught that if they have enough candy to share then they must share it. They may not eat it publicly and be envied by non-candy-owners. They must share school play equipment, and they are supposed to share their own playthings. Children are expected to learn to hold their own property *tentatively*, so to speak. It is not wholly their own, since it must be "shared" under some circumstances. "Sharing" is not a complicated idea, nor is "ownership"; but the idea of sharing one's own property is complicated, at least from the point of view of a little child. So, commonly, children learn to distinguish what is theirs long before they learn to share what is theirs. And, of course, there is many an adult who has not achieved this second learning.

Another complication arises from the conflict of "character traits" that are cultural values: independence and obedience. In a way, two other terms reflect the same fundamental conflict: responsibility and dependence. We expect children to learn that they are supposed to behave in an independent, responsible manner under certain circumstances, to be obedient to and dependent on adult authority under other circumstances. Even an adult has trouble distinguishing between the circumstances that call for independent and responsible behavior and those calling for obedient and dependent behavior. Children frequently confuse these situations, and are punished. It is often difficult, also, to be obedient and responsible at the same time.

This analysis of cultural value conflicts might be extended quite considerably. Much of what we report in later chapters of this book is such an extension. It will suffice here merely to remind ourselves of the fact that these conflicts exist, and that they greatly complicate the subject matter of the learnings we wish the children to make about cultural values.

CONFORMITY PLUS UNDERSTANDING

We have seen that the values and aversions we are dealing with here arise in large measure from the culture into which we wish to introduce the children. Furthermore, we have noted the learning method that the culture seems to suggest. We noticed that the effect of the poor learning method and the complicated subject matter of cultural demands is bound to be bewildering to a thoughtful child. One further aspect of this matter should be commented on, and then we can proceed to consider such ways as are known for meeting this problem.

The teacher, being an agent for communication of culture to the young, is ordinarily a person who has himself successfully learned what some aspects of the culture demand. He has achieved these learnings without very much specific attention to the way he learned them; he probably managed, in the long run, actually to learn virtues by avoiding vices, to value the rewards of compliance with the culture's standards *after* having learned to avoid its punishments. Teachers, especially, have learned to value compliance with cultural demands. They probably conform with the culture as thoroughly as any identifiable group within it. It is not suggested here that they should not conform. Conformity, plus understanding, is precisely what is required.

However, the teacher is a problem with respect to the development of social attitudes because he learned to conform in the culture's way. The teacher's normal tendency, then, is to repeat the culture's learning pattern in the course of working with children: to reward quietly and punish dramatically; to require arbitrary completion of learnings by set times; to overlook the complexity of the standards being taught. To do otherwise is impossible for many teachers; they have become personally committed to the culture in a deeper sense than many other people. It is very much easier for a teacher to accept the fact of children's differences in progress in arithmetic, for example, than it is for him to accept as a fact children's differences in understanding cultural standards. Yet, in the abstract, both propositions are equally valid.

Furthermore, the teacher who attempts to apply this kind of thinking to the social behavior of children runs a severe risk of being punished, himself, by the culture. People who are not teachers cannot be expected to understand a teacher's failure to punish severely a child's violation of the cultural value–aversion system. The use by the teacher of some other approach to the problem is likely to bring accusations from laymen that the teacher himself has negated the culture and is not a proper person to teach. Thus, the frequent accusations that teachers "coddle" the children; and thus, similarly, the frequent accusations that modern penologists treat dangerous criminals too gently.

IMPROVING THE TEACHING OF CULTURAL STANDARDS

We are critical of a simplified reward–punishment approach to the building of culturally acceptable attitudes. But the reward–punishment approach to learning can be used constructively. While it is not the only possible approach, and perhaps not the best, it is the one that is available most easily; it is the approach that is most consistent with what most people do anyway.

Let us, therefore, consider how we may employ it intelligently. One of our criticisms of the approach has been that the mild-reward–severe-punishment situation leads to confusion in a child's mind. This confusion could be reduced if we (*a*) increased the visibility of the rewards associated with compliance with cultural standards, and (*b*) helped children to see the positive nature of the standards, rather than merely their negative nature—to see what to do, not merely what to *avoid*.

To make the culture's rewards more visible, we should help children see the relationship between what they do and the rewards that they receive. It is not, of course, always possible or profitable to analyze for children the rewards inherent in a certain kind of behavior; but we can help them to understand the tremendous importance of acceptance by others —the culture's basic reward for behaving in accordance with the values and aversions the culture is made of. Most children want the liking of other children; we can help them to be articulate about it, and to understand that it is admissible to talk about the ways friendship is won and held. Discussions of the bases on which children and adults learn to like one another have proved helpful in our classes. We found it important to talk about the culture's own reward— acceptance—rather than to offer arbitrary rewards unique to our classroom situations. When we could point out the cultural reward, we could assume that the children would be likely to see it in other social situations than those we as teachers controlled.

Discussions of the bases on which friendships were formed helped, too, toward the children's understanding of the positive nature of the cultural expectations. When we pointed out that children liked other children who smiled a good deal, we were by implication pointing out a definite, positive thing to do—smile. When we pointed out (or, better, when children in our classes pointed out) that "tit for tat" was as true for considerateness as for inconsiderateness, we were suggesting something positive, too. That is, we were suggesting that kindness begets kindness as surely as aggression begets counter-aggression.

But such discussions stopped short of what we knew about the way people learn. They were based solely on the culture's reward–punishment system of learning.

There is another explanation of learning that emphasizes the ability of the learner to see things whole. This approach to understanding learning takes advantage of the fact that people are influenced by the way they see the field of operation—by what they think is involved, or pertinent. A field of learning can include many elements; according to the learner's way of organizing these elements into a pattern, he decides what action is required.

Let us contrast the simplified reward–punishment approach we have been discussing with this field approach. Let's assume that we have a wooden box, one end open, the other screened. We have placed some attractive food in the box, at the screened end. Now place a hungry chicken outside the box so that it can see the food through the screen. The chicken will go directly toward the food, run into the screen, and be puzzled. It is unlikely that the chicken will ever solve the problem; it will jump against the screen until it is tired, and give up. The chicken is acting on the basis of a simple perception of what is involved; it feels its hunger, sees the food, and strikes the screen. To solve the problem, it would have also to see the box as a whole, including its open end. Failure to include these elements in its perception leaves the chicken unable to solve the problem.

Now place a small, hungry child in the same situation, with food attractive to the child in the box. The child may be puzzled, too, momentarily, but he will rather quickly look at the box as a whole, and reach around for the food. He acts on a perception of a larger field than the chicken apparently can.

Now suppose one attempted this experiment with a child, and instead of taking the food, he reached toward it, then stopped and wept. To understand his behavior, it would be necessary to know what he saw in the field. Perhaps his perception included elements like these, more or less consciously recognized: *Food, screen, box, open end of box. A box is to play with. Last time I reached into a box like this one, I scratched my hand on a nail. Mother scolded me. Mother is standing here. I'm hungry. If I reach for the food, I may hurt myself again, and be scolded, and I'd still be hungry.*

So he weeps. He can't put these elements together in a

way that suggests a clear-cut action that would achieve the goal.

If this seems complicated, consider how complicated a classroom situation is for a child! Thirty other children, each representing a battery of experiences of some kind, a teacher who holds great power, parents and their expectations, the child's social habits and attitudes—all these elements themselves complicated, and many more, operate as more or less contending forces in the child's field of social behavior.

This emphasis on the wholeness of learning situations has proved helpful for a generation to those who try to understand learning. According to this point of view, one behaves less in terms of specific rewards than in terms of a field of activity, and the behavior of a person is directed not so much toward a single reward as toward a goal. A goal is complicated and must be defined in context. A reward is often viewed as single and simple. This is especially true of the cultural punishments discussed above. Too often, the cultural punishment is profoundly irrelevant to the motive of the one punished—as when a child's mouth is "washed out" for what he means as mere experimentation with a new word.

In practical terms, using this field approach to learning social attitudes would involve frequent attempts to help children to analyze social situations as wholes. Such analyses, carried on in the classrooms, might help the children to seek more and more adequate goals for their own social behavior, and to make their behavior increasingly appropriate to the goals they seek. For example, some children think that the only way to resolve a conflict is to fight. Some other children realize that fighting is only one of several ways to resolve conflicts. Social growth in this case might result from analyzing "fight" situations until other ways to resolve conflicts were learned.

Improved teaching of social attitudes means that teachers must help children to develop more adequate perceptions of social situations. The teacher's job is to help children to understand what our moral and spiritual ideals imply for day-to-day behavior, and thus to help children to act consistently with these ideals.

But to do this, the teacher must have an accurate picture of what the children perceive in the social situations they live in. Failure to obtain this information would (and often does) leave the teacher merely being "preachy"—that is, missing the child's learning level.

To achieve an accurate picture of the child's perception of social situations, it is necessary to be systematic; we must use some research techniques as part of our teaching.

The idea of using research techniques may seem a little formidable. It is less so, however, when we recall that standardized tests and other devices for measuring mental growth are actually research techniques. Any systematic observation of a child's behavior is, likewise, a research technique. What is required is simply that, as teachers, we learn to use ways of estimating the status of a child's social attitudes with something like the same regularity with which we use the better-known ways of estimating the status of other aspects of his growth.

The fact that cultural standards are actually rather complicated and sometimes in conflict with one another makes it even more important that teachers be systematic in estimating children's social development. The conflict between property rights and generosity, for example, requires different kinds of resolutions in different situations. What the teacher must understand in order to know how to help an individual child is the status of the child's understanding of the two values involved and also his understanding of the ways in which the seeming conflict between them may be resolved. This requires studies of three types: studies of the child's perception of the nature of property rights, studies of his perception of the nature of generosity, and studies of his understanding of the ways of resolving conflicts between the two.

These Ideas and the Study

In Springfield, most of our work had to do with finding ways of understanding the children's perceptions of social situations. To do this, we had to spend a good deal of our time together learning how to think about social attitudes. In each school, we started with a practical concern, and rendered it into problems that could be studied. The effect of this approach upon us was exceedingly wholesome, and it will be described. However, when our actual studies are compared with the theoretical framework of the preceding section, it will be apparent that we achieved only fragments of understanding, which are put into relationship in this report for the first time. The rest of this report, then, should be regarded as a series of pieces more or less like those of a jigsaw puzzle from which most of the pieces are missing. The pieces reported here are placed in a proper relationship with one another as nearly as our own knowledge permits, but between them there exist many gaps which require further filling in. It is the hope of the writers of this report that other teachers will undertake experimentation which will make the picture more complete. A proper understanding of what follows requires some participation in it by the reader, who will wish to test for himself both the rationale underlying our studies and the appropriateness of the interpretation made of them.

CHAPTER 3

The Method of Study and How We Feel About It

ACTION RESEARCH may be defined as research undertaken at the action level to improve practices. It is characterized by a design which evolves as the process moves forward and in which intermediate results influence the unfolding design as much as does the original purpose.

The teachers who participated in the various cooperative action research projects reported in this book define action research less abstractly. They describe what it means to them as participants and how it functions in their teaching. If ways are to be developed for helping teachers conduct cooperative action research to improve classroom practices, it is important to understand the relationship they see between the research process itself and such research as it functions in their work with children. We shall endeavor here to establish this relationship by describing, first, the process of research used in the schools participating in the study and, second, the ways in which the teachers themselves describe cooperative action research.

The Action Research Pattern

Action research can be described as an evolving plan of research and action. Beginning with a problem in a specific situation, action researchers proceed to study the situation, identify the factors with which they will deal, and devise a plan of action to study and work toward a solution of the problem as they see it. The plan of action is usually stated in the form of an "action hypothesis," which predicts that certain desirable consequences will result from specific actions. This hypothesis is then tested as the plan of action is tried out and data are secured on the success or failure of the plan. These data are carefully evaluated, and if the plan of action needs modifying, the necessary changes are made and the revised plan is tried out. Again data are collected and evaluated and necessary revisions made in the action.

In this way each step in the evolving plan is built on the results attained in the preceding step. Such a procedure allows for the use of new insights gained at each step of the study in improving the situation in which the original problem appeared. The action research in the schools studied followed closely this pattern of identifying and defining problems, formulating a plan of action (including plans for evaluating results), putting these actions into effect, collecting evidence in order to evaluate the consequences, and then modifying the action plan in light of this evaluation.

IDENTIFYING PROBLEMS

In each of the schools the total staff participated as a group in the entire action research process, delegating responsibilities to individuals and small committees as needed. Teachers considered the participation in the design of the action research of all persons involved to be an essential part of the research process itself. Although all of the schools were concerned with the problem of the development of desirable attitudes and values in children, each school group developed a research design which seemed best for its school. The decision by each staff to participate in the study had been based on the teachers' understanding of the way in which the proposed research area applied to their particular problems. The understandings of the separate staffs differed somewhat. Therefore, the designs differed too.

Each staff chose the specific social attitude it wished to study, and proceeded to define the attitude in terms of behavior which the group thought reflected it. This initial definition of the value or attitude in terms of behavior differed from school to school according to the problems existing in the respective schools. In one school, for example, the attitude of "responsibility," through a behavioral definition, became "follow-through-on-plans." Teachers in this school felt that they needed, more than anything else, to help children carry out plans. They chose, therefore, to study ways to develop responsibility for carrying plans through to completion. Another school also chose to study "responsibility"—but in this school it became "self-initiated action to meet personal and group needs." The teachers in this school were working toward helping children develop responsibility for meeting their own and group needs; so the attitude was defined in terms of this problem. The remaining schools chose other attitudes which seemed important to them, and defined them accordingly.

Having defined an attitude behaviorally, the teachers were able to analyze the type of situation which provoked this behavior and to identify factors which seemed to influence it. For example, the group studying the self-initiated action of children identified a number of factors that they felt might influence the extent to which children assume responsibility for their own and group needs. The idea that initiative increases as age increases is one which many people accept readily. However, this group questioned the reasonableness of expecting more self-initiated action from eleven-year-olds than from six-year-olds just because the former had lived more years than the latter. They were anxious to gather data which would show whether chronological age was or was not a controlling factor in self-initiated action. This group also discussed the possible influence of the classroom situation and of pupil–teacher relationships on self-initiated action.

Formulating a Plan of Action

The identification by teachers of factors influencing behavior resulted in a number of hunches concerning the causes of the behavior which reflected the attitudes being studied. The hunches were stated as hypotheses which suggested a relationship between observed behavior and certain factors which might influence that behavior. The teachers interested in self-initiated action attempted at different times in their study to test the influence of age and of certain teacher behavior. Another school group sought to test the relationship between "sharing" behavior and economic status, and still another looked for a relationship between a child's follow-through on planning and his feeling of belongingness in the group.

In order to formulate a plan of action, the school staffs had to state their problems in such a way that action was implied. It was necessary to *predict* that specific desirable consequences would result from certain practices. It was then necessary to devise ways of trying out the practices and of measuring the consequences. For example, the school which was interested in the development of initiative and responsibility in children at one stage in their study formulated this hypothesis: "The fewer action decisions the teacher makes in a planning situation, the more action suggestions will be made by youngsters." In this hypothesis the implied desirable goal is more action suggestions from children. The practice is that of having the teacher encourage children to make more decisions by making fewer himself. The plan for testing this hypothesis consisted of ways of procuring evidence to determine the ratio of suggestions made by children to decisions made by the teacher. The plan also involved providing as many opportunities as possible for children to plan their activities in order that the effect of certain teacher–pupil relations might be observed.

COLLECTING EVIDENCE

The methods of seeking evidence for testing the hypotheses were different in each school. Teachers developed inventories, indexes, projective devices, and observation forms which were suitable to the particular behavior being studied. Use was made of psychological measuring instruments when those instruments would best serve the purpose. It was at this point that use was made of existing educational research in securing help with methodology and in checking certain findings which seemed to be coming from the action research studies.

Teachers compiled and analyzed the data collected in terms of the hunches being tested. When a certain factor was found to have a definite relation to a particular behavior, the study was continued to further clarify the relationship. In such a case, the teachers developed new hypotheses and proceeded to gather data necessary to test them. At each successive step in the action research process, teachers gained new insights which gave rise to further questions which in turn required extended research and which in turn developed new insights. This cycle of developing hypotheses, testing, and evaluating was typical of each phase of the cooperative action research project. In this way, the design of the study evolved as the teachers moved through the planning and research activities. There was no preconceived plan which groups felt obligated to follow.

A description of the methods which the group studying self-initiated behavior of children [1] employed in testing one of their hypotheses will serve to illustrate the ways in which teachers gathered evidence. Early in their study this group of teachers decided to explore the result of certain practices of the teacher on pupil initiative. The hypothesis which was mentioned in the preceding section of this chapter was formulated for testing: "The fewer action decisions the teacher makes in planning situations, the more action suggestions will be made by youngsters." The plan developed for testing this hypothesis involved a number of steps, which were described by the teacher as follows:

I. A training period for each teacher as a first step.
   A. During planning sessions each teacher will write down all action suggestions, indicating whether they were made by child or teacher.
   B. Repeat this process until it becomes easy to spot action suggestions.
   C. Repeat the above process writing down group- and teacher-made decisions.
II. Secondly, having trained ourselves, we will start tallying. We have worked out a simple tally sheet. We have spoken of the importance of tallying every action suggestion and decision.
III. The last step of our plan is to set up tally teams in which an observer would also tally, later checking his observation against the participating teacher's tally sheet. When both tally sheets are quite similar, a fair degree of accuracy will have been achieved.
IV. Some agreements in the matter of classification were made.
   A. Many action suggestions are stated as questions. (Are we going to have a Halloween Parade?) Such questions will be included as action suggestions.
   B. Decisions will be tallied only if they have somehow become explicit. That is: rejected by class or teacher, or,

[1] See Chapter 5 for our report of other aspects of this study. The emphasis there is on what we found out. The emphasis here is on how we went about it.

accepted by class or teacher. These rejections or accept-
ances may be either verbal or tacit.[2]

During the training period a number of things were done
to help teachers gain confidence and skill in tallying action
suggestions and decisions. During classroom discussions,
each teacher attempted to write down action suggestions
and decisions that were made. These were brought to the
group meetings for discussion, but many of the teachers
were not clear as to what should be recorded. It was felt that
this confusion would be eliminated if all teachers could observe the same planning session with each person tallying all
suggestions and decisions which he heard. It would then be
possible to check the accuracy of the observations by comparing the tallies. In order to do this a tape recording was
made of a planning session in one of the rooms. The recording was played in a group meeting while the teachers listened trying to identify action suggestions and decisions.
The tape was stopped often and agreements were reached.
Each person attempted to tally on the second running of the
tape. (Tally sheets had a column for suggestions and a
column for decisions.) The tallies were compared to check
the results and a high rate of agreement was found. The
teachers felt that they were now ready to proceed with the
collection of data to test the hypothesis.

The tallying of action suggestions and decisions after the
training period was accomplished by teams of teachers. One
teacher kept a tally while the other conducted a planning
session with his own youngsters. This proved to be a very
efficient way to work; and teachers soon overcame their reluctance to have another person observe their teaching.

At the end of this study teachers reported a high percentage of both suggestions and decisions made by children and
a low percentage by the teacher in all classrooms. They also

[2] Taken from the consultants' memo, summarizing one of our planning
conferences.

reported that they had gained new insights into ways of improving cooperative planning and into the values of such planning. It was their feeling that because they were concerned about the children's part in planning they had provided more opportunities than before for youngsters to plan their own activities and make their own decisions.

(It should be noted that they drew no conclusion concerning the effect of teacher decisions on child decisions. The observations they carried on suggested that the field was broader than they had thought it was; they therefore chose to overlook their original hypothesis and to study the whole matter of child participation further. Actually, their finding was that when they paid close attention to suggestion- and decision-making, their classroom cooperative planning improved. They had found "points of focus," previously overlooked.)

Emphasis on Action

At each stage of the on-moving action research pattern, implications of findings for changed classroom practices were emphasized by all of the teachers. Interest in the research activities was highest when implications were most clearly seen. The preceding account of the activities of one school group shows the way in which change was inherent in most of the hypotheses developed and tested by teachers. Another example of this is the school group which had a hunch that counteraggression (getting even for a wrong done) is greater in youngsters with a low degree of self-esteem. The teachers felt that if this were shown to be true, they could reduce the aggressive behavior of many children in their school by helping them to raise their self-esteem. Still another group found that what they described as positive democratic behavior was related to the security of the youngsters. As a result of this understanding, they developed many teaching procedures for building security in children as a means of helping them behave more democratically. These examples were typical of the stress most of the school groups placed on the instructional consequences of action research.

Validity of Action Research Findings

There are some educational researchers who are skeptical of the contribution action research can make to curriculum development and to knowledge. Because of the concept of research which they hold, they feel that action research is less scientific than the type which makes use of the standards and procedures of research in the physical sciences. For this reason they question the validity of the findings and generalizations resulting from action research. Lewin holds such attitudes to be unwarranted. In discussing this problem, he says that it is by no means true "that the research . . . is in any respect less scientific or lower than what would be required for pure science in the field of social events." [3]

The skeptical attitude toward action research exists because the generalizations developed are applied only to the population studied. Generalizations derived from action research are usually based upon population samples that are not randomly selected. It is not possible in action research to set up a rigid control of variables in the classic manner, so that results can be verified in repeated studies under similar conditions.

Such objections have merit. However, there are many factors in cooperative action research which compensate for these conditions. Action research findings achieve an actual validity because the studies are conducted in real classroom situations where the effects of many factors operating in such situations can be studied. As a result, the findings are often more realistic than those obtained in an artificially con-

[3] Kurt Lewin, "Frontiers in Group Dynamics, Part II," *Human Relations*, 1 (1947), pp. 150-151.

trolled setting. Action researchers [4] recognize that when cooperative action research techniques are employed it may be difficult to isolate and verify the effect of any one factor. But they believe that the lack of precision in any one aspect is overbalanced by the greater precision achieved through study of the situation as a whole. This is to say that when the researcher, through a rigid control of variables, seeks precision which can be verified through repeated experimentation under similar conditions, he does so at the expense of validity in a broad sense. Rigid control of variables is rarely possible in a social situation. Therefore, the results of such research too often cannot be applied in a normal social situation. For this reason, action researchers seek greater validity by operating in a research setting which is whole. The results of such research carry more meaning for action in normal social situations.

The opportunity to test the propositions with the same children and in the same situation which gave rise to their formulation is another important advantage of action research. This practice of keeping research in a setting where action can be taken directly to improve teaching is of paramount importance to action researchers. They work hard to develop defensible generalizations but their major interest is in applying these generalizations to subsequent classes they will be teaching.[5] They are not interested primarily in establishing generalizations that apply to all children in a given grade in the United States. They realize, however, that by combining the results of action research undertaken in many places and under varying circumstances the base for

[4] Cunningham and Miel, *op. cit.*, pp. 370-371.

[5] See Stephen M. Corey, *Action Research to Improve School Practices* (New York: Bureau of Publications, Teachers College, Columbia University, 1953), pp. 132-139, for evidence supporting the contention that generalizations from investigations undertaken by a teacher to provide a better basis for decisions and actions concerning his present pupils can be extended to his future pupils in the same school and at the same grade level.

generalizing will be broadened and each study will take on an added significance.

Action Research from the Teachers' Viewpoint

When teachers who participated in cooperative action research were asked about the process, their replies usually fell into three areas. They often discussed how action research differed from other methods of study which they had encountered; they never failed to point out that the methods used were closely integrated with their regular classroom activities; and they frequently mentioned the satisfactions which they experienced in conducting action research.

It is different from other study methods

Many of the teachers who participated in the cooperative action research project described it as different from other ways in which they had studied professional problems. The "other ways" are the procedures usually employed in curriculum improvement programs: discussion groups to discuss professional problems and professional readings, committee work to prepare curriculum materials, system-wide meetings to hear speeches by curriculum authorities, classroom visitation, case studies of children, and so on. The teachers say that this way is unique. When they were asked in individual interviews to indicate ways in which the research was different from other methods of study, a number of aspects were mentioned.

—more than reading about solutions to problems

Teachers said that the research they conducted was more vital to them because they were studying problems firsthand, and not just reading about the way someone else solved his problems. Study and research have come to mean looking at vital teaching problems and attempting to do something about them by bringing to bear insights gained from reading, from studying children, and from sharing ideas with others on the problem under consideration.

One teacher remembered:

Research to me used to be mostly reading—not doing much about what we had read—just compiling all we had read and drawing our conclusions from that. . . . We would come across something in our reading and say, "Well, I bet I could use that when I get back to my children." But when we did, we forgot it or we didn't carry it out. But now we are using these things we are learning right in the classroom with the children because that's where we learn them. It is much more vital. Now we can see results of it, and before we couldn't.

Another teacher told of study in which he and other teachers engaged before becoming involved in cooperative action research:

I can remember that before we started this, we thought it fine professionally to do something or other to improve ourselves. Someone would read an article on education and then report on it, and once in a while I would get a spark as something would happen to strike my individual case. Then I would listen. Now, we are all concerned personally with the problems we are studying, and because human nature is as it is, we are more interested in things that vitally concern us. . . . We had a committee once of which I was a member. It was called "The Professional Growth Committee" and we struggled valiantly. We brought speakers in and we showed moving pictures. Right at the end of a school day we would say, "Now if you will come over to the auditorium, we will show you a movie that will help you improve professionally." You see, that was another way that we tried and because it wasn't vital and purposeful, it didn't go over. We don't have a professional growth committee now.

Comments from other teachers reinforced these statements that there was a difference between study methods that had been used previously and action research which makes the latter more significant to teachers. Another teacher pointed out that research had always previously been something that was done by someone else, and about which he read if it seemed to apply to his problem. He added that even after reading, the application of the finding from another's research to his problem was not always clear to him. He felt that his group was actually involved in analyzing real problems and collecting evidence as to the effectiveness of their efforts to do something about them. In this same connection, another teacher suggested that action research is "like the new ideas of education. You are actually doing your research instead of just seeing it done." To these statements can be added a comment by one other person:

This [developing their own study] meant more to us than if we had taken someone else's plan and checked it. It was our own brain-child. With all of its weaknesses and all of its bad points, it was ours. We had a feeling . . . that we had done something, and that it hadn't been handed out to us by someone else.

—starts with children

Some of the teachers felt that a fundamental difference between their action research and other methods of study was that the research began with firsthand contact with children in the classroom—with the real problems they face in teaching children. They stated that they had seen implications of what they could do for children more clearly because in this activity they had studied children and worked with children in terms of specific teaching problems. One teacher pointed out, "In the past, we just studied *about* children—*about* teaching. Now we are studying teaching. We are studying children and trying to make some changes in their behavior as we study them."

Another teacher elaborated this difference in greater detail:

We [formerly] took some of those things we read, and discussed them, and tried to apply them in our schoolroom. It seems to me this way of working is just the opposite. We have started in the schoolroom with children and are working with them. The information we get isn't just theory. We have a hunch and we try it out. If it doesn't work out, we try another hunch, but we are studying the children to begin with. . . . As I look back now on the notes I took—the volumes of notes I took on those professional study meetings—I realize how far removed it was from what I was doing in the classroom. Now all my volume of notes are on the children—with implications for what I might do for the children.

—more systematic than other methods of study

Teachers felt that the action research project gave them a framework for their study. The research began with problems which the teachers themselves identified as important in their classroom teaching. Their study of children, their reading, and their experimentation with new procedures were all directed toward the solution of the problems. They gathered evidence and kept records as a means of checking the effectiveness of their efforts and to make modifications intelligently in their procedures. Teachers appreciated the purposeful activity which resulted from this method of study.

A teacher discussed this point as follows:

Now we have a framework for our study. We know where we are going and if we run into something we don't understand, we go down to the curriculum library and get a professional book and find out about it. Before this, our study was sort of haphazard because we felt that if we didn't have enough business to fill up faculty meetings we should improve our minds a little bit.

One teacher said that even though the staff of his school had attempted for a number of years to study specific problems, they had never been systematic in the collection of evidence to prove or disprove ideas they might have had.

IT IS PRACTICAL FOR BUSY TEACHERS

Most of the participating teachers felt that the cooperative action research project contributed to an increased understanding and skill in teaching. They stressed the fact that they were able to use the findings directly in their own classrooms. To many of them, this was the feature that would cause them to recommend action research to other teachers as a very desirable way of studying professional problems. Several practical aspects of the procedures used were mentioned frequently by teachers:

—related to classroom procedures

Teachers are busy, and are quite justifiably reluctant to undertake in-service professional study which they cannot see contributing directly to their teaching problems. This accounts for the aversion of many teachers to participation in curriculum study programs as conducted in many school systems. Teachers who participated in the action research said that the way in which the research had been related to classroom procedures and problems was a factor that had made it possible for them to carry on the study without jeopardizing the quality of their teaching. Even though they felt that time to carry on the study had been a problem, they were pleased to discover that, in one teacher's words, it is "possible to find out things you do not know within the stream of ordinary classroom work." Another said:

It seems to me that one thing I have seen happening in Springfield that might be worth reporting to other people is that there are kinds of research and there are ways in which we can relate ourselves to it which really makes that research an integral part of the responsibilities we now have.

In discussing reasons why busy teachers have found it possible to carry on the research, someone stated:

We are working, right along as we are teaching. We are getting our information as we go along. There is no separation from the teaching. The research is all a part of our teaching as I see it.

Some of the teachers accounted for the high degree of interest in the study by pointing out that the research had centered on classroom problems and had been a part of the on-moving work:

It was just a part of our regular work. It wasn't something detached from our classrooms. It was a study of the kinds of things that go on in our classroom day in and day out that we need to know about . . . If it had been something away from the children and away from our work, I don't believe I would have been half so willing to work as I was.

—helps with ways of working with children

Many teachers felt that the study had been very valuable because it had directed their attention to better ways of working with children. The fact that the emphasis had been on finding better procedures for teaching youngsters had helped the teachers make direct applications of improved methods to problems as they arose. One teacher commented on the help that teachers in her school had been able to give specific children. She added that they wouldn't have been able to make adjustments in situations to increase a feeling of belongingness in children had they not been studying that very problem and had they not possessed the information about the relation of belongingness to the development of desirable behavior.

—causes change

There was a feeling on the part of many teachers that the mere use of the methods of study which they employed caused them to change their ways of teaching. They felt that the findings resulting from their study contributed to increased knowledge of the need for change, but they credited the process of study with causing them to change as they worked. An example of this was found in the school which was studying the choices youngsters make (see Chapter 5). The group decided to observe and record the kinds of choices children made in various situations during the school day. The teachers pointed out that, because of this method of study, they put forth an effort to create more and more situations in which children had opportunity to make choices.

A teacher of third grade children commented:

I know now that when I face a situation instead of saying, "I want children to do this in this situation," I say, "Maybe I could offer these alternatives or maybe I could say something that would help children to think through the situation and to offer better suggestions than I could offer myself." For instance, . . . the problem has come up as to what we are going to do for Easter. Friday is the day when the children would normally want to have an Easter Egg Hunt, but that is the day our music supervisor comes, so what I plan to do, is put the situation up to the youngsters and explain the problem, and help them to work out the solution to it.

Another example of change resulting from the process of study came from a school where the staff was studying planning.[6] The teachers were investigating the extent and quality of children's participation in planning and they found themselves seeking more opportunities for children to plan in order to have situations for observations. A teacher from this school remembered a specific incident where an opportunity was seen for additional planning:

For years the children have run through the shrubbery in front of the school, and we have put up signs, and tried to do things to help them see that it is a beauty spot and should be kept beautiful. Then, this last year the children themselves took it up. They secured shrubs from their neighbors and visited green-houses and nurseries, and now we have little shrubs in all those bare spots. I think we have learned that when you involve children and let them feel they have had a share in the planning, they take more responsibility.

Another teacher from the same school credited the process of study as having contributed to his security in planning:

I like what we have been doing because of the fact that we planned with children, looked at the observation sheets made by

[6] See the parenthetical note on page 62.

others, and then tried it again. We gained confidence that we could do the job as it should be done. It helped to look at the record of the planning session, and then to look at the results. After you had done that several times, you began to see that you were not wasting time when you planned with children.

One teacher thought that the process of making use of new insights in the situations in which they had been acquired was very valuable. He contrasted this method to the method of studying all the aspects of a problem before attempting to make use of new understandings. He said that in the present way of working "we are learning to study and use what we learn and move along into a better program. We will just never get to the place where we have all the pins in place before we begin to work."

Another teacher reinforced this same idea:

It seems to me that the process itself is valuable enough because as we go along, we change our procedures in light of the evidence we have about the problem. It is valuable to have discovered that technique for handling problems.

Summary

Teachers who participated in the cooperative action research projects studied described the process as very different from the kind of curriculum study they had known before; as a practical means of professional study for busy teachers; and as a very satisfying experience. Because action research involves more than reading about solutions to problems, and because it enables teachers to study at first hand their own problems and to do something about them, teachers would recommend this type of research as a very satisfactory way of improving teaching practices. The fact that action research starts with the child in the classroom and that it provides a framework for study and a systematic approach to seeking evidence makes it a valuable means whereby teachers may gain new understandings and new insights, according to the teachers who participated in the research projects.

Teachers felt that action research was practical because it was closely related to their classroom responsibilities. They were pleased to discover that it was possible to find out things one does not know in the course of ordinary classroom work. Participating teachers also pointed out that the action research process caused them to change their ways of teaching as they studied.

PART II

WHAT WE LEARNED
ABOUT CHILDREN'S SOCIAL ATTITUDES

Introduction

I̲N THIS SECTION, we shall report what we learned about children's social attitudes. In each of the chapters that follow, we identify an attitude as it appeared to us, then indicate what we studied that had to do with it, and finally report what we learned.

In each case, we shall stress two things: first, that what we learned suggests to us some conclusions we can act on, but that we should like to know much more; second, what the reader can do to test our findings in his own class. The second of these emphases is more important, for the purpose of this report, than is the first.

Our main purpose in reporting these short studies is that other classroom teachers may test our findings in their own classrooms. The conclusions we have reached are true for our children, and we are busy trying to apply them. We don't know whether they are true of children generally, or of other specific classrooms. That judgment is one other teachers must make for themselves. To help them make it, we have taken pains to indicate how they may repeat what we did, so that other classes may be compared with ours.

The form to be used in each of the chapters that follow, then, is as follows:

1. A discussion of the social attitude in question.
2. The hunches we tested, and what we found out.
3. The implications for teaching of what we found, as they appear to us.
4. How these experiments may be repeated.

Our tendency to call social attitudes "intangibles" reflects the experience of every teacher who has felt baffled by the problem of pupils' character development.[1]

When the participating members of the present study first met, the question was asked: "Just what are these intangibles?" We responded rather quickly with a number of names: responsibility, dependability, initiative, follow-through, cooperativeness, independence, sharing, honesty. Many others, of course, might have been added—critical thinking, open-mindedness, reverence, kindness, to mention only a few. All these represent cultural values to which most of us subscribe without much thought. It is surprising, in a way, that things we refer to so often should be thought of as "intangible." One would suppose that these cultural values were such an intimate part of our lives that we would be

---

[1] See Chapter 2 for a discussion of the sources and referents of attitudes. In view of our previous definition of attitudes as predispositions to act toward or away from referents, it needs to be reiterated that in practice we also used the term "attitude," as here, to mean a predisposition to behave in a certain way toward referents such as ideas, named beliefs, and courses of action. "Initiative," then, would be the name we give to one of these courses of action; and it would also be the name we give to an *attitude* toward—a predisposition to take—this course of action. In some cases it might be defined as "an attitude toward opportunities for acting without the direction of others," the referent (course of action) here being something the person is aware of as a value, if only as a means to another value. Behavior thought of as revealing such attitudes often represents the individual's reactions to *many* referents which he sees in a situation but which he may or may not identify consciously. Since we were concerned with identifying those which tend to produce more or less consistent social behavior of a certain kind, we postulated them, so to speak, by calling the behavior the sign of an attitude.

able to be explicit about them. Still, we called them "intangibles."

In the course of examining our own ideas and feelings about this situation, we discovered that these things were not so "intangible" when we thought of our own actions. As individuals, we knew which actions we intended to be kind, courteous, considerate, and so on. However, as teachers, we had doubts about classifying children according to these traits. There was entirely too great a chance that we were basing judgments on vague impressions, not on real evidence.

We tested this out a little bit among ourselves.[2] Several teachers who were well acquainted with certain children asked themselves which of these values particularly fitted those children. They had done this before—in informal lunchroom talk, and in more formal conferences on the welfare of particular children. When they compared their impressions, they found a surprisingly high degree of agreement concerning the "intangibles" ascribed to a particular child. However, this did not seem to change the intangibility of the traits—the teachers felt they were simply pooling subjective impressions that had no more validity collectively than they had individually. There was, however, more to be thought about before we could dismiss this subject.

The fact that we were in substantial agreement about some children whom we had never discussed before required some explanation. We were, after all, a group of experienced teachers. Most of us had been teaching in Springfield for more than ten years; each of us individually had dealt with many hundreds of children. When we said of a particular child, "He is an uncooperative youngster," or "He is very dependable and responsible," the chances were that we were not speaking carelessly. The fact that we had built up sim-

[2] The discussions on which this section of the report is based took place in individual school buildings, one staff at a time.

ilar impressions of children, independently, tended to support this conclusion. Apparently we were looking at the same things in these children, or at least looking at the children in a substantially similar way. Otherwise, we would have disagreed. Of course, we might all be wrong, and merely in agreement in our error. But even so, this agreement suggested that we were responding, wrongly or rightly, to the same things in children.

When we considered the way these similar judgments were formed, we hit upon the source of our feeling that the whole matter was "intangible."

What had happened was this: as experienced teachers working with groups of children, we constantly noted little cues in a child's behavior that experience suggested were closely related to some social attitude—his cooperativeness, for example. In the course of the first few months of our acquaintance with a child, we saw him do one thing after another, each of which indicated his cooperativeness. As time passed, these observed incidents were stored up in our minds and began to accumulate in such a way as to cause us to make a judgment concerning his cooperativeness with increasing firmness.

The difficulty came later. While we could remember the judgments, and while we were aware of the increasing firmness of these judgments, as the days passed, the incidents, or cues, on which these developing judgments were based had never been systematically noted, and were forgotten. Although evidence had been used to form these judgments, it was lost. What we remembered was the judgment, but not the evidence on which the judgment had been based.

If, a few months later, someone were to ask one of us whether a certain child was cooperative, we could report our judgment with considerable certainty. However, if we were asked to prove that our judgment was valid (and such proof could only have been offered in the form of records of observation) we were at a loss. We remembered the judgment, but had forgotten the evidence.

Now, this forgotten evidence had once been tangible. A child helping a teacher to straighten up a bookcase, or going out of his way to cooperate with his classroom group, is doing something concrete and tangible—as concrete and tangible as is any human behavior. These bits of observed behavior were the tangible elements on which the teachers' judgments were based. The teachers considered these judgments "intangible" because the tangible evidence on which they were based had been lost.

Our first task, then, was to go back and re-examine these tangible behaviors, and to see whether we were in substantial agreement about their significance. If we were, the problem of intangibility would disappear. Since the behaviors were tangible, and since we could agree about their significance, we would know in the future what it was that underlay our judgments.

To restore the tangibility of these traits, then, we had only to look at the behavior on which we usually based judgments of character.

For this reason, the patterns of the studies reported in the chapters that follow had a common feature. In each case, having decided to study one of the "intangibles," we began by looking for behaviors which in our opinion showed the trait in question. In so doing, we were restoring the tangibility of these traits.

We were doing something else, too. We were giving behavioral definitions to educational objectives of supreme importance. All of us were familiar with the axiom, "Learning is changed behavior." The clear implication of this definition of learning is that educational objectives, to be achieved, must be stated in terms of behavior. Teachers must be able to say what it is that they wish the children to *do*. This is as true of a trait like cooperativeness as it is of a skill in arithmetic, say. Until we are able to describe the behavior we seek, we do not have an attainable or even a describable educational objective. Therefore, the attempt, here, to find what behavior illustrates these character traits was of fundamental importance to an understanding of how children's social attitudes may be improved in school.

The attempt to give behavioral definitions to social attitudes has one other significance. Ultimately, we hoped to be able to describe the amount or degree of change occurring in a child with respect to these social attitudes. We hoped to carry on evaluative studies which would allow us to come to a better understanding of the school environment as it affects the development of such attitudes. But, in order to do this, it was essential that we find means of describing social behavior in definite, concrete terms. Until this could be done, we could not hope to compare a child's behavior at one time with his behavior at another, or to compare the behaviors of different children, in any meaningful way.

By describing these "intangible" social attitudes in tangible, concrete, definite statements of children's behavior, we got rid of the feeling that these attitudes are hopelessly beyond our reach, and, at the same time, provided a basis on which we could erect real educational objectives—not vague statements of illusory ideals. Thus we hoped to bring some of our most cherished values into tangible, practical reality.

CHAPTER 4

Follow-Through and
Group Acceptance

ONE ATTITUDE we want to develop in children is a willingness to do what they have agreed to do. Whether this is called dependability, or responsibility, or "follow-through" (as *we* called it), we want children to have it.

The fact that follow-through involves a *social* attitude was less obvious to us [1] when we began our work than it is now. At the outset, we saw the problem as an individual matter. Whether or not a child followed through on his commitments seemed to depend on the individual child in question. However, the school situation out of which commitments to *others* arise is clearly social, as most school situations are. And the more we studied this kind of follow-through, the more convinced we became that the social climate of the classroom is a significant factor in it.

We had for some time been using cooperative procedures in our classrooms. It seemed obvious to us that in the degree

---

[1] The staff of the Phelps Elementary School, where there were 345 children, carried on this work. In this chapter, "we" is the Phelps staff and two Institute consultants.

that children learned to plan and carry forward their own educative activities, they would reap a rich harvest: they would have a clearer understanding of the purpose of what they did at school; they would learn more and more about how to solve their own problems; educative activities at school would be more appropriate to the children themselves; the children, having made plans, would follow through on them more consistently than if the plans had been made for them.

Cooperative planning had long since passed the test of our experimentation with it. We were satisfied that the ideas behind it were sound, and that it actually achieved the results we anticipated from it, and more. However, some aspects of cooperative planning puzzled us. Follow-through was one of these.

In spite of our best efforts, some children didn't follow through. A class might have planned for arithmetic, an excursion, the preparation of social studies notebooks, or a play period. The children really had participated in the making of the plan. It had not been one of those fraudulent "We decided . . ." affairs in which the teacher does all the talking, here and there introducing directives in the familiar "Shall we . . . ?" disguise. No, we thought we had learned to avoid fooling ourselves (we knew we couldn't fool the children) and that the children's participation in the planning had been real and genuine. But even when the children had done most of the talking during our planning sessions, there were some who simply failed to follow through on their plans. What did this mean?

What Is Follow-Through?

Before we could go very far in our thinking, we had to make certain we were all talking about the same thing. To see whether we were, we observed the children for two weeks, collecting examples of "follow-through" and "non-follow-through" behavior. If we agreed that these were examples of what we meant, then we could go ahead.

Here are some examples we agreed on:

Grade 6

The class agreed to use a particular library period either to read library books they already had or to begin writing book reports. Joe wrote one book report and had me check it. Then he talked quietly to the librarian while selecting another book and spent the rest of the time reading it. (Follow-through.) Wanda took ten minutes to select a new book, spending most of this time talking to a friend of hers. She spent most of the rest of the time rearranging her desk and talking to her neighbor and had scarcely opened the new book when the period ended. (Non-follow-through.)

Grade 4

The class had planned an excursion by automobile and had assigned themselves to the various cars. There was a list for each car. When it was time to go, Boyd wasn't in the car he belonged in; he was in another car. He hadn't followed through on the plan.

Grade 2

We spent some time talking about how to behave in the hall. I really believe the children understood the reasons behind the rules; at least, they suggested both the reasons and the rules. I didn't have to. Next day, Billy used the hall as a race track and cheered himself all the way to the boys' room. By itself, this is nothing to worry about—and I'm not much worried about Billy. But Billy had been one who had taken a very prominent part in the discussion of the previous day.

All told, we collected more than fifty examples like these. "Follow-through," to us, simply meant doing what one had agreed to do. "Non-follow-through," for our purposes, was failure to do what one had agreed to do. (Of course, we might have given different meaning to the term "follow-through." We might, for example, have defined it as be-

havior going *beyond* the original commitment. The important thing to us at this stage, however, was that we come to
an agreement on terms, rather than that we conduct an ex-
ploration of other possible meanings.)

Having reached agreement in this manner, we were in a
position to begin studying follow-through. We had suc-
ceeded in the first task of the researcher—we had found a
way of making our observations comparable. We had,
through practice, found that when we reported follow-
through behavior, we were talking about the same thing.

How Could We Explain Differences?

Now we were ready to study the question we had asked at
the outset. How was it that some children did not follow
through, while others did? Plainly, the children differed
from one another in a great many ways, including this one.
How could we explain this difference? Were there any reasons for this failure to follow through that were independent
of such reasons as home background and general ability? It
wouldn't do us, or the children, much good to blame it all
on the home. Many of us had taken that convenient exit
from trying to influence character in the past. While we supposed that follow-through, like other social behavior, did
stem in large measure from family-bred attitudes, we
thought that we teachers, too, had some influence on it.
Each of us had known the thrill of success as an occasional
upset, fearful child responded to our work and "found himself."

What we were after now, however, was somewhat different from what we had sought through studies of individual
children. We sought, now, to learn whether any aspects of
the school environment were consistently affecting the follow-through of many children. If we could detect any, and
if we, as teachers, could influence these aspects of the school

environment, we could hope to have a desirable effect on the follow-through behavior of many of our children, thus diminishing the seriousness of some of the problems of individual children. What is more, we might hope to find ways of helping many of our children to recognize and understand the value of follow-through as such.[2]

Verbal Participation and Follow-Through

When we thought about it, we found that we had based our original statement of the problem on a questionable assumption: that a child would have a feeling of personal commitment to a plan if it were developed in class cooperatively. Such a plan might not have any meaning to a particular child. We pursued this a little further. When a classroom plan is developed through discussion, not everyone in the class actually participates orally in the discussion. Usually, in a class of 35, only a few of the children actually speak during such discussions. The class plan is actually made by the teacher and this minority of children.

Was it possible that the youngsters who were following through on cooperatively made plans were chiefly those who had spoken while it was being made? Were the non-following-through children the ones who didn't take a verbal part in the making of the plan? If this were so, we would have something we could work on. By experimenting with ways to increase the spread of verbal participation, we might see whether there was a cause-and-effect relationship between verbal participation and follow-through. Moreover, we might help the children to see follow-through as something that begins at the point of commitment—while the class plan is being made. They might see the importance of taking re-

[2] See Chapter 2 for a discussion of the necessity of teaching children to place higher personal value on the social values of our culture. Follow-through is such a value.

sponsibility in the *making*, as well as the carrying out, of plans.

Our hopes ran high, but our study showed us that this line of thought was inadequate. We still think that the argument we used was plausible, and we mean to test it further. However, the test we developed, which we shall report now, caused us to look beyond verbal participation as an invironmental factor in follow-through.

Testing the Verbal Participation Hypothesis

To test our hypothesis (that follow-through on cooperatively made class plans is positively related to verbal participation in making them) we gathered the following information:

1. We identified, after two weeks of observation, four children in each of our elementary classes: two who usually followed through on class plans, and two who usually didn't.

2. We kept a record of the participation of each of these four children in three classroom planning discussions.

3. We examined the data we had collected, to see whether the relationship we had predicted would appear.

Our prediction had been that children who consistently followed through would talk more during plan-making—make more contributions, have more ideas and suggestions—than would the children who consistently did not follow through.

Our prediction was not supported by the facts we gathered. The data we gathered, insofar as we accepted them, forced us to conclude that, for our children, *there was little or no relationship between verbal participation in classroom planning and the tendency of individual children to follow through on such planning.*

Although the data on which this conclusion is based are somewhat fragmentary and incomplete, they convinced us. They exist in the form of a large number of anecdotes describing the participation of the children in classroom planning situations, indicating that the child in question was usually "high" or "low" in follow-through. Sometimes the "high" children talked; sometimes they didn't. Sometimes the "low" children talked; sometimes they didn't. But their habit of following through, or not following through, seemed to bear no consistent relationship to their tendency to make verbal contributions to the class plan.

Some examples of the anecdotal material we gathered follow. It will be noted that in some cases, a reason for the child's follow-through rating is strongly suggested by the anecdotal material itself. In no case did the mere fact of his verbal participation in the planning seem to have much to do with his follow-through.

Mary. Grade 1. No participation; high in follow-through.

It was during our planning meeting for trimming our Christmas tree. Several children suggested what they could bring, and were so excited over all our plans. Mary, during all of this, seemed to have no interest—chewed her hair-ribbon and gazed out the window. No one had volunteered to bring lights.

The next morning Mary came in with a bounce and a smile all over her face. She came up to me and said, "Look, Mrs. B., I have brought two strings of lights for our tree."

Wirt. Grade 3. No participation; high in follow-through.

When we planned what to do after the play period that was about to start, Wirt said nothing, but gazed at one after another of those who spoke. We agreed to rest first, then to get ready for a spelling test.

He came in from the play period, went to the Boys' Room, got a drink, came into the classroom, sat down, arms folded on desk. After a short rest, he took out his spelling notebook, removed a sheet of paper from his looseleaf book, and continued with preparations for the spelling test as planned.

Larry. Grade 4. Forced participation; low in follow-through.

Larry was chosen on a committee to investigate the building of some new houses near our school. He had not been interested in the planning session, and did not participate in the discussion. When asked what he thought of the plans, he said, "O.K., I guess." The other children were not pleased with his attitude, and said so. One boy said, "Maybe if Larry was on the committee he would be more interested." Because of this suggestion, Larry was chosen on the committee.

When the group started on their investigation, Larry did not cooperate. He threw snowballs, ran across peoples' yards, and did not take any information. When the group returned, he had nothing to report.

Gary. Grade 6. No participation; low in follow-through.

Gary took no part in our discussion while we planned a reading period.

When the time came, Gary got one of the new books that he had started reading yesterday. He went to his desk, put the book down, and took his paste bottle out. He took off the lid, then turned to talk to Barry. Then he leafed through his book, looked around the room, snatched Barry's box of pencils. Then he put his head on the book, raised up, turned to a story in the book beyond where he had read, looked at some circus pictures in book, meanwhile chewing something. He put his hands over his eyes, shut the book, and rocked in his chair. . . . later he brought the book to me and asked, "Is this far enough for me to read?" I said, "Did you read that far?" He smiled, hesitated, and said, "Well, I read part of it." This is an old story for Gary, who needs constant help and encouragement in reading.

The other anecdotal material we gathered at this time was similar to the samples given here. We had several examples of good participation for "high" follow-through children, and several of good participation for "low" follow-through children. Our conclusion remains that factors other than oral participation in planning seem to determine follow-through.

Follow-Through and Belongingness

We had to try again in our attempts to find general class-room environmental factors that might help explain the follow-through behavior of individual children. Generally speaking, we had the impression that the children who consistently followed through on class plans were the happier, better-accepted children in their classrooms. Similarly, the children who did not follow through well were those who were less happy and less well accepted by others in the class. This impression suggested another line of thinking to us.

Was it possible, we asked ourselves, that following through on class plans was in some sense a function of the child's feeling about how well he was accepted by his classmates? If follow-through and acceptance by others were positively related, we might hope to influence follow-through by influencing the acceptance of individuals in the class. This possibility interested us. For a long time, we had noticed that children seemed to choose their friends on a somewhat superficial basis. A child might be accepted by the group simply on the basis of his athletic skills, or (especially in the primary grades) merely because he happened to have something, such as candy, that the others wanted.

Once more, we had a hypothesis: the higher the level of the child's acceptance by the group, the more likely he would be to follow through on group plans. To state it another way, the degree to which a child habitually follows through on class plans is directly related to the degree of his acceptance by others in his class.

Testing the Belongingness Hypothesis

To test this idea, we had to gather two bodies of evidence: (1) evidence of group acceptance of individuals; (2) evidence on the follow-through behavior of these individuals.

We used two means of gathering evidence on acceptance by the group—the Classroom Social Distance Scale [3] and sys-

[3] See Horace Mann–Lincoln Institute of School Experimentation, *How to Construct a Sociogram* (New York, Bureau of Publications, Teachers College, Columbia University, 1947), for a description of this scale. For fur-

tematic observation. Data from the Scale would enable us to rank children according to the degree of their acceptance by the members of their classroom group. Systematic observation was based on the following "dimensions of belongingness":

1. The nature of the child's participation in observed activities and situations.
   a. Did he offer suggestions in class in a self-depreciating manner?
   b. Did he seem to speak with a good deal of self-assurance?
   c. How did the others respond to his comments? Did they accept them? Ridicule them?
2. The nature of the child's feeling about his belongingness in situations under observation.
   a. Did he seem drawn to the situation?
   b. Did he initiate his own activity?
   c. Did he seem happy as he worked in the activity?
   d. What did he do with the result of his efforts? Destroy it? Hide it? Display it?
   e. Was this an activity he carried on frequently?
   f. Would he like to repeat it?
   g. Did he do it at odd times on his own initiative?
3. The nature of the child's acceptance by the group.
   a. Did other members of the class show any evidence that they were glad to have this child do the thing he did in the class situation?
   b. Was the activity delegated to him by other members of the group?
   c. Did the activity involve a voluntary grouping (e.g., a rearrangement of seats)? With whom did the child sit, or did he sit alone?

ther suggestions on interpreting it, see Ruth Cunningham, *et al.*, *Understanding Group Behavior of Boys and Girls* (New York, Bureau of Publications, Teachers College, Columbia University, 1951).

4. The degree of the teacher's confidence in the child's ability to succeed in the observed activity. (That is, did the teacher believe that the child was being given a task he could actually carry out?)

The idea that belongingness could be observed systematically was new to us. We had watched children "choose up" baseball teams, form committees, sit together to read, and choose companions to go home; but the fact that such choices could be recorded systematically, on a sociometric basis, was one to which we had paid little attention. When we stopped to think of it, however, it seemed obvious enough. The possibility that a child might display his feeling of acceptance or rejection by his classroom group through his responsible participation in group activity was what we were trying to explore. We planned to look for such feelings of acceptance or rejection by gathering evidence of "dimensions of belongingness."

We used the results of the administration of the Classroom Social Distance Scale, and of the observations of the "dimensions of belongingness," conducted according to the plan above, as bases for the selection of children to be observed for follow-through. Each of us now chose two children (we could observe two, and still do our regular class work): the one who was highest in group acceptance and the one who was lowest in group acceptance. We observed these two children in each of three planning situations, and paid particular attention to their follow-through on the planning done in these situations. This time we found a pronounced and consistent tendency. *In every case the child who rated high in group acceptance was also high in follow-through. In every case the child who rated low in group acceptance was also low in follow-through.*

Here, we had something we might use in our classrooms. The existence of this consistent relationship might mean that attempts to influence one of these factors would affect the other. (Moreover, we believe that the same relationship exists as between the three or four highest and the three or four lowest children, too. The reader might see whether this is true of other classes.) It was at least conceivable that if we could do things that would help a child to achieve a greater acceptance by his classroom group, he might actually follow through on group plans better. Possibly we had found a point of leverage, so to speak, toward producing better follow-through. But the apparent relationship between these two factors did not of itself mean that one caused the other. Before we could make such an inference we had to test the relationship a little further.

Further Tests for Belongingness

A further test of any cause-and-effect relationship between belongingness and follow-through was to be found in the minds of the children. We had to find ways to look at the problem through their eyes. To do this, we asked the children to interpret some of the anecdotal material we had collected about their own follow-through behavior, with the names changed and the situations slightly altered.

By presenting the children with anecdotal material of this type, and asking them to explain why the children in the anecdotes did what they did, we would obtain from the children *their* explanations of what was involved. We would obtain from the children *their* perceptions of these social situations. If the children perceived belongingness as a major factor in determining follow-through, they would be likely to mention some aspects of belongingness in order to interpret these anecdotes which have to do with poor follow-through.

Here are the anecdotes we used for this purpose:

The "Poster" Story

Each room had been asked to make a poster to advertise the flower show. Sue Ellen asked if she might make the one for her room, and the children agreed that she should make it. She collected the materials and then stopped. When a boy came from the office to pick up the poster, the children said, "Sue Ellen, where is our poster?" Sue Ellen said, "————."

The "Playground" Story

The boys and girls had talked about how important it is to help people to have pretty yards. They planned ways they could help, such as staying on the walk as they came to school and as they went home. Bert helped in the discussion, but when he went home he ran up and down the terrace where Mr. Randall had just planted new grass. When his teacher asked him why he did this, Bert said, "————."

The "Reading" Story

The group planned a free reading period, and the children had selected books they wanted to read. Sid put his book on his desk, took out his tablet, tore three or four sheets out, took his paper to the waste basket, and sharpened his pencil. He did not read. Why didn't Sid read his book?

The "Car" Story

Plans had been made to go in cars for an Easter egg hunt. Eldon had been chosen to go with Sam, but instead he ran and climbed into Boyd's car. Why did Eldon do this?

To see how the children would interpret these anecdotes, each of the ten of us involved in this study selected two children, one who was consistently low in follow-through, and one who was consistently high. First, we practiced the anecdote–interview situation among ourselves as a staff. One of us took the part of a child, the other of a teacher. The "teacher" read the anecdote, with its concluding question, to the "child." The teacher who was playing the role of the "child" responded as she felt the child might respond, and the "teacher" followed this response with additional questions. Others of us listened to this role-playing, and took our turn playing one role or the other. Following each practice interview, we commented on the "teacher's" questions and the responses they seemed to draw from the "child." What we sought was skill in asking questions that would lead a child to talk freely, without either suggesting pat answers to him, or suggesting that the teacher expected any particular answer.

Having done this, each of us selected one or two children (some of us tried it with three or four) other than those we intended eventually to interview with respect to these anecdotes, and practiced further with them. We recorded two or three of these practice interviews on tape, and played the tapes at a faculty meeting. Again we studied the apparent consequences of certain kinds of questions from the teachers. We learned to avoid some pitfalls; we learned not to ask a child what the child in the story *should* have done, or whether what he did was bad. Whenever these questions were asked in our practice sessions, the child answered moralistically, and had no more to say. All the children knew what *should* have been done. But this was not what we were after. Our purpose was to find out how children explained these situations, not to find out whether they could say the proper words about what should have been done.

We had found, while we were practicing obtaining children's interpretations of these anecdotes, that it was very difficult to conduct the interview and at the same time to keep a record of the questions and answers. As we finally worked it out, the teacher and her selected child sat together and talked, and a second teacher sat out of the way and wrote down what was said. We found various ways of making this whole procedure understandable to the children. It was easiest to explain this novel activity by saying that we were trying to find out more about some things that children often do, and that we needed help. With such an explanation, the children responded eagerly to the invitation to take part in these interviews. Some of them who were not included in the practice session later came and asked to be interviewed, and we granted such requests when they were made.

After this fairly lengthy practicing, we felt ready to use our anecdotes with the children we had selected. There were ten of us teachers in the school. Each of us tried to use all five anecdotes with each child. In a few cases, the children were absent, or there was some interruption which prevented us from using one or another of the anecdotes. Each child, then, interpreted four or five of these anecdotes, and each anecdote was interpreted by from 13 to 20 children, in a total of 88 interviews, one for each anecdote.

When we had finished these interviews, we had the records that had been kept by the recorder–teachers. These records, usually not more than a page or a page-and-a-half in length, were what we analyzed.

This is what we found:

1. Most of the children first explained the behavior of the child in the anecdote by offering some "common sense" reason for his behavior. The most common of these explanations were: the child simply did not know how to do the thing he was expected to do; he had misunderstood the plan; he was distracted by something else; he forgot. This "common sense" explanation of the behavior in question we came to call a "first level" response.

2. If the teacher was successful in getting the child to offer other explanations beyond the first-level explanation, the children suggested as a "second-level" reason *some aspect of the interpersonal relationships in the classroom* as having determined the non-follow-through behavior in the story.

We thought that this was a finding of real consequence, tending to support what we had found through a comparison of the group acceptance of our children and their follow-through as observed and rated. We concluded that the children, too, in their own way, saw personal relationships (which are central to acceptance by the group) as a major factor in determining whether or not children followed through on group plans.

To test our interpretation of the children's responses to these anecdotes, we asked three other people to interpret them, including a teacher from another school system. These people interpreted this material in the same way we had.

Here is a portion of an interview with Mary, who was in the fourth grade, and who was interpreting the "poster" story.

Mary: Oh, she'd say, "I wasn't supposed to make a picture. I forgot." She might say, "I had no time. I had to get my arithmetic." (A first-level response.)

Teacher: But she had been chosen by the group to do it in a certain time.

Mary: Maybe she didn't want to do it by herself. Maybe she wanted *her best friend* to help her. (A second-level response.)

In the balance of this interview, Mary mentioned *friends* several times, and then talked about *the other children teasing* the child in the story.

Here is another example from the "poster" story. Jim was classified by his teacher as low in follow through, and he was in the fifth grade. Jim's first-level response was that Sue Ellen didn't have the time because she was interrupted. His second-level response follows:

Teacher: She had made posters before.

Jim: Yeah. Maybe it wasn't as hard as this one looked. If she asked other kids to help her it might be they would ruin it, or they might be *someone the kids don't like to work on this poster.*

Teacher: How did the others feel when she didn't have the poster?

Jim: They felt bad and teased Sue Ellen and she got mad.

Our point here is that Jim did not fail to include something about the relationship of the children involved. Notice his comment about "someone the kids don't like" and the reference to teasing.

Here is another example of the interview material and the way we analyzed it. The teacher told the "reading" story. Sparky, who was thought of as low in follow through, was in the fourth grade.

Teacher: Why didn't Sid read his book?

Sparky: Well, I guess he didn't like to read. (A first-level response.)

Teacher: He said he wanted to read when the plans were made.

Sparky: Oh sure, he said so. But he never did intend to go through on the plans.

Teacher: Why did he say he wanted a reading period if this were true?

Sparky: That's easy. He said that so as *to make the others think he wanted to do what they wanted to do.* He just didn't like to read. (A second-level response.)

Teacher: Suppose he did like to read. What reason could there have been then?

Sparky: He didn't like the book and didn't have enough of a chance to choose another second book. Or if he did have a chance he chose the book too quickly. Didn't take enough time. (Another first-level response.)

Teacher: How did he know he didn't like the book if he didn't read any of it?

Sparky: Didn't like the title. He thought he did at first, but when he got back to his seat he decided he had made a bad choice. Then there were other things he liked to do better—draw, look out of the window. He said he would read—sure. *You have to say things like that to fool the others.* Just like a bunch of gangsters—they act like they're going to be good citizens to fool the public. Then when the time is ripe—bingo!

Teacher: You think that he wanted the other children to think he wanted to read a book?

Sparky: Sure.

We have selected responses to these two anecdotes rather than the others because the "poster" and "reading" anecdotes are less obviously connected with human relationships in the classroom than are the other anecdotes. The children's explanations of the other anecdotes all clearly imply that some aspect of human relationships operates to determine follow-through.

What We Think Our Conclusions Mean

We drew two main conclusions from our work, and a number of implications. The main conclusions have already been stated, but we will restate them here: (1) Verbal participation in the classroom planning bears little relationship to the tendency of individual children to follow through on classroom planning. (2) Follow-through on classroom planning seems to be closely related to the human relationships among the children in the classroom.

We think that the evidence we collected gives considerable support, so far as our children are concerned, to these two generalizations. The implication is clear that we, as teachers, should try deliberately to improve the human relationships in our classes, to see whether our children will follow through better. Now, we do not think that we have shown that good human relationships, of themselves, *cause* follow-through. However, the children talk as if there were some cause-and-effect relationship here, and we have found that some relationship exists, through our direct observation and our sociometrics. The next step for us is to see whether the cause-and-effect relationship which is so strongly suggested is real. We think it probably is.

That the social status of a child with his classmates is closely related to his follow-through is, in a way, obvious. But it had not been obvious to us when we began. We had been in the habit of explaining all such behavior on an individual basis—that is, through case studies of the individual children. The evidence we have summarized in this chapter has led us to add group study to child study. We are persuaded that such group phenomena as the friendship patterns in our classrooms, and the implied human relationships, probably have a perceptible effect on follow-through. So, in the last analysis, our present conclusion is this: to understand follow-through behavior, we must examine both the individual and the group of which he is a part.

How to Verify Our Findings

We cannot say whether what we found concerning our children would apply to other children. If you wish to see how it applies to yours, we suggest that you undertake the following steps:

Step 1. Observe. Look for follow-through behavior, and jot down what you see for a week or two. At the end of that time, look over your records and see whether you still think that everything that you recorded is follow-through. If you do not think that it is, select those few examples that you think do represent follow-through or lack of it, and observe again with them in mind. Repeat this process until you feel at ease in observing follow-through. (This took us only two rounds of observation of two weeks each.)

Step 2. Now observe again, and select two children (or more if you wish), one of whom is "high" and the other "low" in follow-through.

Step 3. Administer such an instrument as the Classroom Social Distance Scale to your entire class, if your class is above the third grade.

Step 4. Determine the social distance of your "high" and "low" follow-through children. (When we did this, we found that the "high" follow-through child was generally one with high group acceptance, and conversely for the "low" follow-through child.)

Step 5. Now take two or three of the anecdotes that you collected in step 1, change the children's names, and try having a number of your children explain them to you. If you wish to practice this as we did, try it out first with some children in another classroom. Remember, your object here is to get the children to talk freely. If you suggest answers, or show your disapproval of some of the answers you get, the children will stop talking freely and you will defeat your own purpose. When you have practiced until you feel confident that you are getting really free responses, ask your "high" and "low" children to explain these anecdotes. (If your results are like ours, the children will give first-level and second-level responses, and the second-level responses will tend to have to do with some aspect of classroom human relationships.)

CHAPTER 5

Independence and Initiative

THE DEVELOPMENT of independence and initiative among growing children is recognized as important by everyone who gives any thought to the matter. When two elementary school staffs [1] sought to study initiative and independence, their problem was not so much that of persuading themselves that these attitudes are important, as it was a problem of coming to some agreement about what *behavior* the words "initiative" and "independence" connote. We had to restore the tangibility of the "intangibles." That is, we first had to come to some agreement on the behavioral meaning of the "intangibles" we sought to study.

For purposes of this report, the studies of these two staffs are being reported simultaneously, although they were conducted separately. The "intangibles" studied seem to us to have a great deal in common. The teachers of the six-grade elementary school studied "initiative"; the teachers of the primary school studied "independence."

[1] The staffs of Tefft and Sunshine elementary schools carried on the activities reported here. At the time, the Sunshine school consisted of the first three grades only (149 children). The Tefft school enrollment was 285. "We" in this chapter were the members of one or the other of these staffs, and the Institute consultants.

The Values and the Implications

We think we should observe at the outset that what we were attempting to study here is deeply rooted in the beliefs of a great many people concerning the purpose of education and the nature of child development. Most people agree that the school's fundamental purpose is to contribute to the maturing of children. The ultimate goal of education is the development of a mature person, equipped with skills and attitudes suitable for a citizen in our country.

We have all heard a great deal about the nature of maturity. We are quite persuaded by the arguments of those who suggest that maturity is largely a matter of increasingly taking to oneself the initiative for solving one's own problems. In this sense, and especially if the word "problems" is thought of in the large, a mature person is one who shows initiative: he is often described as one who has a high degree of personal independence and emotional security. Children ordinarily depend heavily upon their parents for their own emotional stability. As they progress through childhood, they become more independent of their parents, but they depend more and more heavily upon the approval of their playmates and other children for their personal security. Maturity consists, in a measure, of achieving a balance between independence and the necessary dependence upon others. A mature person, from this point of view, is one who has successfully achieved interdependence with his fellows, without losing his individuality. In this sense, some grown-ups are far more mature than others.

This aspect of maturity, which is concerned with dependence, interdependence, and initiative, was on our minds as we began our study. We wished to make an appropriate, and reasonable, and right contribution to the growing independence of the children who were in our care. We had seen the children doing things which suggested to us that they were not taking initiative at some times when we thought they could and should. We had seen them doing things that suggested an overdependence upon us as teachers. These were the kinds of thing we had in mind:

A second grade child, who had to use the public bus to ride home from school each day, frequently became distracted by other things, and missed his bus. He reproached the teacher for having failed to remind him that he had to catch the bus, in spite of the fact that he had twenty minutes after the end of the school day before the bus came by. The teacher thought that he should not have to depend on her to remember the bus, especially since it was an everyday affair.

Some of us in the primary school had the impression that first, second, and third grade children were asking us questions about their school work which they should have been able to answer for themselves. When we gave them a degree of freedom to carry on their own work in class, most of the children seemed to thrive on it. Some, however, seemed to us to be at a loss, and to depend constantly on us to tell them what to do.[2]

As an elementary school staff (this was the staff of the six-grade school) we frankly did not know how much initiative to expect of our children. If we didn't expect enough, they would not grow. If we expected too much, they would be bewildered. How could we find out how much initiative children ought to be

[2] It should be observed again that our interpretation of these and similar anecdotes was intended to help us understand whether any general controllable aspects of the school environment were contributing to this kind of behavior in many children. Anyone trained in child study will see in these anecdotes, and many others we collected, symptoms of difficulties we have not reported. In this case, the child's failure to catch the bus might have been symptomatic of his unwillingness to go home, for example. Unwillingness to go home, in a six- or seven-year old, might be the result of something quite seriously wrong in the child's life—something, perhaps, that a teacher and parent should work on. We are not ignoring such important possibilities as we study our children's social attitudes, but we have chosen in this report to concentrate on general environmental considerations—such as the ways a teacher handles children's questions—rather than on the problems of deepening our understanding of individual children. Our broad assumption is that in the degree that we make the general school environment better for all children, the difficulties of children will be lessened. This is not an either–or affair. It is a both–and affair. We must study *both* individuals *and* how to make our general school environment as good as we know how.

expected to have? We constantly attempted to offer the children practical problems to solve, on the assumption that by solving such problems they would grow in self-confidence and in initiative. How wide open should we leave these problems? How much of the analysis of these problems (into the details that required action) should we do for the children? How much analysis should we explicitly help the children to make? How much should we leave for the children to make on their own?

These impressions and sources of concern had been on our minds for quite a long while. They all related in one way or another to the problem of freedom and authority in the classroom. We wished the children to have as much freedom as they could handle, on the assumption that disciplined behavior is largely a matter of handling freedom wisely, and that one must practice this art if one is to learn it. Our experience indicated that this was a valid assumption. However, we wished to know far more about it in detail. There were children for whom this kind of treatment seemed to be inappropriate. What could we do to help these children grow up?

From our point of view, this whole matter had serious implications. If we left our children dependent upon us with respect to matters which they should have been able to handle for themselves, what would happen to these children when we were no longer available to tell them what to do? How would they handle themselves later in the somewhat less closely supervised activities of the secondary school? If they did not learn how to handle themselves, would they not tend to accept the leadership of anybody who seemed dominating? As adults, would not these children be fair prey to any demagogue who came along? We thought we had here, in small, a problem fundamental to the maintenance of our political liberty. In the unknown world that lay ahead of our children, many people would attempt to capture their minds. In the degree that we could help them become independent, we would be contributing our share to the future independ-

ence and maintenance of liberty of the people of America.
We said these things to one another, and although we did
not always think in such broad terms, none of us thought
that we had gone beyond the plain truth in the discussion
that led to this serious conclusion. We were convinced that
we were dealing at this point with the very vitals of education in our society. We sought to insure that the children
who had gone to school under our care would themselves be
the makers of their society, and that they would not be the
easy captives of any shouting would-be dictator or conniving
revolutionist. We hoped in the elementary school to lay the
foundation for a reasonable and tough-minded approach to
the problems of living which would lead our children to have
the courage of their convictions. We wanted them to be sufficiently independent to think for themselves, to resist pres-
sures, and to stick firmly to what is right. We were sure that
in making this our aim we were supporting all that is best
and most important in our American tradition.

Independence

When those of us in the primary school sought to give behavioral definition to "independence," we acted on the comment of one of us that the children were "always asking us
questions that they ought to be able to answer for themselves." This suggested that the questions the children asked
were an indication of their dependence on teachers. If we
studied their questions, we might learn something of significance about their independence.

CHILDREN'S QUESTIONS

Accordingly, we arranged to pair ourselves off, each member of the pair observing the other's class for five periods of
one hour each. The observing teacher recorded all the questions the children addressed to the class teacher during

these periods of observation. The questions the children asked were then brought together, categorized, and tabulated according to the number of questions in each category. These were the categories we developed:

1. Permission to carry out decision already made by child. (May I finish my paper cutting after lunch?)
2. Information. (Where is Panama?)
3. Help in carrying out a decision already made by the child. (Will you help me with my problem?)
4. Request to make decision for the child. (Is that too little?)
5. Verification of a decision that a child had made. (The turtle's back is round, isn't it?)
6. Approval. (Is that a good picture?)
7. Personal curiosity. (Mrs. B., what are you here for?)
8. Attention. (Me?)

If the children actually were depending on us to make too many decisions for them, or were otherwise overdependent on us for their security, most of their questions would fall in categories 4, 6, and 8 (request for teacher to make a decision for a child, request for approval, request for attention).

We analyzed 293 questions. Shown below is the number of questions asked for each category.

1. Permission	30
2. Information	74
3. Help in carrying out decisions	63
4. Make a decision for the child	43
5. Verification	42
6. Approval	9
7. Curiosity	10
8. Attention	14

When we looked at this tabulation and noticed that the largest number of children's questions fell in categories 2 and 3, which had to do with information and help, we thought that our original hypothesis had been based on an underestimation of the children. True, there were forty-three questions in category 4, but categories 6 and 8 (approval and attention) had very few entries. The ten questions that fell in category 7, we thought, were simply the product of the fact that observing teachers were present, writing down these questions. Accordingly, we concluded as follows: *Most of the children's questions have to do with permission, information, or help in connection with carrying out decisions that the children have already made.* The children were already exercising considerably more general independence than we had assumed. They were already carrying on intelligent, self-directed activity. What they wanted from the teacher, basically, was either help or permission to go ahead. The great majority of these questions were neither requests that the teacher make a decision for the child concerning what he should do, nor requests for approval or attention.

This study of the children's questions led us to shift our attention from overdependence to the problem of giving the children still more opportunities to make decisions for themselves. We had underestimated the children's independence in the first place. What they really needed was more opportunity to exercise the independence they already had.

We turned, therefore, to a study of what actions of ours might have a discernible effect on the independence of the children. We decided to analyze the way the teacher might deal with these questions. We thought that if the teacher responded to these questions in such a way as to give the child the help he wanted, his independence would be fostered, yet the teacher would have given him the guidance that he really needed.

TEACHERS' RESPONSES AND CHILDREN'S ENSUING BEHAVIOR

To study our own responses to children's questions, we repeated our observational pattern (that is, we paired off, each member of the pair observing the other's class); but this time our records included two items instead of one. The two items were: the teacher's response to the child's question, and the child's response to the teacher's response. We were looking at the second and third items in a series of three behaviors. The first behavior we had already studied: the child's question. Each of the four of us recorded nine observations. When we had gathered our records together, once more we categorized both the teacher's action and the child's response.[3]

The categories that were developed for *teachers' responses* to children's questions are as follows:

1. Discuss the purpose and reason. (Answer the question, "Why?")
2. Point to the problem.

[3] *A Note on Categorizing.* The way to categorize such unstructured, open material was something that we had to work out. Essentially, what we did was to take all of the material we had gathered, place it before us, and simply go down the list of observations in the order in which they happened to appear, until we found two or three items that seemed to be so similar that they belonged in a category. We considered this as a trial category, wrote down whatever name for it seemed to make the best sense to us at the moment, and continued in the development of other trial categories. When we had gone through all of the records, we often found we had developed four or five categories which themselves could be grouped together without doing violence to the material being categorized. We then took these trial categories, set them up on sheets of paper, re-examined the anecdotal material, entering tallies underneath each of the categories to show how many of the anecdotes or observations we had collected would fit in each category.

We then tested our tentative categories by asking other people to take the same material and categorize it according to our tentative categories. In our study of children's questions, this testing of categories was carried on by two of our Horace Mann–Lincoln Institute consultants, each of whom categorized the material independent of the other, and then compared the tabulations. The tabulation which we reported on page 108 represents an agreement reached after discussion among the two Institute consultants and the school staff concerning how the material should be categorized. The agreement was reached only after the material had been categorized three times, independently. In the case of the study of teacher's responses to children's questions, the material was categorized independently by our two Institute consultants. In this case, the school staff could not participate because the school year was coming to an end.

3. Point to the purpose.
4. Point to the consequence.
5. Indicate the factors involved.
6. Ask the child (or children) to indicate the factors involved.
7. Give suggestions.
8. Ask the child (or children) to give suggestions.
9. Set the physical stage.
10. Ask provocative questions.
11. Offer alternatives.

We found the following categories of *children's ensuing behavior:*

1. Independent.
2. Agreeing with the adult.
3. Agreeing with other children.
4. Group consensus.

We wished to discover whether any relationships existed between what the teacher did and the kind of response the child made. The child's response that was most desirable, from our point of view, was what we called "independent" (category 1 above). The category that would represent greater dependence upon us as teachers was number 2 ("agreeing with adult"). Category 4, "group consensus," was a desirable behavior for other reasons. Acting on the consensus achieved by a group is a form of independence of the teacher; the development of the skill of acting on group consensus is an important one in any social situation. Action on group consensus is a desirable form of interdependence. Category 3, "agreeing with other children," was a form of dependence. As we thought of our earlier description of maturity, we thought that the first and fourth categories were the most mature responses, and that the second and third categories were somewhat less mature.

We do not think that these types of responses should be thought of as good or bad. There obviously are situations in which what we call a "dependent" response is the best one. However, what we were paying attention to at this time was the possibility that we could, through our responses to children's questions, encourage whatever independence the children could handle. The broad purpose of this study was to learn more about what kinds and degrees of freedom the children could handle in the classroom. This study of our responses to their questions, and of their ensuing behavior, was an aspect of this broad problem.

The 46 responses of the children to our answers to their questions are tabulated in Table 1.

TABLE 1

First, Second, and Third Graders' Responses to Teacher-Answers
to Their Questions

	CHILD'S RESPONSE TO TEACHER'S RESPONSE			
Teacher's Response to Child's Question	Independent	Agreeing with the adult	Agreeing with other children	Group consensus
1. Discuss the purpose and reason (Answer the question, "Why?")	1	1	1	1
2. Point to the problem	5	1	1	4
3. Point to the purpose	1	1	0	1
4. Point to the consequence	0	0	0	0
5. Indicate factors involved	3	4	1	2
6. Ask the child (or children) to indicate the factors involved	2	0	0	1
7. Give suggestions	1	0	0	0
8. Ask the child (or children) to give suggestions	3	0	1	0
9. Set the physical stage	1	0	0	0
10. Ask provocative questions	5	1	1	0
11. Offer alternatives	1	1	0	0
Total	23	9	5	9

When we looked at this analysis, we paid particular attention to our first category, "Independent." What kinds of responses to the children's questions led to independent behavior by the children who had asked the questions? Our analysis indicated to us that when the teacher responded by indicating the central problem involved in the question (category 2), when she asked the child or children to give suggestions (category 8), and when she asked provocative questions (category 9), the children tended to behave in a more independent manner than when she responded with comments represented by our other categories.

—provocative questions

The category "provocative questions" was one that interested us considerably. Here are some examples of provocative questions by the teachers that led to independent behavior by the children.

Child asks, "Where is the paper cutter?" Teacher answers (taking care that the expression on her face indicates that she does not mean a rebuff), "Isn't the paper cutter where it usually is?" Child goes to investigate (his investigation is independent).

Child asks, "Where is Panama?" Teacher answers, "How can we find out?"

"May I draw this picture in the morning?" Teacher: "What else do you have to do tomorrow morning? Have you time?"

The purpose of the provocative question, we thought, was to provoke a child to solve his problem for himself. However, there are two serious risks in the use of provocative questions in class. One is that answering one question with another can be construed by a child as a rebuff to his question. However, we thought that the frequent assurances of high esteem that experienced teachers offer children should be satisfactory protection against this kind of risk. The twinkle in the eye, the smile, the careful avoidance of ridicule, the quick offer to help if the child seems hesitant, frequent assurances that the questions are valued by the teacher, and the like—all of these were ways that we used to make certain that the children did not feel rebuffed if we answered their questions with a question that put them back on their own.

The other risk that accompanies answering with a provocative question is that we may miss the child's purpose. If the child who asks, "Where is Panama?" merely wants to use his answer to crush another child who was asserting that Panama was in the Arctic, the teacher's provocative "How can we find out?" might simply be annoying. The child's real purpose was to get a quick rejoinder to his neighbor, not to know where Panama is. To guard against this kind of possibility—that is, that of missing the child's actual purpose by giving him knowledge or provoking action that he doesn't want—we had to make certain we knew why the question was asked. We would ask, "Why do you want to know?" and if the child's purpose is simply to crush some other child with a fact, he is likely to show this purpose by this rejoinder: "Well, Jeanie says that Panama is near Alaska, and I know she is wrong but I can't prove it."

There is one kind of question for which we are quite certain that a provocative question from the teacher is usually inappropriate. This is the child's question, "Is my picture any good?" We think this ought always to be treated as a crisis question. A child's picture, especially when it is the freely expressed product of his own imagination, is very much a part of himself. There are few objective things in the world with which a child so thoroughly identifies himself as with a picture he has made. When he asks the teacher, "Is the picture any good?" he has laid himself open to deep hurt. We were very sure that under these circumstances the teacher should neither answer "yes" or "no" nor answer with a provocative question unless she is prepared to follow it up with a fairly lengthy discussion. If the child doesn't already know whether his picture is "good" or not then the problem lies in his lack of means of knowing, not in anything objective about the picture. The teacher's task, under these circumstances, is to help the child in the immensely important process of developing means of self-evaluation. For it is precisely evaluation of himself that the child is asking for. (Many a child's artistic impulses have been crushed beyond revival by the teacher's evaluation of his artistic product—even when the evaluation is an approving one. Too often, children have failed to progress beyond a rudimentary skill in art work because the teacher has evaluated in too indiscriminate a manner the first explorations of the budding artist.) The provocative question, of course, is "How can you tell whether a picture is good?" However, the answer to this provocative question is not one that the child who asks the question in the first place can work out for himself. Unless the teacher is prepared to take the time that is necessary to help the child develop a way of evaluating his own work, then and there, the question should not be answered at all, but deferred to a specific time when she and the child can work together on this exceedingly significant problem. Probably, under most classroom conditions, the best answer to this question is "I like to look at your art work [a little reassurance is offered]. Can we talk about it at [teacher names a time when she is free to talk for at least ten minutes with child alone]."

—point to problem

The other responses to the children's questions, we thought, were somewhat less complicated than the response called "provocative questions." Our category "point to problem" included typically, "I think you have to pay attention to . . . to answer that question." For example, one child's question was, "Wouldn't we need seventeen nickels?" Teacher: "I think we have to decide how much we want to buy first."

—ask children for suggestions

The category called "ask the child for suggestions" is relatively easy to use. For example, one of the children asked,

"Can we keep care of the seed or do we have to decide in committee?" Teacher: "Jerry has asked an interesting question. Does anybody have any suggestions?"

We have discussed three of the teacher-responses that led most frequently to independent action by our young children. Now let us give examples of children's questions and teachers' responses for each of our eleven categories of teacher-responses.

Category 1 (discuss purpose and reason). Child: "Shall I put a big letter on the poster?" Teacher: "We were trying to make a poster big enough so that you could see it from the door."

Category 2 (point to problem). Child: "Wouldn't we need seventeen nickels?" Teacher: "I think we have to decide how much we want to buy first."

Category 3 (point to purpose). Child: "Do you think my pencil is sharp enough?" Teacher: "It has to be very sharp if we are going to make fine lines, doesn't it?"

Category 4 (point to consequence). Child: "Is that too high for the stem of the flower?" Teacher: "If you make it that long will you have room to draw the flower on top?"

Category 5 (indicate factors involved). Child: "Wouldn't we need seventeen nickels?" Teacher: "To decide that, we'd have to think of how many children there are, how much we want to buy, and whether we want any to be left over."

Category 6 (ask the children to indicate the factors involved). Child: "I don't know what to write." Teacher: "What was it we said we were going to write about?"

Category 7 (give suggestions). Child: "I don't know what to write." Teacher: "Well, you might write about. . . ."

Category 8 (ask children to give suggestions). "Can we keep care of the seed or do we have to decide in committee?" Teacher: "Jerry has asked an interesting question. Does anybody have any suggestions?"

Category 9 (set the physical stage). Child: "We should announce about the stamps, shouldn't we?" Teacher: "I have the chart here that the children need to see."

Category 10 (provocative questions). Child: "Where is the

paper cutter?" Teacher: "Isn't the paper cutter where it usually is?"

Category 11 (offer alternatives). Child: "Would I have time to make something with clay?" Teacher: "You could do that, or you could straighten your desk, or you could take another look at the list of spelling words we worked out yesterday."

SOME IMPLICATIONS

This analysis suggests strongly that our responses to children's questions function as one important control on what the children do. Of course, control in the classroom is a function of the whole classroom situation, not simply the product of the direct words the teacher uses. For example, in one of our observations, the teacher said, "Boys and girls, it is time to go outside. What could those who haven't finished their cards do?" The children put away their cards and left. The time to play and the need to finish their cards were aspects of the total situation. These elements of the situation had fully as much to do with what the children did as did the words the teacher happened to use.

Moreover, direct control by the teacher is necessary for good learning in some situations. While a second grade was working, several first grade children moved around the room while waiting for their bus. The teacher said, "Will the people who are waiting for their bus sit down quietly? Get a book or something you want to be doing, but sit down quietly." The first grade children had to be quiet if the second grade children were to finish their work. Also, the teacher's direct control reminded these first graders that there are ways of keeping themselves busy doing something constructive when there is time to fill.

However, there is a kind of teacher control that gives children an opportunity to develop the social attitude that we call "independence." This kind of teacher control is not offered when the teacher remains in direct control of what the children do. In spite of the fact that direct control is often necessary, we sought every opportunity we could find to place the children on their own. We had found that when we responded to children's questions by asking them to make suggestions, by asking provocative questions, by indicating the factors involved, and by pointing to the problem, then we led the children to be self-directive (independent) in their own problem-solving activities. *We had found that the interaction between ourselves and our children was a powerful force in helping our children to be self-governing individuals, at least so far as classroom behavior is concerned.*

Initiative

The eight of us who taught in the six-grade school studied initiative. The discussions that led us to this study are, we think, of some interest. We shall sketch our line of reasoning very briefly here.

We had first said that we wished to study responsibility. For two years before we began this work, we had been trying a form of student government in our school, with a council made up of elected representatives from each classroom, and council officers elected by the student body. We had found (as many an elementary staff has found) that the council idea was essentially sound. It was unquestionably a valuable experience for the children who were members of the council. The problems arising from a representative system, while not always fully understood by all the children, nevertheless had been fruitful sources of significant learning about self-government in general and representative self-government in particular. Furthermore, the student council served to keep us teachers aware of school problems we might otherwise have overlooked. The council served quite well as a means of bringing about increased unity within the school, and a feeling of school pride.

However, good as it was, the council plan did run into

some difficulties. One of the difficulties arose from what we teachers called irresponsibility. Generally, decisions made in the council went into effect rather easily. However, as might have been expected, decisions were too often not carried out properly by those who were supposed to carry them out. Sometimes children in whose names the decisions were made, and who were responsible for their execution, apparently had not accepted the responsibility.

This whole matter of giving and accepting responsibility was one we talked about at some length. We heard about the study of follow-through (reported elsewhere in this book) and thought that the staff working on that topic might well be of help to us.

And so they were. Their study suggests to us that we look to see whether even the members of the council all accepted the responsibility implied by their own planning—that is, whether among the members of the council themselves, "follow-through" is a function of personal relationships. Perhaps we should pay more attention to the personal relationships developed in our school council.

However, we did not wish to duplicate their study, which was just beginning. We sought instead to find some examples of responsibility which were central to its meaning in our school.

When we looked at the many examples we collected, we found that they had one thing in common. In each case, the child had either taken initiative, or had failed to take initiative, for carrying out some job. The more we talked about it, the more we tended to use the term "initiative" to describe the behavior we were really looking at. Initiative, we said to ourselves, is certainly an important aspect of responsibility. The behaviors we actually found seemed to us to have more to do with what we called initiative than they did with the larger concept that we called responsibility. Why not, we said to ourselves, agree to study initiative? Such a study would have the advantage of being in fairly clear focus, and since, in our view, taking initiative was central to taking responsibility, by studying the one we might learn much more about the other. Accordingly, we decided to study initiative.

How much initiative?

We wished to encourage the children to take initiative in solving their purely personal problems, as well as in applying the school rules and in applying decisions made in their classrooms and in the school council. How much initiative of this kind should we expect of the children? How wide open should we leave classroom planning? Should we as teachers see to it that classroom planning is continued until the details of action involved were all worked out and assigned? Or would this be undesirable? Would we be thinking for the children in a field in which they should be learning to think for themselves? We assumed that children grew in initiative as they grew in other ways. What did this growth consist of? Were there real differences in initiative between first graders and sixth graders? If so, what were these differences?

We study initiative

It seemed very probable to us that children *grow* in initiative. We first sought some means of describing this growth in a way that would make it easier for us to be realistic in our own expectations of the children. To look into this matter, we adopted a design for our work which we shall report now. The results of our work were rather surprising to us.

We defined initiative as action a child committed on his own volition, with no apparent prompting by anyone else. For our purposes, a child was showing initiative whenever he did something on his own. This meant that much of the ordinary trivia of living fell within our definition, and we had to rule out of our observations such behavior as scratching one's nose and picking up a piece of paper. In order to avoid being distracted by these, we attempted an analysis that would name those aspects of initiative that in our opinion would probably develop as children grew older. We hoped, by observing initiative with this analysis in mind, to locate aspects of initiative that actually grew, and thus to achieve a somewhat better understanding of what initiative we ought to expect of our children.

Our analysis suggested to us the following five categories, which we presumed were developmental aspects of "initiatory" behavior:

1. *Consequences.* Was the self-initiated behavior apparently directed toward consequences of value only to the person himself, or did it also include in its consequences something affecting another person (or group of persons)? We thought six-year-old children would show little, if any, behavior involving consequences to large groups, six-year-olds being more self-centered and lacking much experience with large groups.

2. *The number of people involved.* How many people were involved in the observed behavior? One, two, thirty, five hundred? We thought that as children grew older, they would involve more and more people in behavior resulting from their own initiative.

3. *Complexity.* How complex was the behavior itself? How many steps did the child have to complete to carry out his intention? Was it possible that as children grew older, the behavior they initiated became more complicated in the sense that there were more steps involved in it?

4. *Content* (concrete–abstract). Did the observed behavior tend to deal more with things, or with ideas? Our guess was that as children grew older they were more prone to deal on their own with ideas. When they were younger we thought that they tended to devote their attention more to tangible, concrete things.

5. *Time involved.* How long did it take for the behavior to be carried through? A few minutes? Several days? Our guess was that little children would not undertake behavior with consequences deferred for very long. We assumed that older children would initiate behaviors taking a longer time to carry through.

THE DESIGN OF OUR STUDY

In order that we not be misunderstood, it is necessary that we explain rather carefully the way we gathered evidence concerning these categories. A thoroughgoing test of the various hypotheses we had expressed would have required that we gather examples of all the initiative that took place within our classes for a long enough time to give us a fair sample of the actual initiative being shown. Or, we might have taken one of these categories and kept records of all of the behaviors in a given length of time that fell within it. We did neither of these things, not because we doubted that they would test our ideas, but because they would have interfered with our teaching.

Specifically, the prediction we actually tested was this: that with a week's observation the most extreme examples of each category we could find in each of the grades would differ according to the grade in which the observation was made. Thus we expected to find that the largest number of people involved in self-initiated activity by a first grader would be smaller than would the largest number of people involved in a self-initiated activity by a sixth grader. What we are reporting here, in each category, are two behaviors at either end of an assumed continuum. We are reporting, for example, under the category "time involved," the self-initiated behavior that took the *shortest* time that we saw in a week, and the self-initiated behavior that took the *longest* time to carry out, for each grade. The test of our hypothesis (that as children grow older they will undertake self-initiated behavior of longer duration) would come when we compared the longest behavior seen in the first and sixth grades, during the week of observation.

Our findings, then, would have to do, *not* with what we ought to expect of *all* our children, but with what potentialities certain children have. If, in our category "complexity," we found individuals in the first grade doing things as complex as anything we saw undertaken in the sixth grade, the implication would be that in our first grade classes we could act on the assumption that at least some of the children could initiate quite complicated behavior. If, on the other hand, the most complicated behavior we saw in a week in the first grade contained far fewer steps than the most complicated behavior we saw in a week in the sixth grade, then our original hypothesis would be supported in some degree—that is, that we ought expect less complicated behavior even from our exceptional first grade children than from older children. We were carrying on here a study of exceptional behavior. We wanted to find what the ends of the range looked like, in each category. We did not, in this study, try to find out what lay between these ends.

Our plan of study

At this point in our work a plan for the study began to appear. We put this plan on paper and agreed to its feasibility. This was the plan:

Step 1. Set up some categories of self-initiated action. (We had already done this.)

Step 2. Make a "trial run" of observations of our children to see if the categories were descriptive of the actual behavior of our children.

Step 3. Clarify (by comparing and discussing observations) each teacher's judgment concerning specific behaviors observed in this "trial run," so that the entire staff would arrive at a common interpretation of these behaviors.

Step 4. Collect from our 285 pupils many examples of self-initiated action in anecdotal form.

Step 5. Analyze anecdotal records and categorize them according to categories set up in step 1 above.

Step 6. Draw conclusions concerning the accuracy of our predictions.

Step 7. In the light of our conclusions, state implications for improved classroom procedures.

THE PLAN AT WORK

Since the categories were already set up (and step 1 was already taken) before the total pattern for the study emerged, we were ready to go to work on step 2 of the plan, that is, to make a trial run. Each of the eight teachers made a record of five behaviors which reflected the kind of action we were agreed was self-initiated. Using these records as samples, we categorized them (step 3). The records of behavior we had collected seemed to fit into the categories and to describe the aspects of initiative we had named in the categories.

For example: At one end of the "complexity" scale was the one-step behavior of the eight-year-old who pulled off the calendar sheet, while at the other end of the scale was the seven-step behavior of the eight-year-old who cleaned the locker and table.

Moving to step 4, we collected about two hundred examples of self-initiated action. These observations were made at two different times. The first collection was made between nine and ten o'clock each morning for one week. Eight of us did this. This hour was chosen chiefly because the same kinds of planning and activity were likely to be going on in all the classes: caring for personal needs and property, taking lunch and stamp orders, making the day's plans, talking about solving group problems. Assigning ourselves a specific time had the effect, too, of reminding us of our commitment. None of us forgot to do it.

Our second collection of observations was made at various times chosen at random during the school day, but during the same week as the first. This meant that the kinds of activities observed would not be limited in any way, and the evidence collected would not be arbitrarily restricted.

We were ready for step 5. After the evidence was collected we categorized the observations for each age group.

LIMITS OF OUR STUDY

This study has certain limits beyond which our conclusions do not go.

First, the children involved. Our school enrollment was approximately 285 children, between six and twelve. We do not know in what way these children are representative of children elsewhere. They are, however, representative of the children we have had in our school, and of the children we are likely to have in the future.

Second, the number of observations recorded for this study. Our conclusions are based on approximately 200 anecdotes. We do not assume that another 200 would necessarily give identical results.

Third, the behaviors reported for each category. We have not described the whole range, only the extremes. Thus, in the category "time involved," we are reporting the range as being from two minutes to seven days for the six-year-olds we observed. We are not reporting the behaviors that took thirty minutes, twenty-four hours, two days, or five days.

Fourth, no attempt was made to tabulate the frequency of similar behaviors. Thus, we do not report what behavior is typical of a particular age group.

Fifth, the categorizing of behaviors here rests on the pooled judgment of nine people including the principal, all experienced teachers.

OUR CONCLUSIONS

Within these limits, we are confident of the conclusions we have drawn from the observation reported below. We are reporting observations for each category.

Consequences. We found instances in every classroom of initiative clearly intended to have consequences for the entire classroom group. We could make no distinction here according to the grade membership of the child observed.

Number Involved. For the first and second grades, the largest number of people involved in the self-initiated behavior we observed was 30 (the whole class); for the third and fourth grades, 35 (the whole class); for the fifth grade, 268 (several classes); for the sixth grade, 60 (school stamp order).

There was a slight tendency here for the older children observed to undertake activities that required the participation of several classes. However, we saw examples in every grade of children initiating activities that required the participation of their whole class for their completion.

Complexity. For the first and second grades, the range in number of steps required to complete self-initiated activities was 1–5; for grade three, 1–7; for grade four, 1–6; for grade five, 2–5; for grade six, 2–4. There was no consistency here. The most complicated behavior observed in a week in grade six had fewer steps than the most complicated behavior seen in grade one.

Content. We found examples of both "concrete" and "abstract" behavior (behavior involving manipulation of concrete objects, as contrasted with behavior involving non-concrete data) in every grade except grade three, in which all observed initiative dealt with concrete objects.

Time Involved. The time required to complete various self-initiated activities ranged as follows for the grades indicated:

Grade 1	2 minutes to 7 days
Grade 2	10 minutes to 3 days
Grade 3	30 minutes to 1 day
Grade 4	5 seconds to 7 days
Grade 5	5 minutes to 30 days
Grade 6	2 minutes to 1 day

The greatest length of time required to complete an act initiated by the child himself fell in grade five (30 days). There was no pattern here. The length of time involved was not related to grade level.

An examination of the data given just above will suggest our basic conclusion immediately. What we found was that *no aspects of initiative as we categorized them were closely associated with age or grade level.* We conclude, therefore, that so far as the upper limits of these ranges are concerned, there is no important difference in the initiative we saw. The six-year-old, as well as the eleven-year-old, was acting with reference to large groups. Children in every class were carrying on activities extending over several days. Some children of each age were engaged in acts that involved many steps for their completion. We could find no single consistent trend, for any of the six categories which we examined, that was closely related to the age of the children.

We do not conclude that age and initiative bear no relationship to each other, however. It is possible that, had we recorded all of the self-initiated behavior in these classes according to these categories, some gross trends would have been apparent which we have not reported. Also, we might have found such a relationship if we had used other categories of initiative.

SOME IMPLICATIONS

The fact that we found some first grade and second grade children doing things on their own initiative that took as long, involved as many people, were as complex, and so on, as anything we saw in the upper grades, does lead us to reconsider what we ought to provide for in the first and second grades.

The chief implication of our findings for classroom experimentation, we think, is this: many opportunities should be provided for children of all ages (including six- and seven-year-old children) to initiate activities which will (a) involve groups as large as their whole class, (b) deal with abstract ideas as well as concrete objects, (c) extend over several days, (d) require six or seven steps for completion.

This means that, at least for some of our younger children, we could well afford to raise the level of our expectations. It means that we must provide for a far broader range of individual differences than we have been used to thinking of, especially in the lower grades.

The fact that we did not find pronounced differences between the lower grades and the upper grades may mean that we have not been offering opportunities to children in the upper grades to behave in ways that are as complicated, lengthy, and intellectually challenging as they can handle.

This study caused us to give renewed attention to the exceptional child. We think we may have been underestimating his potential for initiative all along the line. We intend undertaking further study of these exceptional children.

We think, moreover, that the amount of initiative that the children show is probably related to classroom climate. We believe that children have to be relatively free to try things out, and that they have to be quite sure of the teacher's basic support of them, before they will initiate anything of importance in class.

How to Verify Our Findings

The basic material we gathered was all anecdotal. To compare your children with ours, you could follow this plan:

First. Practice observing initiative in your class for a while. Practice looking at your class for a half-hour a day, jotting down examples of this kind of behavior as you see them. When you have gathered ten or fifteen examples of this type, talk them over with a fellow teacher and see whether you and your fellow teachers are in agreement that your observations are examples of initiative. (In our case, this practice period took a total of two hours of observation and two hours of discussion.)

Second. Record as many examples of initiative as you can at a regular time each day for one week. Do not make your recordings lengthy. We found that we seldom had to write more than thirty words to describe adequately the behavior we wished to record.

Third. When you have gathered about twenty such examples, put them together and look them over. (If you can find a friend to do this with you, it will be more interesting and more thought-provoking. In our case this was done by the entire school staff, working first in pairs, then as a whole group.) See whether you can categorize the examples of initiative that you have seen.

Fourth. Draw some conclusions. What do your observations suggest to you? In our case, we found no connection between grade level and incidence of initiation at various levels of length, complexity, and the like. Do you find any surprises in your own class with respect to the amount of initiative that some of the children show? Do your observations suggest that they show initiative at certain times rather than others? (We found very few examples of pupil initiative during reading and arithmetic periods, for example.) Does your anecdotal material suggest anything about how initiative may be encouraged in school?

If you do follow this plan, or one of your own that extends our ideas, we should like very much to hear what results you obtain.

CHAPTER **6**

Considerateness and Aggression

THE ROMANTIC notion of childhood, that children enter the world "trailing clouds of glory," that the innocence of children is equivalent to virtue, beguiles many people. Indeed, it is rooted deep in our culture. The idea that sweetness, kindness, or considerateness must be *learned* by children is hard to accept—unless one deals with children constantly! Even then, the idea that children are often inconsiderate, unkind, even cruel to one another is distressing. But it is so.

Some of us in Springfield, having been distressed by inconsiderateness among children and high school youth, sought ways of studying the matter.[1]

[1] The staff of the York Elementary School (11 teachers, 346 children), and varying groups from the staff of Springfield Senior High School (between 10 and 35 teachers, out of a total staff of approximately 70) were involved in the activities reported in this chapter. The "we" of this chapter refers to members of these staffs, and the three Institute consultants, who worked with the school staffs at different times.

The material that follows was gathered chiefly in the elementary school. We shall report only a small part of the work done in the high school, because circumstances made it impossible for us to bring more than a small portion of our work there to the kind of fruition that would make a report possible.

130

What Is Considerateness?

Like the other staffs in Springfield, we first defined our "intangible," which we called "considerateness," through observing and recording behavior that seemed to us considerate or inconsiderate. Accordingly, both in the elementary school and in the high school, we gathered examples of these kinds of behavior. Here are some examples of considerate and inconsiderate behavior from the elementary school.

GRADE 1

Considerate
Anna helped erase errors on a note that Freddy was trying to write to his mother. (Freddy's eraser is badly worn and makes dirty marks. Anna has a new eraser.)

Inconsiderate
Jackie put his foot to one side to keep Karen from sitting by him.

GRADE 3

Considerate
Rosalind offered to count change in the classroom for Wanda, who could not make change.

Inconsiderate
Merle knocked Robert's coat off the hook in the cloakroom so that he could hang his own on the hook.

GRADE 5

Considerate
Sue helped a new girl with her lunch order.

Inconsiderate
In front of the other children, Buddy said he wished Jimmy were not on his ball team. He said Jimmy was lazy and made an out every time. This happened on the playground.

GRADE 6

Considerate
Jerry requested that the pitcher slow down the fast ball when it was a timid new boy's turn at the bat.

Inconsiderate
Larry tried to make Frank lose a ball game by fumbling purposely.

In the high school, similar observations were gathered. One reported by an eleventh grade teacher will be given here, because it was thought-provoking:

I entered the school at eight o'clock in the morning. Albert, a tall sixteen-year-old, ran toward me from the other end of the long school corridor. He must have run seventy-five feet, bearing down on me like a locomotive. He skidded to a stop, a foot from my nose, raised his hand, said, "Hi!" and then vanished before I could say anything. He knew that this was against the school rules; he scared the wits out of me. This was grossly inconsiderate, and I think he meant it to be.

When we talked about Albert's running down the hall, two of us who knew Albert disagreed sharply about the meaning of this incident. The one who had reported the incident was convinced that Albert's behavior was inconsiderate, though in some ways laughable. The other, who also knew Albert quite well, said, "I don't think he meant to be inconsiderate. I don't think he knew that he was frightening you. I think that boy has to be taken at his word. When he says, 'Hi,' that's all he means. I really believe that all he meant to do was to say hello. I suspect that he darted out of the hall when he saw the expression on your face."

We went on talking. Someone else gave this account of Albert: "Albert really seems to me to have a friendly attitude toward everybody. He's a good deal like a setter pup, loose-limbed and gangling, and friendly and clumsy. You have to take him in stride. Just yesterday afternoon, Miss —— and I went to the soda fountain across the street after school. It was filled with students, laughing and talking and taking it easy in general. When we came in, Albert jumped up on a bench, raised his hand, and shouted, 'Silence! There are teachers present!' So help me, I can't get angry at Albert. I think he's trying to find himself, and that he laughs at himself all the time. I think we ought to laugh with him, not at him; and that's what Miss —— and I did yesterday. We laughed, had our sodas, and that was the end of the matter."

We agreed that either of these explanations of Albert's behavior could conceivably be true. However, more important than our explanation of his behavior was Albert's own explanation of his behavior. Was there any way for us to find whether Albert saw this thing as we did, or whether, in general, the students in the high school saw inconsiderateness as we did?

WERE WE AND THE CHILDREN TALKING ABOUT THE SAME THING?

To examine the possibility that students and teachers interpreted considerateness quite differently, the film "You and Your Friends"[2] was shown to a group of students and a group of faculty members. Each group was asked to indicate the *most* considerate and the *least* considerate act portrayed in the film. Their reactions are shown in Table 2.

An examination of these data suggests that, while there are some minor differences in the order of importance assigned to these acts of considerateness and inconsiderateness, students and teachers tended to mention the same things as being considerate and inconsiderate. "Breaking a date in a considerate way" was relatively more important to the students than to the teachers, and loyalty between the girl and the boy seemed somewhat more important to the teachers than to the students. However, both of these behaviors were ranked high by both groups. Insofar as the responses to the motion picture revealed the real judgments of the two groups, they indicated that teachers and students were talking about the same things.

[2] "You and Your Friends" (7 min. sound film in black and white). Produced by Association Films and Look Magazine. Art of Living Series. Association Films, Inc., 347 Madison Ave., New York 17, New York, 1946.

TABLE 2

ACTS INTERPRETED AS CONSIDERATE AND INCONSIDERATE
BY TEACHERS AND STUDENTS

Acts	Percentage of Teachers (N = 51)	Percentage of Students (N = 31)
Most Considerate		
Loyalty of girl to boy	49%	29%
Breaking a date in a considerate way	21	48
Dependability	8	0
Acceptance of broken date	8	0
Trying to act pleasant	8	3
Starting a conversation (with a girl who seemed left out)	6	6
Interested in others	0	6
Helping a girl with food	0	6
Least Considerate		
Revealing a secret	65	39
Lack of dependability	12	0
Interrupting a conversation	8	5
Criticizing an absent person	6	10
Breaking a date to make another	6	25
Poor table manners	2	11
Not considering the feelings of others	0	5
Talking too much	0	5

CONSIDERATENESS AND POPULARITY

Continuing our examination of this situation in the high school, we were intrigued by the possibility that what we were calling "considerateness" and "inconsiderateness" were actually reasons for popularity and unpopularity among our high school students. Accordingly, we turned to one portion of a reaction sheet for the film "You and Your Friends," and analyzed responses to that. The question asked in the reaction sheet is: "If you want to be popular in this school, what three things are most important that you be or do?" Students who filled out this form were also asked to name three to five students they considered the most popular in school, and to indicate why they thought they were popular. It was possible, by analyzing the students' responses to the first question and to the "Why?" part of the second question, to draw up a list of sixty-one items mentioned frequently as reasons for popularity. The list could then be made into a check sheet, in which students and teachers could indicate those "reasons for popularity" that in their opinion had most to do with considerateness. The form which was developed is given in Appendix B.

This sixty-one-item form was administered to the seventy-one student members of the student council of the high school, and to the sixty-two members of the high school faculty. Those who checked these items were asked to indicate by their response "whether you believe considerate behavior is important to the reason given [for popularity]." There is some reason to suppose that this request was not heeded as the sheet was checked, and that the responses should be read simply as "reasons for popularity." Consequently, we did not base our analysis of the compared responses of students and teachers on the assumption that either group was actually relating these "reasons for popularity" to considerate behavior. However, we thought that it was reasonable to compare the responses of the two groups with respect to their notions of "reasons for popularity."

Before we could make the comparison, however, it was desirable that we test the responses of each of these two groups (students and faculty) for internal consistency. If there was as much or more inconsistency within each group as there was between the groups, we could not consider them as differing. Therefore, each group was divided into chance halves. The two halves of each group were compared with respect to their tendency to rank these items in the same way. The rank-order correlation coefficient for the faculty was .89. The rank-order correlation coefficient for the students was .96. This meant that each group was consistent with itself. Had the groups been internally inconsistent, comparison of the two would have meant little, since to compare groups one must first "pool" the responses of the individuals in a group. "Pooling" means that the responses in a group are similar enough to permit one to treat them as if they were nearly identical. In this case, we found that in each group there was enough similarity (as described by high correlation coefficients) to permit such pooling.

When sixty-two teachers' and seventy-one students' responses were compared, the rank-order correlation coefficient between them was found to be higher than .8. This suggests that the two groups were in substantial agreement concerning the relative importance of the sixty-one "reasons for popularity."

Particularly significant are the items which fell in the first ten ranks of student responses, because the number of responses to the items that fell in these ranks was much larger than the number of responses to the items that ranked lower. The comparison between the student and faculty rank is quite close. The top ten "reasons for popularity" ranked according to student responses are listed below together with the *differences* in ranks between student and faculty responses.

Thinks of others before self	3.5
Courteous	.5
Considerate	11.0
Cooperative	1.0
Friendly with everyone (makes friends)	4.0
Thoughtfulness	.5
Helpful	.5
Kindness	1.0
Good Sport	4.5
Liked by everyone	3.5

The difference between the student and faculty rankings for any one of the items on the check sheet could have been as great as 61. The fact is, however, that the differences in ranking between the two groups were relatively slight all the way down the scale from "thinks of others before self" (rank 1) to "tough" (rank 61). We teachers found this rather reassuring. At least, when we talked about "considerateness" with the students, we tended to talk about the same things. Our agreements certainly outweighed our disagreements. Moreover, the "reasons" considered most important by the students did seem to involve what we were calling "considerateness."

We Study Considerateness in the Elementary School

We have already given examples of the observations made by the eleven of us who carried on the study of considerateness in the elementary school. These sample observations are our behavioral definition of considerateness. To state the definition in more general terms: By "inconsiderateness" we mean being aggressive and selfish toward one another. By "considerateness" we mean being helpful and generous to one another. However, as our study continued, we found it more helpful to use the examples rather than these general definitions.

VERBAL AND PHYSICAL AGGRESSION

As we looked at our collection of examples of inconsiderate behavior, it appeared that there was a tendency for such behavior to take the form of overt physical aggression in the early grades, and to consist more and more of verbal aggression in the upper grades. We resolved to test this impression of ours by seeing whether the children would reveal such a tendency through their responses to an open-ended question. Accordingly, we asked all of the children in the school to list "Things that make me want to strike back." (The first and second graders responded orally.) In Table 3 we offer a summary of the children's responses to this question, categorized according to whether the children named overt physical aggression or verbal aggression. In the category "overt physical aggression" we included such responses as "choke you," "pinch you," "jump on your back." In the category "verbal aggression" we included such responses as "say dirty words," "tattling," "name calling."

TABLE 3

NUMBER OF RESPONSES IN EACH CATEGORY, BY ELEMENTARY SCHOOL CHILDREN, TO "THINGS THAT MAKE ME WANT TO STRIKE BACK" *

Grade	Overt Physical Aggression	Verbal Aggression
1	56	9
2	18	25
3	10	4
4	8	29
6	16	3

* Responses from grade five were not obtained.

What we found when we analyzed the material gathered was that there was no such tendency as the one that had appeared to us when we looked at our observational material. The children in the second grade named what we called "verbal" aggression more frequently than they named "physical" aggression. The children in the sixth grade named physical aggression more frequently than they named verbal aggression. If this was a valid indication of actual aggression, then, verbal aggression appeared prominently by the second grade among these children, and differences in the prominence of verbal aggression among the various grades of our school would have to be accounted for through reasons other than the grade or age of the children.

How I KNOW PEOPLE DON'T LIKE ME

We wished, however, to discover more about the kinds of things children consider aggressive and thus inconsiderate. We asked another open question of the children in the fourth, fifth, and sixth grades: "How I know people don't like me." A tabulation of the children's answers showed the frequencies for each kind of behavior.

Overt physical aggression   66
  (throwing rocks, hitting people, pushing in the lunch
  line, kicking, jumping on your back)
Gossip, teasing, name calling   47
  (mocking, call you cheater, profanity, tone of voice)
Participation in organized games   32
  (refusal to play with one, criticism of failure or mistakes
  during game play, breaking the rules)
Avoidance   30
  (refusal to talk, snubbing people, running off to be with
  someone else)
Treatment of others' belongings   13
  (tear up my games, "swiping" hat or coat, hiding something, ride your bicycle)
Facial expression   13
  (refusing to look you in the eye, making faces, sticking
  tongue out)

An analysis of the data in this table suggested to us a somewhat more detailed version of our original division of "inconsiderateness" into the two categories which we had called physical aggression and verbal aggression. When the upper-grade children responded to our question, "How I know people don't like me," overt physical aggression continued to occupy a prominent place. This was not surprising. After all, communication with a rock or a fist is quite obvious and easy to understand.

What interested us even more, however, was the subtlety of the several varieties of nonphysical aggression that emerged from our analysis of the children's responses. Gossip, bad treatment of others' belongings, refusing to look someone in the eye, and the like are actually quite aggressive behaviors. The sum of the frequencies for these was greater than the frequency for overt physical aggression. All of us remembered from our own childhood experience that gossip, avoidance, and facial expression were very real means of expressing aggression. There are a great many substitutes for a poke in the nose, the children seemed to be saying. These include openly avoiding another person, offering to play with one and then running off to play with someone else, and other such snubbing and cutting.

How much inconsiderateness does a teacher see?

When we compared our own observations with the children's responses to these two open questions, it appeared to us that in our elementary school, as in the high school, we and the children were talking about the same thing when we talked about inconsiderateness and considerateness. That is, we were talking about the same thing *insofar as we talked about the behavior we teachers could see.*

Most of our observations in the elementary school would fit into the categories named by the children in the first and second ranks of the children's responses to "How I know people don't like me." Most of what we saw, that is, was either overt physical aggression or overt verbal aggression. The nonverbal inconsiderateness that the children described in the comments we classified as "participation in organized games," "avoidance," "treatment of other's belongings," and "facial expression" appear very rarely in our observations of the children's behavior. Had we been looking for this kind of "inconsiderate" behavior, we might have reported more of it in our observational material. However, the fact that we did not report it means that we did not see it and that we were not in the habit of looking for it.

From this situation, we drew a conclusion of some importance to us. We concluded that *what we were calling "inconsiderate" amounted to only a fraction of all that the children recognized as "inconsiderate."* Our observations, which fit into the first two ranks of responses to "How I know people don't like me," would account for only 56 per cent of the items of behavior that the children suggested. The other 44 per cent were apparently out of our sight. At least they were sufficiently well out of sight that we did not report them when we were looking for inconsiderateness.

It was useful, therefore, for us to remember that although we and the children agreed about what kinds of behavior were "inconsiderate," we teachers actually observed only about half of the total picture as the children saw it—only the half which includes *overt* behavior.

Considerateness and Belongingness

Early in our work together, one of us had reported this incident of "considerate" behavior: "Instead of leaving for recess, Sue Ellen stayed in the room and helped Nancy to straighten up her desk." Elsewhere on the sheet of paper used to report this incident, the teacher had written, "Sue Ellen is always going from one friend to another."

This suggested something to us: perhaps Sue Ellen's behavior should be thought of as part of her quest for friends, not just as considerate behavior for its own sake. In fact, Sue Ellen's teacher was strongly persuaded that Sue Ellen was not "fundamentally considerate." Her purpose in recording this incident, in fact, was to raise a question with all of us about the meaning of this kind of behavior and the possibility that we were seriously misinterpreting it.

Perhaps much of the "considerate" behavior we had observed was related to friendship-seeking. We wondered whether we could find any consistent relationship between the acceptance of children in their classes (their group acceptance) and their tendency to behave in a considerate manner. To find out, we outlined our plan of work into a series of steps as follows:

Step 1. Each of us would gather examples of considerate and inconsiderate behavior, making sure that we noted the name of the person initiating the behavior and the name of the person toward whom the behavior was directed—the "initiator" and "receiver," so to speak.

Step 2. Each of us above the third grade would use the Classroom Social Distance Scale to get a measure of group acceptance for each child in our classes. Below the third grade, we would observe children's choices of classmates and friends in an effort to form some judgments about children who were consistently well accepted and children who were consistently lonely in our classes.

Step 3. We would examine our observations of considerate and inconsiderate behavior and our records of group acceptance of each individual, to see whether there were any consistent relationships.

Our report of what we found is given in Table 4, following. To read this table, note that we are attempting here to state the relationship between the person who initiated the considerate or inconsiderate behavior and the person who received it. There are four possible relationships: 1) the initiator can have higher group acceptance than the receiver; 2) he can have equal group acceptance with the receiver; 3) he can have lower group acceptance than the receiver; 4) one of the two can be new to the class. We have categorized the relationship between the two children involved according to the group acceptance of the person who was on the receiving end of the considerate or inconsiderate behavior.

TABLE 4

CONSIDERATE AND INCONSIDERATE BEHAVIORS CATEGORIZED
ACCORDING TO GROUP ACCEPTANCE OF RECEIVER

Group Acceptance	Considerate Behavior	Inconsiderate Behavior
Initiator has *higher* group acceptance than receiver.	1	14
Initiator and receiver have *equal* group acceptance.	10	6
Initiator has *lower* group acceptance than receiver.	3	3
Receiver *new* to the class.	7	0
	21	23

The comparative group acceptance of initiators and receivers of considerate and inconsiderate behavior is described in the first column ("Group Acceptance") of Table 4. Thus, when Billy snatches away Jerry's notebook and throws it on a high shelf (and we call this inconsiderate) we look at the *comparative group acceptance* of Billy and Jerry as indicated by our sociometric device. If Billy is higher than Jerry (is mentioned as a friend by more children in his class) we would record the behavior in the first row of the table, under "inconsiderate." If, on the other hand, Billy and Jerry are substantially the *same* (that is, either both relatively high in group acceptance, both in the middle of the class with respect to group acceptance, or both relatively low in group acceptance) we would record the behavior in the second row of the table, in the "inconsiderate" column. And so on. We did not think, in the case of children new to the class, that their "low" group acceptance as measured by the Classroom Social Distance Scale should be taken at its face value. Children who are new to the room, we said to ourselves, have to find their way into the social structure of the classroom. Until they have been in the classroom for a month or so, it is not possible for the teacher to find out what level of group acceptance they will attain. Therefore, we included a separate category for considerate and inconsiderate behavior directed at new children.

WHAT WE FOUND

Now let us interpret the table. The figure that stands out is in the first row—the 14 inconsiderate acts, more than half of all we recorded, initiated by a child who had greater group acceptance than the child toward whom the inconsiderate behavior was directed. This observation seemed to indicate that *inconsiderate behavior tended to be directed downward in the scale of group acceptance.*

The other portion of this table that interested us was in

the second row, in which the initiator and the receiver have equal group acceptance. While the difference in numbers of behaviors is not very striking (10 considerate acts and 6 inconsiderate acts), nevertheless the fact that nearly half of all the *considerate* behavior we saw took place between children who had approximately equal group acceptance, seemed to us to be significant. Moreover, these 10 considerate acts greatly outnumbered the considerate acts we saw taking place between children who were unequal in group acceptance. The fact that 7 of the 21 observations of considerateness were directed at children new to the room, that only 3 were directed "upward," so to speak (that is, toward a child of greater group acceptance), led us to conclude that, for our children, *considerateness tended to be directed toward social equals,* and to be withheld from social inferiors.

There are some additional interpretations of this material which are not supported strongly enough for us to report them as conclusions. However, we think that they are sufficiently interesting to be reported as questions: Is considerate behavior directed at new children as a means of winning their friendship? Is there any pronounced tendency for children who have generally high group acceptance to commit more considerate acts than inconsiderate acts? Does considerate behavior tend to take place among people of equal and relatively low group acceptance? In a number of cases (but our records are not complete on this point) the considerate behavior directed at children new to the room was initiated by children who had low group acceptance. One example of this was found in the anecdote that led us to study this matter in the first place—the one in which the child who went from one friend to another helped another child during the recess period. The child helped was new to the class. What did this mean?

THE CLASSROOM "PECK ORDER"

In our discussion of this material we came back again and again to this: most of the inconsiderate behavior we saw was initiated by people who had higher group acceptance than did the people on whom it was inflicted. What we thought we saw here was a sort of "peck order" in the classroom. In the barnyard, some chickens can peck other chickens without reprisal, and they get the preferred place at the feed box. In the classroom, some children can be inconsiderate to other children without apparent reprisal.

The additional fact, that almost all of the considerate behavior we saw took place between equals, or was directed toward new children, tended to support this "peck order" conclusion.

The more we thought about this, the more we tended to reinterpret what we were calling "considerate" and "inconsiderate" behavior. Possibly "inconsiderate" behavior was actually an expression of differing group acceptance. Perhaps the child's "code" demanded of him that he maintain his status in class, at least in part, by being inconsiderate to certain people. (If we had found many examples of considerate behavior directed from children of low group acceptance to children of high group acceptance, we would have worried still more. Such behavior would have been "toadying.")

On the other hand, we thought that a good many of the youngsters who had low group acceptance were thought by the others to be actually obnoxious much of the time, and that they brought the "inconsiderate" behavior upon themselves. The fact that a child of high group acceptance had initiated some inconsiderate behavior against the youngster of lower group acceptance did not necessarily mean that the inconsiderate behavior was unprovoked.

But the nagging fact remained that most of the inconsiderate behavior we recognized was directed downward in the order of group acceptance. Whatever lay behind it, we certainly were faced with the probability that our interpretation of the meaning of "inconsiderate" behavior had to be re-examined. We concluded by agreeing that *"considerateness" and "inconsiderateness" are so closely related to group acceptance as probably to be an expression of it.*

BUILDING GROUP ACCEPTANCE

Acting on this conclusion, we resolved to examine the means through which children could achieve group acceptance. If considerate and inconsiderate behavior were considered as expressions of group acceptance, then if we could do things that would make children in the group more acceptable to one another, we might hope that they would be more considerate of one another. (We did not think that we had established a cause-and-effect relationship through our observations as reported in Table 4. However, the relationships seemed so close that we thought a cause-and-effect relationship was at least possible. That is why we now turned to a further study of group acceptance.) What were the means through which children could increase their group acceptance? Which could we help them with in school?

Presumably, children like one another because they find one another attractive in some way. If we could discover what made our children attractive to each other, we might help our less attractive children to become more attractive. First, though, we had to know more about what was considered attractive by the children. To gain information from the children about this, we employed another open question: "Things that make me feel important."

WHAT MAKES CHILDREN FEEL IMPORTANT?

Our reasoning here was as follows: "Things that make me feel important" in all probability meant to our children the same things that we were calling "factors leading to group acceptance." We thought that there was likely to be a very strong positive relationship between the things that the children would identify as making them feel important and the things which they recognized in others as symbols of high group acceptance (or, in other words, high prestige) in the classroom. We thought that we would attack the matter in this oblique fashion in order to avoid what appeared to us to be the rather superficial findings of studies of factors influencing children's friendships, usually based on direct questions asked of children. Briefly, we thought that those things which children found attractive in themselves would be much more likely to influence their actual choice of friends than would things that they might attempt to identify in someone else as being significantly related to choice of friendships.

In Table 5 we have summarized the 185 responses of third, fourth, fifth, and sixth grade children to the "Things that make me feel important" question.

As we examined Table 5, we noticed that the first three categories, "academic," "playing games," and "help the teacher," accounted for 67 per cent of all the responses made by the children. The numbers of responses in the other categories were very small.

We had assumed that those things which the children valued in themselves, they would also value in others. Thirty-four per cent of all their responses had to do with academic achievement and the rewards associated with it. Twenty-three per cent of all their responses had to do with the ability to play games well, and being chosen to play games. Ten per cent of all of their responses had to do with helping the teacher in one way or another. Could these and other acts that the children mentioned actually be considered as symbols of the prestige of children in school?

We thought they could. The high frequency of "academic"

TABLE 5

RESPONSES BY 90 CHILDREN IN GRADES 3-6 TO
"THINGS THAT MAKE ME FEEL IMPORTANT."

Category and Descriptions of Items	Frequency	Percentage of Total
Academic (Doing well in school subjects; getting high marks)	63	34
Playing games (Play by the rules; play skillfully; being chosen for a team; people play with me)	42	23
Help the teacher (Run an errand; carry things for the teacher; bring the teacher a gift)	18	10
Class chores (Straighten books; take stamp order or lunch order)	12	6
Help another child (Help with school work; be "big sister" to new child)	8	4
The teacher calls on me (Praises me; displays my work; calls on me in history)	8	4
Gifts (I give and receive gifts and thanks for them)	8	4
Music (Singing; leading the class in singing; play the piano)	6	3
People say kind things to me	6	3
Be nice to (obey) the teacher (Obey the school rules)	5	3
Help the group	3	2
Be chairman	3	2
Have new clothes or shoes	3	2

The following were mentioned once or twice: only 5 more weeks of school; just to come to school; rest, have a party at school; bring something to school; to be trusted; have good ideas; when I went to the dentist; excursion; get in a fight; don't tattle; people come to my house; we have a new baby; eat lunch; buy own clothing; tell the truth.

comments, upon second examination, seemed to us to relate closely to marks of approval by the teacher. What was strongly suggested here was that the teacher's approval, especially as expressed by high grades, actually did contribute something to the status of the children with their peers.

We listed the children who had high group acceptance. Did they actually receive these marks of teacher approval? There were two or three striking exceptions; but we found that, by and large, they did. The children who enjoyed high group acceptance were the same ones who tended to receive better-than-average grades. (We wish we had kept better notes at this point. We remember having discussed this matter, and having agreed on this point. However, we cannot find the data that would support it. We are reporting it, nevertheless, because we are convinced of the truth of it, generally speaking, for our children.)

By itself, teacher approval would not account for high group acceptance. However, as we looked at the categories called "teacher calls on me," "be nice to (obey) the teacher," and "help the teacher," the children's responses seemed to imply that the teacher's approval should at least be considered as a major factor in their feelings of personal worth, and therefore in their judgment of the worth of others. When we added up the percentages associated with the four categories in which the teacher figured prominently, we found that 51 per cent of all of the responses had to do with these direct indications of teacher approval.

We did not think that teacher approval accounted for 51 per cent of all of the group acceptance of the children. This would have been pushing the significance of the percentages too far. However, the prominence of this type of response made it obvious that overt teacher approval of individual children was, to say the least, a factor of real significance in the self-evaluation of these children and consequently, in all probability, an important factor in their evaluation and acceptance of one another.

WHAT DO CHILDREN LIKE ABOUT THEMSELVES?

Having touched on the crucially important matter of self-evaluation, and having found this evidence that we as teachers were important factors in the children's lives, we resolved to find out more about what children valued about themselves. To do this, we asked these third, fourth, and fifth grade children two more open questions: (1) "What I like about myself" and (2) "What I don't like about myself."

Our purpose here was simply to gather further information about the data the children used in their self-appraisal. We still assumed that those things which they valued in themselves, they also valued in others. The children's responses to these two questions, and their responses to the question "Things that make me feel important" should, we thought, be considered as supplementary to one another. From the responses to these three questions we could develop a sort of inventory of the symbols of self-importance that the children were employing. We did not assume that these symbols would amount to a complete list of the factors that actually contribute to a child's feeling of personal worth, or to his means of evaluating the worth of others. However, we did think that we could gain through these questions some notion of the factors that the children were able to put into words. Conceivably, if we knew more about what the children could be articulate about, we would be in a better position to help them deepen their own understanding of themselves and thus of others. It was on the basis of this reasoning that we now proceeded to obtain the responses that are summarized below. The responses themselves were of this type: "my hair," "the way I read" (classified as "academic"), "my coat" (classified as "clothing"), "my ways" (classified as "personality").[3] These were the categories for responses to "What I like about myself":

---

[3] The categories given here account for all the children's responses. We are neither ranking the categories nor reporting the frequencies, because of a discrepancy in the directions we gave the children. Some of us told the children to state as many things as they pleased. Others restricted the children to one statement. This meant that we could not pool the frequencies.

Physical characteristics:
  (hair, eyes, figure, face, height, teeth, complexion)
Academic
Clothing
Helping parents
Possessions
Personality

And these were the categories (typical responses are also given) for "What I don't like about myself":

Physical characteristics:
  (face, hair, height, figure, complexion, health, color of eyes, eyes, feet, hands, legs, teeth, hearing)
Temper
  (my temper, get mad too easily, I lose my temper)
School subjects
  (grades, spelling, reading, painting)
"The way I act"
  (my ways, habits, the way I do, I absolutely hate myself)
Play skills
  (the way I catch, the way I hit, run fast)
Speech
  (the way I talk, I say ain't, cussing, bad English)

When we examined the children's responses to the questions "What I like about myself" and "What I don't like about myself," we noticed first that the negative question ("What I don't like about myself") led to more detailed responses than the positive question did. Then, we noticed the striking similarity between the responses to the two questions. In each case, physical characteristics appeared prominently, and in considerable detail. In both cases, academic proficiency was mentioned frequently. The categories called

from the classes. Therefore, we have reported here the categories we developed and tested. The actual frequencies are high in all the categories.

The reader will be interested in comparing the responses of our children with the responses of children to the same questions, as reported in A. T. Jersild, *In Search of Self* (New York: Bureau of Publications, Teachers College, Columbia University, 1952). The categories we obtained are very similar to those reported by Jersild, to whom we are indebted for the suggestion that we employ these questions.

"temper" and "the way I act" we thought to be similar in meaning to the category "personality" for "What I like about myself." It was interesting that "play skills" appeared in response to the negative question only and that "clothing" appeared in response to the positive question only. However, we thought that differences of this type between the two tables could not easily be interpreted, and that we would do well simply to take all of the categories that appeared in both tables and to interpret them as fairly representative of the things children like and don't like about themselves. We could generalize this, we thought, into a statement that the categories that emerged from the responses to these two questions were legitimately representative of those things the children were articulate about when they evaluated themselves.

THE CONSCIOUS DATA OF PRESTIGE

Our conclusions can be put together to explain the conscious elements of classroom prestige, and how they are expressed.

First, we assumed that whatever is consciously used in self-evaluation is also used in evaluating others. We found that in evaluating themselves, our children consciously use the data reported in their responses to "Things that make me feel important," "What I like about myself," and "What I don't like about myself."

Second, we found that the group's acceptance of individuals in it is expressed through considerate and inconsiderate acts, and that inconsiderate acts are catalogued in the children's responses to "Things that make me want to strike back." They are also indicated in the records of our adult observations of considerate and inconsiderate behavior.

The children, having formed judgments about one another partly on the basis of such elements as teacher approval, clothing, play skills, and physical appearance, gave expression to these judgments through such inconsiderate and considerate acts as overt physical aggression, snubbing, name-calling, helping each other, "tempering the wind to the shorn lamb," and complimentary remarks.

We thought we were dealing with two kinds of symbols here. One, the considerate or inconsiderate act, symbolized acceptance or rejection by an individual and ultimately by the class group. Others, the characteristics mentioned in the last three tables above, were the consciously employed symbols of prestige which underlay many of the acts of considerateness and inconsiderateness we saw.

Unmentioned bases for self-evaluation

It was important that we recognize what the children were recognizing. It was equally important, however, that we not assume that these consciously recognized symbols were of themselves a sufficient explanation of the considerate and inconsiderate behavior we had been observing.

One big gap in the children's responses to the questions about their feeling of self-importance and personal worth (possibly a consequence of the questions having been asked in school rather than somewhere else) is the infrequent mention of family. In the three tables having to do with self-evaluation, parents appear in only one category, and that category is not mentioned nearly so frequently as are others that are purely personal or that relate to marks of school approval. It is unlikely that our children's feelings of personal worth and their judgments of the worth of other children are actually influenced as slightly by family membership as their responses suggest.

Another gap is the children's failure to mention physical health. While attitudes toward physical health might be inferred from their responses dealing with play skills and their physical appearance, not a single child ever talked directly about health or illness, fatigue or abundant energy. It is likely, however, that the status of a child's health has considerable influence on his feeling of personal worth and his judgments about the worth and prestige of others.

We were dealing here only with those personal characteristics and behaviors about which the children were specific and articulate. We knew very well that there are other important factors that help to determine the prestige system of the classroom and the feeling of the individual worth of the children in it.

IMPLICATIONS FOR TEACHING

How, then, should we use the information we had gathered? We thought the use of it was suggested by a phrase we adopted and have placed at the head of one part of this discussion: "the conscious data of prestige." When a child deprecates his own appearance, we know now that he is talking about a factor that is of great importance to his feeling of personal worth and to his prestige. Similarly, when children ask questions designed to elicit from us as teachers some expression of approval or disapproval of their school work, or of themselves as persons, we now treat such questions very seriously. We assume that our judgmental statements have a substantial effect on the feeling of personal worth of the child and on his prestige in the classroom. We have learned, too, to pay more attention to game-playing situations than has been our habit.

The net effect of all this has been to make us far less casual in carrying on routine classroom work. These data remind us of something we tend to overlook—that, from the point of view of children in our care, every classroom moment may be crucial to somebody.

—the prominent place of the teacher

We were particularly interested in the indications that we teachers occupy a prominent position in determining children's feelings about themselves. They do and say so many things that suggest that they are not paying much attention to what we say, or that they are scoffing at us or ignoring our marks of disapproval, that this evidence that they take us so seriously was somewhat surprising.

When we stopped to think about it, we remembered from our many studies of individual children that scoffing, "stubbornness," and "stupidity," are very often best understood as attempts by a child to defend himself against attack. We knew from many a conversation with individual children that at the very moment a child was thus fending off our wrath, he was taking what we said very seriously. The responses to these open questions suggest that this is true of our children generally. We will do well to remember that when we give a child a high grade, send him on an errand, ask him to lead the class in some way, or even when we thank him for doing some little chore, we are contributing significantly to his feeling of personal worth.

—the importance of even-handedness

The clear implication of this line of thinking is that we have to learn to be even-handed in our dealings with the children. We all mean to be even-handed all the time, of course. However, when we think of the ordinary school day, we know that often we give marks of teacher approval or disapproval on an utterly casual basis. Yet our children suggest, through their responses to these open questions, that we ourselves contribute heavily to the prestige system in the class, and thus indirectly to the acts of considerate and inconsiderate behavior that we had been observing throughout our study.

It is our moral responsibility, since this is the situation, to keep the classroom prestige system as wide open as possible. The clear implication for us as teachers is that we neither give nor withhold indications of our own approval of the children's behavior on an accidental basis. Our ideal, as teachers, is that we accept all of the children as valuable, worthy individuals. We are obliged to give all our children equal opportunities to rise in the class prestige system, insofar as we have influence on it. This means that we shall overlook no opportunities to praise children for work that is praiseworthy, and to call the attention of the class to good work wherever it appears.

As we try to imagine how to make our approval generally available, we run afoul of the "teacher's pet" idea. We think that a teacher's pet is found only in a class in which the teacher has closed the prestige system. The children's resentment against the teacher's pet arises precisely from the fact that the teacher is inequitable in granting marks or indications of approval. By granting prestige symbols to one child rather than another, the teacher withholds from some children something they require for their feeling of personal worth. Thus, the children resent the teacher and scapegoat the teacher's pet. To avoid such a situation, then, the teacher must maintain an open prestige system in the class when it comes to doing those things the children have indicated to us represent teacher approval.

What are these indications of teacher approval? Our children told us: school marks, running errands, being asked to lead the class in singing, helping the teacher, being praised for school work, being called on in class and so forth. Our tendency, we thought, had been to be very fair and equitable in the granting of school marks, but to be far less equitable in these other ways that the children indicated were important to them.

Children's Interpretations of Stories About Considerateness

The observations, responses to open questions, and sociometric material had all been gathered and interpreted by adults. It remained to check these explanations of "considerateness" against the children's own explanations. This behavior had been explained as it appeared to us adults. Possibly what we called inconsiderate was not so thought of by the children. We now attempted to look at it through the children's eyes.

To do this, we changed the names and otherwise disguised some of our anecdotal material, and asked the children to interpret the anecdotes to us.

These are the anecdotes we used: [4]

THE "SCRIBBLE" STORY

Claude and Ralph were in the same grade in school. One day when Claude went to the pencil sharpener, Ralph turned around and made scribbling marks on Claude's clean paper that was ready for work. Why did Ralph do this?

THE "FIRST IN LINE" STORY

It was time to get ready for lunch and the children all went to the rest room to wash their hands. Jack hurried to the rest room, turned on the faucet, dipped his fingers quickly in and then right out again, and then dried his hands on a towel and hurried out of the rest room as fast as he could. He hurried back to the room to be first in line. Why did Jack want to be first?

THE "MILK" STORY

This is a story about Laura. She is in the fourth grade. In the lunchroom a second grade boy spilled his milk. Laura quickly went to the kitchen, got some paper towels and went right in to help him clean it up. Why did Laura do that?

[4] The titles of these stories are given only so that they can be identified in the discussion that follows. If the reader wishes to use any of these stories with children, we would suggest that no title be used. If it seems necessary to use a title, call them "The Story of Claude and Ralph," "The Story of Jack," and so on.

The stories are reproduced here very nearly as they were first written in the observational records. There is a certain wordiness to some of them, and others are definitely inelegant, if considered from a literary point of view. However, the style in which they are written is the same chatty, informal style we usually adopt when talking with our children. To the children, the stories sounded like us, not like some impersonal writer of tests.

THE "READING CIRCLE" STORY

The children were coming up to make a circle in front of the room. John sat at one end of the circle. He put his foot out to one side like this so that Ella couldn't sit down beside him. Why did John do that?

THE "HAT" STORY

One wet day, Dick and Jerry were walking to school. Dick took hold of Jerry's hat and gave it a jerk. What happened then?

THE "LUNCH PAIL" STORY

Sally was coming to school. She was going up the steps one morning on her way to her room. She was carrying her lunch pail, overshoes, and a box of crayons. She stumbled and fell on the steps and dropped the things she was carrying, and the crayons all rolled out of the box. Now Leonard came along right behind her. What could he say when he came along? [Children give "nice" answer.] Now let's suppose that Leonard did not stop to help Sally. Why didn't Leonard stop?

THE "RECESS" STORY

The children were having recess period. Robert kept stamping on Alice's toes. Why did Robert keep stamping on Alice's toes? What do you think Alice thought about that?

Five pairs of children in grades three to six were asked to interpret each of these stories to us. The interviews were conducted as follows: the teacher sat with two children in her class, and conducted the interview. The entire interview was recorded on tape, and the tape recording was transcribed.

We selected two children in each class, one we thought of as "high" in considerateness, and the other "low." However, when we examined their interpretations of these stories, we could see no particular relationship between the responses of our "high" and "low" children, nor could we find anything consistent that had to do with grade membership of these children. This may arise from the fact that we used such a small number of children. In any case, we shall not discuss the grade membership of the children. We shall, instead, interpret only the social mechanisms that the children seem to imply by their responses.

What quickly appears from the children's responses to these stories is this: there is a kind of back-and-forth to these inconsiderate behaviors. The first thing that the children saw in these stories was a situation involving aggression and counter-aggression. If A did something to B, then B did something to A. In order to understand what happened to Sally, the children turned to Sally's past relations with Leonard, or looked forward to some retaliatory behavior on Sally's part. The children report, we think, an "eye for an eye" kind of social interaction.

For example, let us consider this response to the "scribble" story:

TEACHER: Well, what do you think that Claude would do if he came back and saw that Ralph had scribbled on his paper?
                                              [An eye . . .]
BILLY: I'd scribble on his paper.   [. . . for an eye.]
TEACHER: What do you think, Jerry?
JERRY: I think he wouldn't. I don't think he'd like it.
TEACHER: What do you think you can do about it?
JERRY: Go tell the teacher. I think I know what the teacher would do. Send Ralph back in the corner.   [Hit back.]

Here are the responses of two other boys to the "scribble" story.

TEACHER: Why do you think Ralph did that?
ELDON: Maybe he thought he was just showing off.
TEACHER: Well, what do you mean by showing off?
ELDON: Well, you just go and scribble or just do anything like a show-off—well, you get it right back cause they can do it and not tell the teacher. If they tell the teacher, then they'll be a tattle-tale and they'll get a spanking too.
                                    ["You get it right back."]
TEACHER: We don't give spankings very often here do we?
                                    [Teacher on the defensive.]

ELDON: No.

TEACHER: We don't, do we?

ELDON: No. Get a guy home that tattles.

TEACHER: Oh, you get it at home sometimes for tattling?

ELDON: Usually. My little brother goes and gets some water, and I tell on that and get spanked.

TEACHER: Willard, why do *you* think Ralph did that?

WILLARD: Might be mad at him.

TEACHER: Well, this is just suppose. What do you suppose he might have done that got him mad?

WILLARD: He pushed his sister down.

[Child uses only physical aggression to explain this.]

TEACHER: Do you think that maybe he pushed his little sister down? On the way home or to school? What do you think, Eldon, might have happened?

ELDON: I think he might have scribbled on his paper for that.

Let us consider one more of these interviews, this time in response to the "hat" story:

TEACHER: What happened then?

DONALD: Pulled it off.

TEACHER: He did what?

DONALD: Pulled it off and threw it in the water.

TEACHER: Why do you think he did that? Do you have any idea why he'd do a thing like that?

DONALD: No.

TEACHER: Do you, Chris?

CHRIS: No.

TEACHER: Well, what makes you think he pulled it off and threw it into the water?

DONALD: Because maybe he wouldn't play with him.

TEACHER: Would that be a nice thing to do if he wouldn't play with him?

DONALD: Because maybe the other fellow had his cap off and wouldn't give it back to him, but he didn't throw it in the water, so he threw his in the water and this other guy, he took the other fellow's cap off and he threw it down in the deeper water.

[A "spiral" of aggression and counter-aggression is suggested.]

TEACHER: You mean Dick threw Jerry's cap in the water?

DONALD: Yes.

TEACHER: And then Jerry took Dick's cap and threw it in the deeper water? Is that what you mean?

DONALD: Yes.

KEEPING EVEN

In every case in which the story involved what we had called "inconsiderate" behavior, the children's explanation was based on an assumption either that something had happened in the past for which the child was getting even, or that he would have to get even in the future for what had been done to him. For another example, consider Eldon's explanation of the "lunchpail" story:

ELDON: Well, maybe he just didn't like her because she goes by his house, and they play together, and when his mother calls, well, he don't wanta go home, and she tells him he'd better go home or his father will whip him, and then he says "shut up" to her, and then he goes in.

If considerate and inconsiderate behavior were expressions of the prestige system in the classroom (and we thought they were), then the children's interpretations of these stories suggested that the prestige of an individual was maintained in part by keeping even in the face of aggression. Now, our comparison of group acceptance and observed inconsiderate behavior suggests that most of the inconsiderate behavior we had observed was directed downward in the prestige system of the classroom. Yet the children implied that it was crucially important to keep even in the face of aggression and counter-aggression. If inconsiderate behavior was usually directed downward, then either some of the children consistently failed to keep even (which might explain their low prestige), or our observations had not revealed the whole situation to us.

The "keeping even" situation suggested by the children's interpretations of these anecdotes was fully as likely to be true as the "peck order" situation which our own observations had implied. If they were both true, then the inconsiderate behavior we had observed was likely to have been part of a back-and-forth series of aggressions in which the child committing the inconsiderate behavior we saw felt that he himself was keeping even. It did not quite add up, however. We still had an impression that a good deal of the inconsiderate behavior we saw was actually initiated by the children we saw doing it. We wondered how the victims of it could keep even. As a matter of fact, they were *not* keeping even, if the results of our sociometric questions were to be trusted, except in the sense that the peck-order status quo may not have been disturbed, but actually maintained, by some aggressions.

Our conclusion was that if aggression and counter-aggression are expressions of prestige in the classroom, then the children who were not accepted by the others were actually out of balance with respect to the aggression–counter-aggression pattern. We supposed that the children of low group acceptance either commit too many aggressions (possibly out of our sight) or fail to commit enough counter-aggressions. In either case, the penalty for failing to keep even would be a loss of prestige in class. In a sense, what was exchanged in this "give and take" was prestige.

We thought of it this way. When A hits B, he has taken away some of B's prestige. In order to get it back, B must hit A back. If he does this, they are "even" and the matter comes to an end. If he hits back too hard, then they are out of balance, B having taken away more of A's prestige than was his due. A, then, must hit back again.

Actually this A and B business seemed to us to square with the facts of a great many playground squabbles. When boys start roughhousing, their roughhousing often spirals into a "mad" fight, with thirty other children surrounding them making hysterical noises. We try to prevent such fights on our playground; but they happen on the way to and from school, and sometimes they happen on the playground despite our efforts.

"An eye for an eye" and the teacher

We wondered what our role, as teachers, should be. Here was the situation, as the children reported it—an "eye for an eye" sort of thing.

It was possible that we were sometimes involved in this spiraling, trading, primitive social mechanism, without knowing it. An incident in the school yard one morning illustrated this situation to us. Here is the teacher's report of what happened:

During recess two fourth grade boys caught hold of Willa Jean, backed her up against a tree, and kissed her. Cora, who saw this, was outraged. She ran into my room and reported the incident to me. I agreed with her that this kind of thing was intolerable on the playground, called in the two little boys and scolded them for their behavior. After school the two little boys caught Cora and engaged in quite a rough scuffle with her. Cora went home crying. She told the whole story to her mother, and her mother said, "That's what you get for tattling."

The teacher had been caught squarely in the middle of a spiral of counter-aggressions. The effect of her calling in the two little boys and scolding them had been to get things so "out of balance" that the boys committed aggression against Cora. The series had come to an end only with the mother's rebuff. How might the teacher have avoided being caught?

There was a way to handle this situation that would have dealt with the disciplinary problem on the playground and yet not left Cora "out of balance" with the two little boys. The teacher somehow had to break the spiral of aggression and counter-aggression. The teacher might have broken the spiral by accepting Cora's report of the misdemeanor, but not reacting to it instantly. Rather, the teacher might have waited for an opportunity to put this event with others and discuss the whole matter with the two boys, or in a general way with the whole class, at a later time. Her immediate response to Cora might have been, "Thank you very much, Cora, for reporting this to me. I'll look into it." The teacher's mistake had been made when she immediately went out and called in the two boys for their scolding. In a sense, she simply added velocity to the spiraling aggression and counter-aggression by what she did, and Cora's treatment after school was predictable.

In Summary

We have reached some conclusions based on the evidence we collected, and think that there are some important implications that grow out of these conclusions.

First, we think that considerate behavior and inconsiderate behavior are thought of in a substantially similar way by our children and by us teachers, insofar as we are talking about the overt behavior we teachers have customarily referred to in these terms. This was true in both the high school and the elementary school. However, the children identify a great deal of covert inconsiderate behavior (in naming "things that make me want to strike back") that we have not usually seen.

Second, we believe that in our elementary school there is a pattern of considerate and inconsiderate behavior which is an expression of the existing social structure of the classroom as revealed through sociometric questions. This leads us to re-examine the significance of such behavior.

Third, the group acceptance of individuals in the classroom depends (among other things) on a number of consciously recognized factors—"things that make me feel important," "things I like about myself," and "things I don't like about myself." These symbols we regard as the currency or data of prestige. We think that these consciously recognized symbols of individual worth should be taken into account by teachers in our school who wish to have a deliberate desirable effect on the children's feelings of personal worth, and consequently on their feelings about the worth of others.

Fourth, we believe our children, who maintain the prestige system in our classroom by means of what we have been calling "considerate" and "inconsiderate" behavior, actually see themselves as keeping a sort of balance with one another when they commit what we call "inconsiderate" behavior. Their interpretations of this behavior strongly imply that, from the child's point of view, most aggression is counter-aggression.

Fifth, the teacher's approval or disapproval is a very important contributing factor in both the personal feeling of worth of our children and the system of aggression and counter-aggression, considerateness and counter-considerateness, that exists in our classrooms. With respect to "inconsiderate" behavior, it is very important that we teachers avoid being caught in a series of aggressions and counter-aggressions of which we are not aware. This bears particularly on what we do about "tattling," and on what we think about the "teacher's pet" situation.

How to Verify Our Conclusions

If you wish to see whether what we found in our classes is true in yours, we suggest that you short-cut our procedure in some ways and go through the steps given below.

Step 1. Observation. Jot down as many examples of considerate and inconsiderate behavior as you can during one week. You will find it a little harder to find examples of considerate behavior than of inconsiderate behavior, primarily because most of us are not in the habit of looking for considerateness. However, if you put your mind on it, you will find quite a large number of them. Ten or fifteen anecdotes of each kind are enough.

Step 2. Examine the records of your observation. We found that working together on this material was very satisfying. If you can, sit with a fellow teacher (or, desirably, with your whole school staff who have made similar observations), look over your records of observations, and see whether you agree that all of them should be called either "considerate" or "inconsiderate." Discard those about which you have doubts.

Step 3. Observe again. For a period of one week, record every example of considerate and inconsiderate behavior you can, making sure to include in each anecdote the name of the person who initiated the behavior and the name of the person toward whom it was apparently directed. You will find that in some cases the considerate or inconsiderate behavior is apparently directed at the entire classroom group. We have not reported our observations of this kind of behavior, because we found only a few examples and because we were more interested in examining other behaviors. However, you may find it interesting to notice which children direct their behavior at the entire group. Categorize the observed behavior according to whether it is considerate or inconsiderate. *Be sure* to get the names written down in each case. We often forgot to do this.

Step 4. Try to explain the behavior. We suggest that you short-cut what we did at this point, by getting the material from all of your open questions in a brief time. That is: (*a*) Administer the Classroom Social Distance Scale or some other sociometric device to all of the children in your class. (These devices are useful only above the third grade.) (*b*) Obtain the children's responses to "Things that make me want to strike back," "Things that I like about myself," "Things that I don't like about myself," and "Things that make me feel important." We suggest that you ask these questions one at time, on separate days; but there is no reason why you cannot do all of them within a two-week period. You may think of other open questions that you would like to ask at this time—questions such as "What I like about my three best friends," or "A considerate (or inconsiderate) boy or girl is somebody who . . ." There are numberless open questions that one *might* ask. The only limit we are aware of is the children's patience. By the way, we found that a discussion of the results of these questions in our classes was very worth while. The children often supplemented our interpretation, and obviously benefited from the sharing of ideas.

Step 5. Ask the children to interpret the anecdotal material. Select four or five anecdotes like those we used, change the names so that no name of a child in your class appears, and ask the children to explain the behavior. We found that it was important in using these anecdotes to select names that were a little unusual. Names like Billy, Jimmy, Mary, Alice, and the like seemed to be so similar in the children's minds as to lead them to confuse one character with another. Names like Eldon, Ralph, Jennifer, and Sue Anne, were better. Try, too, to select anecdotes that do not suggest pat answers to the children. We found that the only way to make this selection was to try out anecdotes on a few children. The purpose of the anecdote is to get the child to talk freely about the general situation. In our "hat" story, for example, we were not particularly interested in hats. We were interested in the inconsiderateness involved. To record the children's discussion, we used a tape recorder. We did not find that the tape recorder made the children any more self-conscious than they were without it. In a few cases we found it helpful to allow the children to play with the tape recorder—to hear their voices back and to make some strange noises—before we began our interviews. Also, we liked our way of interviewing our children in pairs, rather than alone. We thought that the fact that there was another child present was reassuring to the children.

Step 6. Analyze the material. Our way of analyzing the material we gathered has been explained in detail in this chapter. We compared the results of the sociometric question with our observations of considerateness and inconsiderateness, noticing the relative group acceptance of the children who initiated and received the considerate or inconsiderate behavior. Our analysis of the responses to our open questions took the form of developing trial categories of the responses, testing these categories by asking someone who was not participating in the study to sift the children's responses into the categories, and then comparing these independent categorizations of the children's responses. We based our conclusions, not on the rank order in which the frequencies appeared, but merely on the fact that some kinds of responses appeared rather frequently. It was from the responses to three of our open questions, put together, that we developed our conclusions about "the data of prestige." This is not the only way that this material might be analyzed. Other ways will occur to you as you read the responses of your children to questions of this type. One difficulty we encountered was the result of our failure to make absolutely certain that we all administered these questions in the same way. If you are going to work with someone else, you cannot spend too much time making certain that you are in complete, detailed agreement concerning the directions that you are going to give the children. If your directions are not identical, it becomes very difficult to pool the responses of your children or to compare them with the responses of the children in some other classroom.

If you do carry on this analysis, or any part of it, in your classroom, we would be very much interested in your results.

CHAPTER 7

Ownership and Sharing

As CHILDREN go through their early years, the culture demands that they learn two different attitudes toward property. In the first place, parents and teachers ask that they learn to observe the rights and obligations of ownership, to recognize the difference between "mine" and "thine." Little children are not allowed to appropriate things that do not belong to them. The punishment for taking things that are not theirs becomes more and more severe as they grow older. We commonly expect four- and five-year-old children to have a rather clear-cut notion of what is their own and what is not their own. By age seven or so, infantile "swiping" is severely punished, if detected.

But at the same time that we insist that children learn ownership, we also ask that they learn to *share* the things they own. Middle-class Americans, especially, bestow praise and other rewards upon children who will share their toys. We ask that by the time children have finished kindergarten they learn to "take turns" (a form of sharing), and that they become increasingly generous with their possessions as they grow older.

There is a superficial value conflict here which is bewildering to a small child. How can a thing be mine, and yet be shared? Well-adjusted adults understand the difference clearly. The value, generosity, is expressed in the maxim, "It is more blessed to give than to receive," which functions as a rule for much of our conduct as adults. Private, anonymous giving is widely considered to be one of the most praiseworthy kinds of social behavior. There is no adult problem as between ownership and generosity. But it is often puzzling to young children.

As teachers, we are trying to teach these two values, "ownership" and "sharing," to the children. These two values do not have equal intensity. The difference in their intensity is indicated by the maxim quoted above, "It is more blessed to give than to receive." According to the Biblical injunction, "sharing," or generosity, is a more important, more intensely valued referent than is the value "ownership."

Now, everyone who has dealt with children understands that they have difficulty learning to share what they own. There are many reasons for the difficulty, for values associated with the ownership of property occupy a central place in our culture, and therefore in our social behavior. In adult society there are a great many more laws about property and property rights, for example, than about libel, slander, and other violations of individual integrity.

We Study Sharing

With this on our minds, we [1] undertook to study sharing. Some of our children come from families that live in very poor houses. The children do not have many very valuable possessions. It seemed obvious to us that the frequent quarreling over possessions, for these children, arose from the fact that possessions were rather hard to acquire. Whether

[1] "We" were the staff of the Robberson Elementary School in Springfield, and two Institute consultants.

or not this was the chief reason for the problem, we agreed that the problem existed; and it was on the basis of this agreement that we decided to study it.

We began by observing "sharing" behavior for two weeks. What we sought and found were examples of "sharing" behavior: a child brought something to school, gave something to someone else, or loaned something to another child. We made an attempt to distinguish between sharing things and helping people. We agreed to consider only the sharing of tangible property, as contrasted with "sharing" an experience (telling the class of an experience) or "sharing" the door (holding the door open for someone else).

Here are some examples selected from a total of 74 observations which all of us agreed should be called "sharing."

GRADE 1
Gave some candy to another child.
Let another child look at his book.
Let some others play with his new truck.

GRADE 2
Brought his corn popper to school.
Gave another child a sheet of his paper.
Brought a "get well" card from home to be sent to a sick classmate.

GRADE 3
Gave away part of his spending money.
Brought some outgrown shoes to school for a classmate.
Gave away a ruler.

GRADE 4
Brought a checker game to school for the others.
Loaned a jumping rope to another class.
Brought candy for the other children.

GRADE 5
Brought materials (cloth, and so on) for class project.
Brought some sea shells.
Photographed the class and put the developed pictures on the bulletin board.

GRADE 6

Brought stamps to school.
Brought moths from own collection.
Baked some cake and brought it to school.

These behaviors, for our purposes, were "sharing." What was involved, usually, was some tangible bit of property which was either given or loaned to someone else, or divided with someone else. This was what was tangible about our "intangible."

How Could Sharing Be Explained?

A number of possible explanations of the behavior that we had observed occurred to us. We listed factors that might be closely related to sharing, in order to select some among them for further study. Here is our list:

Popularity (acceptance by the classroom group)
Age
Socio-economic status of the home
Size of the family (that is, number of brothers and sisters)
Academic achievement
Emotional security (measurable by the use of personality tests and other devices, plus observation)
Physical health
Intelligence quotient
Recent serious illness (removal from classroom group)
The school situation (e.g., classroom, party, playground, lunch line, and so on)
The receiver of the sharing behavior
The thing being shared
The influence of home-bred habits
Variety of interests

Of this list of possibly related factors, we studied two: the economic status of the family, and the thing shared.

Economic status of the home

We shall report our study of the relationship of economic status and sharing status rather briefly and quickly, because it was easy for us to carry out and led quickly to a negative conclusion. First, we re-observed our children for sharing. On the basis of two weeks of observation (this seemed long enough), each of us selected two children: one who seemed consistently to be quite generous, another much less so. Then we attempted to see whether there were any appreciable differences in economic status between the homes of these children. We took into account as many of the following factors as we could get information about:

Father's occupation (and thus probable income)
Mother's income (if any)
Number of people to be supported by the income (average income per family member)
Any recent or chronic heavy expenditures for health
Location and maintenance of the home

We did not need to use more factors than these to establish whatever purely economic differences existed among our children's families. We used three classifications of economic status, "low," "medium," and "high," all within the rather limited economic range represented by our school neighborhood. Some of our children, as we have pointed out, came from low-income families. Others came from families with a good, steady income, but none of the children was from a well-to-do family.

We can report the results in a sentence: we found no consistent relationship whatever between economic status and sharing behavior as we observed it. Some very poor children were very generous; some were not. Some children from families that were better off were generous; some were selfish with their possessions. Sharing behavior seemed to depend on factors other than the economic status of the child's family.

THE THING SHARED

We turned now to the study of one class of referents of the children's sharing—the things they shared. We realized that sharing behavior involved an attitude not only toward the thing shared but toward the person with whom it was to be shared. However, we chose to restrict our study at this time to the child's attitude toward the thing he was sharing. Other staffs in Springfield were studying the human referents, so to speak, of behavior much like our "sharing." [2] Anything we could find about the children's attitudes toward the physical things they were dealing with would be supplementary to these other studies.

It was a safe assumption, we thought, that children value some things more than others. We thought, too, that the things the children value most are probably the things they are least willing to share.

First it was up to us to find out what the children valued most. Therefore we asked all the children in the school an open question: "What I want most." In the first, second, and third grades, this was done orally, and the teacher wrote down what each child said. In the upper grades, the children were asked to write their responses. We assumed that what they wanted would reflect what they valued. We then categorized the children's responses. We shall first report the totals by grade and category, in Table 6. Then we shall report, in Table 7, some of the most frequently mentioned "things wanted" by grade. An examination of these tables will reveal some patterns of "want" among our children.

[2] The reader will notice a striking similarity, for instance, between "sharing" and the behavior studied elsewhere as "considerateness." We do not deny the similarity. It is quite possible that the factors that underlie considerateness also underlie sharing. However, we chose to keep our emphasis on the child's attitude toward tangible things. We think that the studies of "considerateness" and "sharing" actually do overlap quite substantially, and that the two studies should be considered together. We see no inconsistency between what we found and what was found by the staff studying "considerateness."

TABLE 6

RESPONSES OF 451 ELEMENTARY SCHOOL CHILDREN TO
"WHAT I WANT MOST"

GRADE	NUMBER OF RESPONSES	Toys	Cloth-ing	Pets	Money	Family	Sweets	Miscel-laneous
					PERCENTAGE OF RESPONSES			
1	79	68%	6%	1%	5%	4%	10%	6%
2	66	53	17	8	2	9	5	6
3	57	35	5	37	2	21	0	0
4	65	52	11	21	0	8	0	8
5	52	50	2	22	7	14	0	5
6	37	24	8	49	0	13	0	6

Notice, here, the rapid decrease, from grade one to grade six, of "toys," and the increase in "pets." Notice that "sweets" disappears after grade 2. We were interested in the constant appearance of "family" items: "a new house," "a car," even "a baby sister"!

TABLE 7

ITEMS MENTIONED MOST FREQUENTLY BY 451 ELEMENTARY SCHOOL
CHILDREN IN RESPONSES TO "WHAT I WANT MOST"
(Percentage of Responses per Grade)

Item	1	2	3	4	5	6
			GRADE			
Doll	13.0	4.5	0	1.5	0	0
Bicycle	8.0	26.0	23.0	24.0	27.0	16.0
Pony	0	4.5	17.0	13.0	11.0	0
Horse	1.3	0	12.0	3.1	3.9	21.0
Dog	0	0	0	3.0	1.9	16.0

We were interested in these patterns of "wants." The interest of the children above the second grade in means of locomotion was very strong indeed. Their interest in "bicycle," "horse," and "pony" mounted rapidly through the grades. "Bicycle" was the most popular single item of all from the second to the fifth grade (see Table 7), being replaced in the sixth grade by "horse." In the sixth grade, too, "motorcycle" appeared for the first time, being mentioned by one child. We were amused, too, by the rapid increase in the amount of money mentioned, when it was mentioned at all.

It begins at a nickel in the lower grades and increases rapidly to a million dollars in the upper grades!

We had gathered this material in order to see what *things* the children valued most. We had our answers, for each grade and for the school as a whole. While the pattern of things valued varied considerably by grade, there were certain objects, such as "bicycle," that were valuable to almost everybody.

A *Trial Test of Sharing*

Having located these "things valued" we cast about for means of testing the children's willingness to share them. One way of doing this that occurred to us was to make up unfinished sentences, some having to do with these objects, and to see how the children would finish them. We developed the following incomplete sentences for this purpose:

1. When two children were visiting Dora, her mother gave her some money; so Dora . . .
2. Phillip was standing at the back of the group waiting to get on a crowded bus when the bus stopped. Phillip . . .
3. When Steve's mother made him a cake, he . . .
4. Edgar was riding his shiny new bicycle when Bert came to play, so Edgar . . .
5. Stella shares with the kids in her room when . . .
6. Christine had a sack of her favorite candy, so she . . .
7. Kate was helping her mother with the dishes when Gladys came to play, so Gladys . . .
8. When John was passing the books to ten children in his room, there were seven old books and three new ones, so John . . .

First, we tried these sentences with eight or nine children in each of our classes, to see whether they "functioned" well —that is, whether the children finished the sentences in different ways or whether the sentences seemed to suggest pat answers.

We based our selection of sentences to be used on evidence such as that given here for a few of the sentences. No. 6, "Christine had a sack of her favorite candy, so she . . . ," seemed to us to "function" well in the sixth grade, because the children answered it in a good many different ways. Following are the responses of eight children to this sentence:

. . . ate all of it in an hour.
. . . saved it. (Two children said this.)
. . . took it home with her and ate it there.
. . . went home and ate a piece of it.
. . . did not share some.
. . . went home and gave her sister some of it.
. . . gave her friend some of it.

Similarly, our fourth sentence, "Edgar was riding his shiny new bicycle when Bert came to play, so Edgar . . . ," called forth quite different responses from different children in the sixth grade:

. . . took turns with Bert.
. . . put up his bicycle (and played with Bert).
. . . told Bert to get his bike and they would go riding.
. . . asked Bert to take a ride on it and see how he liked it.
. . . put his new bicycle away because he knew Bert would want to ride.

In the second grade, this sentence got responses that differed considerably: "When Steve's mother made him a cake, he . . ." Six children said, "ate it." The following responses also were made:

. . . he said, 'I want to give a piece to my neighbor.'
. . . gave some to his brother and sister.
. . . was happy.
. . . ate part of it and then shared with his brothers and sisters.
. . . iced it and then wrote his name on it.
. . . gave a piece to his mother.
. . . ate half of it and left the rest for another time.
. . . divided with kinfolks.
. . . ate some of it and saved some of it.

We thought that we had found sentences to which the children responded differently. Possibly we could make of these sentences a test that would give us more information on the children's attitudes toward sharing. We approached this with some doubts, thinking that most of the children would try to give us the "right" answers if we gave them a chance to, whether or not their answers matched their behavior.

Our idea was to take some of the typical responses that the children gave on our "trial run" of these sentences, and give all of the children a chance to check them. It would be interesting, we thought, to see how many of the children would check the "good" answers and how many might check the "bad" answers. We did not think that the fact that a child checked a "good" answer necessarily meant that he would behave consistently with it. However, we thought that if any of the children checked the "bad" answer, they either did not know what the "good" answer was, or really were defying the value that we sought to build in them. In any case, we thought the device was sufficiently interesting to try out. The test and the children's responses to it follow.[3] For each grade, the percentage of the children who checked each response is given. Thus, under the first sentence, 14 per cent of the first grade children checked "bought some candy," 50 per cent of the first grade children checked "kept the money and put it away." In the original form of the test, we included a blank space so that the children who did not wish to check any of these responses could write in some other re-

---

[3] First graders responded orally. We used two instruments here; the same incomplete sentences were used in both, but the items offered for checking were different, in some cases, for grades 1-3 from those for grades 4-6. That's why there are blanks opposite some of the items. Thus, "spent the money" appeared in our primary form, but not in the intermediate form. These differences arise from the fact that on our "trial run," the response "spent the money" appeared only in the primary grades. The same explanation applies to the other phrases for which no response is indicated in one grade group or another.

sponse and check that. We have not reported these scattered write-in responses. There were too few of them.

1. When two children were visiting Dora, her mother gave her some money, so Dora . . .

	Grade 1	Grade 2	Grade 3	Grade 4	Grade 5	Grade 6
Bought some candy.	14%	5%	3%	16%	16%	23%
Spent the money.	12	10	9			
Bought candy and gave some to the children.	24	47	59	72	78	65
Kept the money and put it away.	50	38	29			
Got herself something.				12	6	12

2. Phillip was standing at the back of a group waiting to get on a crowded bus. When the bus stopped, Phillip . . .

	Grade 1	Grade 2	Grade 3	Grade 4	Grade 5	Grade 6
Got on the bus.	9%	4%	1%	%	%	%
Waited until his turn and got on.	42	83	79	92	92	94
Did not get on the bus.				5	6	3
Walked around the crowd and got on first.	49	13	20			
Ran through the group to get on the bus.				3	2	3

3. When Steve's mother made him a cake, he . . .

	Grade 1	Grade 2	Grade 3	Grade 4	Grade 5	Grade 6
Ate it for supper with his mother and father.	16%	37%	47%	%	%	%
Ate it.	12	5	9			
Invited some children over and gave them some.	49	49	40	38	56	43
Was happy.	23	9	4			
Ate some of it and saved the rest.				14	6	21
Took his teacher a piece.				48	38	36

4. Edgar was riding his shiny new bicycle when Bert came to play, so Edgar . . .

	Grade 1	Grade 2	Grade 3	Grade 4	Grade 5	Grade 6
Went on riding.	10%	4%	%	%	%	%
Didn't ride on his bicycle and played with Bert.	6	15	11	11	11	6
Took turns riding with Bert.	52	81	83			
Told him to go home.	32	0	6			
Put his bicycle away because he knew Bert would want to ride it.				7	4	9
Let Bert ride his bicycle to see how he liked it.				82	85	85

5. Stella always shares with the kids in her room when . . .

	Grade 1	Grade 2	Grade 3	Grade 4	Grade 5	Grade 6
Another kid shares with her.	6%	7%	9%	33%	14%	3%
She wants to.	8	17	17			
They have no scissors.	20	22	23			
She has some candy.	21	32	33			
The teacher comes in.	45	22	18			
They need paper or something.				48	65	70
She has candy.				16	14	21
The teacher asks her.				3	7	6

6. Christine had a sack of her favorite candy, so she . . .

	Grade 1	Grade 2	Grade 3	Grade 4	Grade 5	Grade 6
Ate it.	16%	3%	5%	%	%	%
Gave some to her mother.	23	23	37			
Gave some to the other children.	31	62	43	51	65	70
Ate half and kept rest.	30	12	15	12	7	12
Gave her mother and father and sister one piece.				28	18	12
Left it in the house when her friends came over.				9	10	6

7. Kate was helping her mother with the dishes when Gladys came to play, so . . .

	Grade 1	Grade 2	Grade 3	Grade 4	Grade 5	Grade 6
She finished the dishes and then played.	14%	28%	18%	30%	36%	29%
She went to play with Gladys.	29	15	6	5	7	6
Gladys helped finish the dishes and then they went to play.	57	57	76	65	57	65

8. When John was passing the books to 10 children, there were 7 old books and 3 new ones, so John . . .

	Grade 1	Grade 2	Grade 3	Grade 4	Grade 5	Grade 6
Gave the teacher, another boy and himself the new books and the rest of the kids the old books.	21%	8%	3%			
Gave the good ones to his friends.	21	14	3	32	19	9
Gave the new books to the other children and kept the old one.	11	19	26			
Passed out the books as they came in the pile.	47	59	68			
Took one of the old books and handed out the others.				65	72	82
Read one of the new ones.				3	9	9

In spite of the fact that in each case we had offered "good" as well as "poor" answers, it was very interesting to notice the number of children who checked the "poor" answers. In the first grade this was particularly noticeable. Forty-eight per cent of the children "walked around the crowd and got on first"; 30 per cent "ate half and saved the rest" of the candy.

This was not confined to the first grade, however. In spite of the fact that instructions for administering the form included the request that all of the responses be read to the children before they marked any of them, many children in the upper grades, too, marked the "poor" responses. One would think that the temptation to mark the "good" response in each case would be overwhelming. The interesting fact is that it was not.

One interpretation of this situation might be that there was a good climate in our classrooms—that is, that the children did not feel constrained to respond in the "nice" way if they did not feel that this was the most honest response. There are some classrooms and some families in which anything but the "nice" response brings such swift retribution that the niceties are observed even at the cost of profound insincerity.

Another possible interpretation is that the children who marked the "poor" responses simply did not discriminate between what we thought of as "poor" and what we thought of as "good." In the degree that this is true, we had turned up through our device a surprisingly large number of children who indicated a shattering ignorance of what is expected of them with respect to generosity and sharing. This demanded further examination.

A Test Situation

We turned now to an examination of ways of testing directly children's actual sharing behavior. Our investigation of the "things valued" by the children suggested to us that if we could find things that children valued in the usual school situation, we would be able to observe the tendency of children to share those things.

In school, a child's personal possessions are, after all, unique to him. Bicycles are valued by children, and can of course be shared; but not all the children have bicycles to share. What was it that all the children had, the sharing of which was available to us for observation? Scarce schoo supplies fit this criterion. School equipment belongs to everyone equally. If the children could be observed in school as they handled scarce school supplies, their sharing might be compared.

Therefore, we spent a little time discovering which supplies and which typical school situations demanded sharing. We selected for our purposes school situations in which the supplies had to be distributed with not quite enough to go round. The following supplies were selected for use: scissors, new books, certain music books, colored paper, play equipment.

We selected children for observation whom we had previously identified as "high" and "low" sharers. We deliberately asked these children, at various times during a period of two weeks, to distribute these scarce school supplies, and we recorded their behavior.

AN EXPERIMENT IN TEACHING "SHARING"

We thought that we had here a sufficiently rigorous test situation to allow us to observe some of the immediate results of any efforts we teachers made to improve sharing. We wished to attempt directly to change the sharing behavior of these children. We did not assume that anything we did would have a very profound effect, especially among the older children. However, we thought that we would do what we could, and see whether there would be any detectable effect whatever.

This is the plan we developed. We had observed our four selected children distributing scarce school supplies. Now, each of us introduced discussions of sharing, the value and importance of it, in class. We did this for a week. In no case did our discussions have to do with school supplies. After this week had passed we re-observed the four selected children for two weeks to see whether we could see any change in their tendency to share scarce school supplies.

We thought that we ourselves, as children, had learned the value of sharing through such discussions as these. We thought that, if any of the children was ready to improve in this respect, a reminder of this type might have the desired effect. Also, we were convinced that some of the children simply had not heard about the value of sharing; at the very least such discussions would bring the important matter to their minds.

Several of us introduced moral homilies into our classroom discussions. In one class, the story of the good Samaritan was read to the children, and a discussion followed it. In other classes, we seized upon instances of good sharing from newspaper or radio stories, or from some reading that the children had done, or pictures they had made, using these as springboards for discussions of sharing.

In every case, we handled the matter on a purely verbal level. It had occurred to us that we might use skits, or examples of cooperation in nature, or call the attention of individual children to the happy consequences of sharing on their part when they happened to do it. However, all of us chose to do the thing that was easiest for us—to talk about it.

THE RESULTS

The results of our efforts were quite surprising to us. Ten of us were involved in this experiment, and each of us worked with four children, a total of twenty "high" sharers and twenty "low" sharers. These were the results:

1. Of the twenty "high" sharers, one became a "low" sharer in the course of two weeks following our discussion.

2. Of the twenty "low" sharers, eleven showed no particular change, and *nine showed a substantial improvement* in the sharing of scarce school supplies in a two-week period following these classroom discussions.

3. The nine "low" sharers who improved were in different

classes. In each class, one "low" sharer improved, the other didn't.

Our school year reached its end at this point, and we could not follow up to see whether there were any relapses among our improved "low" sharers after the two-week period of observation. We would assume that there would be many such relapses, especially if nothing more was done about the matter.

But the thing that impressed us was that our classroom discussions appeared to have made a difference. We had given the children some ready-made attitudes through classroom discussion. There was no question in the children's minds of our own attitude toward sharing. By starting classroom discussions of sharing, we were teaching the children directly what attitude they ought to have. And the encouraging thing to us is that it apparently "took" as well as it did.

We assume that the children who were ready and able to make such a change made it—that is, those who were not too preoccupied with some other aspect of their relationship with other people. Whatever the reasons, the results of this informal experiment suggest that classroom discussions of this type, while not strikingly effective (and evidence elsewhere confirms our own experience that they are not), are nevertheless not totally without value in bringing about such a change in behavior as we sought. The difficulty does not lie so much in the relative inefficiency of discussions as a way of bringing about behavior change as in the fact that in a great many schools this is the only approach used. We have continued such discussions, though not *ad nauseum*. However, we have constantly sought to supplement classroom discussions of sharing with other approaches to this goal.

In Summary

Certain learnings about the children in our school seem valid to us.

1. There is no relationship between the economic status of our children's families and their tendency to share things at school.

2. There is a rather definite developmental pattern of things that our children value: as they grow older they become less interested in sweets, for example, and more interested in means of locomotion. Their concern with family possessions remains fairly constant.

3. Some of our children are either ignorant of the expectation that they should share things under certain circumstances, or they are rebelling against the expectation.

4. Discussion of sharing in class has at least a short-term desirable effect on some of our "poor" sharers. Its effect on the others is unknown to us.

How to Verify Our Findings

If you wish to compare the responses and behavior of our children with those of the children in your class, we suggest that you go through the following steps:

Step 1. Collect ten or fifteen examples of "sharing" behavior, and compare them with the collection of a fellow teacher, or discuss them with a fellow teacher. We decided at this point to confine our observations to the sharing of tangible objects.

Step 2. Obtain responses to the question, "What I want most." You may find it interesting to compare the responses of your children with ours. It would be interesting, too, to compare the responses to this open-ended question with your observations, noticing in particular whether the things that you observed the children sharing are the same things that children mentioned in responding to this question.

Step 3. Make up some unfinished sentences, dealing with the things that children apparently value most. In doing this, be sure that the names used in the sentence are not those of any children in your classroom, and that they are sufficiently unusual to allow the children to distinguish among them easily. Notice that, in our case, we ended each of these unfinished sentences with the name of the person whose behavior we wished to have described. We did this to avoid confusing the children.

Step 4. Administer "What did they do?" We based this test on the typical responses of our children to the unfinished sentences that we developed in Step 3. We were interested in the fact that a substantial number of our children checked what we thought were "poor" responses. We do not think that our study of what lay behind "poor" responses was at all adequate. You may wish to try to explain these responses through careful study of the individual children who made them. Perhaps the children who responded in this way were indicating to us that their relationships with others were poor. It is not likely that their attitudes toward tangible property exist in isolation from other social attitudes. Of course, we never referred to the way these children had checked these items in discussing the matter with them.

Step 5. Experiment. We observed our children sharing scarce school supplies long enough to select two children who consistently shared them even-handedly and two others who were consistently selfish or shared them only with close friends. You can do this in the course of ordinary classroom work, since supplies have to be distributed and picked up many times in a school day. Our attempt to change the behavior of the "poor" sharers took the form of classroom discussions for one week. If you wish to try this, we suggest that you carry on the discussions for a much longer period, and that you observe the effect of the discussions for a much longer period than we did. In addition to classroom discussions, the following other approaches to this matter occurred to us, but we did not try them at this time: (*a*) Have some "poor" sharers write a skit about sharing. (*b*) Have some "poor" sharers play the role of "good" sharers in such a skit. (c) Discuss with some individual "poor" sharers the problem of scarce school supplies, and how we might go about distributing them on a fair basis, and make a point later of indicating that the new plan (when it is introduced) was developed with the aid of these "poor" sharers. (Obviously, we would not at any time indicate that we thought they were "poor" sharers.) (d) Involve the "poor" sharers (as well as others) in writing some unfinished stories in which sharing is the crucial element. (e) Ask many of the children to find examples of sharing and other forms of cooperativeness in nature.

We did not think that these approaches, or any combination of them, would wholly correct the "poor" sharing that we were seeing. We thought, though, that they might have a desirable effect on children who were ready to improve. For children who did not respond to this kind of thing, we were certain that further close study of the individuals themselves would have to be undertaken. We were quite certain that the ultimate causes of "poor" sharing, like those of other poor social attitudes, were complicated and lay deep in the child's emotional life.

CHAPTER 8

Democratic Behavior and Security

I T HAS been observed repeatedly in the course of this report that the social behavior of children as shown through considerateness, sharing, initiative, and follow-through, is related to the child's group acceptance and his feeling of his own importance. Although we have chosen in general throughout the study to emphasize factors in the social environment that affect all of the children, we have not meant to overlook what appeared to us to be a fact from the outset: that the inconsiderate, selfish, dependent, or irresponsible child is also an unhappy, insecure child.

One of the elementary school staffs in Springfield chose to study this relation.[1] From the point of view of those of us who undertook this study, all of the "intangibles" had in common something that we called "otherness." All of them, that is, had to do with behavior which was intended to serve the group good or the good of some other individual. This, to us, lay at the heart of the morality of democracy. Democracy, for us, had at least two dimensions. One was the democratic form of government. Another was something we thought of as the democratic type of personal behavior. It

[1] The Weaver School, with an enrollment of 249 children.

189

was the latter of these, democratic personal behavior, that we selected for study.

By democratic personal behavior, we meant thoughtful behavior directed at the good of the group of which a child was a member.

Observing Democratic Behavior

Before we felt free to begin observing democratic behavior, we analyzed our beliefs about its nature. As we thought of it, these three cultural values seemed central to democratic behavior: (1) freedom to act as a self-directing individual in dealing with peers and peer groups; (2) belief in the sharing of responsibility as a necessary contribution to freedom; (3) faith in critical thinking as the best way to solve a free society's problems.

We tried to make these general statements more specific— to break them down into categories that we could relate to specific behavior. We tried it for the first of them: "Freedom to act as a self-directing individual in dealing with peers and peer groups." This we did in a series of staff discussions, our purpose being to explore our thinking in advance of observation.

In Table 8, we show the result of this staff discussion. We found statements that fell into three categories, to which we thought we could assign what we called "plus" behavior (behavior that implied acceptance of the cultural value in question), "zero" behavior (behavior that implied apathy), and "minus" behavior (behavior that implied an aversion to the cultural value in question).

We tested this analysis by observing children to see whether we could find behaviors that clearly fit these plus–zero–minus categories. We found such behavior. Here are some examples of it. For the "plus" category stated as "consideration for the welfare and convenience of others when personal sacrifice is involved" we found the following anecdote.

TABLE 8

A Concept of Freedom for Democratic Living: Categories for Analyzing Behavior According to Value I, "Freedom to Act as a Self-directing Individual in Dealing with Peers and Peer Groups"

+	0	—
1. Belief in value of another's qualities, contributions, or opinions.	1. Acceptance of contributions of others, but belief in superiority of own contribution.	1. Refusal to accept contributions or opinions of others when in variance with personal opinions.
2. Tendency to consider in advance the probable consequence to others of a proposed action.	2. Willingness to make concessions to restore pleasant relations.	2. Unwillingness to yield to will of majority.
3. Willingness to let others develop even at sacrifice of opportunity for self-glorification.	3. Belief in equality of opportunity for all.	3. Desire for constant personal recognition and gratification at expense of others.
4. Consideration for welfare or convenience of others when personal sacrifice is involved.	4. Consideration for welfare or convenience of others when no personal inconvenience is involved.	4. Lack of consideration for welfare or convenience of others.
5. Ability to recognize and work toward a common group purpose.	5. Willingness to cooperate and accept responsibility when self gain is involved.	5. Refusal to cooperate or accept delegated responsibility.

Jerry (a sixth grader) took a hard fall on the ice slide to keep from hitting Carolyn, who had fallen in front of him. He limped the rest of the day.

For the "zero" category stated as "consideration for the welfare or convenience of others when no personal inconvenience is involved," we found the same sixth grade boy doing the following:

Helen asked Jerry to move down one place at the lunch table so that she could sit next to Shirley, and he willingly moved.

For the "minus" category stated as "lack of consideration for welfare or convenience of others," the same boy

snatched the last of the spool of plastic "boondoggling" material from Danny, saying, "I have to get enough of this red to go with the yellow I already have to finish my lanyard."

For the "plus" category stated as "belief in the value of another's qualities, contributions, or opinions" we noted the following behavior of a fifth grade girl:

The children were commenting on the contestants in an assembly program. JoAnne's comment was "I liked the accordion best of all, but the skates were good. I imagine she could have done much better if she had had more room. The stage was really too small to show her off well."

Here is another fifth grade girl doing something we classified under the "minus" category stated as "lack of consideration for the welfare or convenience of others."

Ellen drew pictures and straightened her desk while the rest of the class did arithmetic problems from the blackboard. When the class had finished, we needed the blackboard for something else, and I began to erase the arithmetic problems. Ellen protested sharply, and said that she was not through.

Here is behavior we classified under the "plus" category stated as "tendency to consider in advance the possible consequence to others of a proposed action."

At the camera club, Billy (fifth grade) wanted another child to keep his money. Then he added, "No, I'd better keep it. If it is lost, you would be to blame. It is my job."

Here is a third grade boy showing "consideration for the welfare or convenience of others when personal sacrifice is involved."

The class was giving *The Three Billy Goats Gruff*. Chuckle, who was not a goat, went far out of his way to the town stock-yard and brought three pairs of goat horns to school to be used as props.

These things that we had seen the children do were either directed toward the group, or directed toward themselves without regard to the group need.

One surprise for us was the very small number of "zero" behaviors we could find. Most of those we found, we couldn't agree on. Eventually, we agreed to disregard this category, and to consider that we were studying democratic and undemocratic behavior—that is, behavior which either accepts or rejects the cultural expectation that, under certain circumstances, one should behave for the group good rather than exclusively for oneself.

The effect of this preliminary analysis and observation was to draw us together on what we meant by "democratic behavior." We could see it; it was no longer "intangible." We now attempted to study it further.

What Is Security?

We had begun by assuming that there was some connection between security and the tendency of children to behave in terms of the group good. We assumed that undemocratic behavior was itself a symptom of some insecurity. What, exactly, did we mean by "security"?

To answer our question, we turned to the numerous tests and other psychological devices that have been published for use in answering just this question. Those we used included:

The California Test of Personality (California Test Bureau, 1942.)

The Wishing Well (Ohio State University, Bureau of Educational Research. Since withdrawn for further study.)

Aspects of Personality (World Book Company, 1937.)

The Springfield Interest Finder (See A. T. Jersild, and R. J. Tasch, *Children's Interests and What They Suggest for Education,* Bureau of Publications, Teachers College, Columbia University, 1949.)

In addition to these, we made and used instruments (see Appendix C) called "Who Would It Be?," "Things I Wish," "Things About Me," "My Problems in Growing Up." All of these offered children opportunities to indicate ways in which they were anxious or insecure.

The interpretation of results obtained from the administration of inventories like these has been discussed in many places, and we will not discuss it here. Generally speaking, we scored the results for each child, and separated those with low scores from those with high scores, noticing the degree to which these different instruments tended to point out the same children as insecure. We found, as we had expected to find, that these instruments again and again indicated as insecure the same children whom we had previously identified as showing "undemocratic" behavior.

If we had had any doubts about the relationship of insecurity and undemocratic behavior, our doubts vanished now. The very symptoms that we customarily identified as pointing to "insecurity" were the same behaviors that we were now calling "undemocratic." After all, it is common enough for a child who is emotionally upset to be aggressive, quarrelsome, and self-centered. This was an old story to us.

From the examination of the children's responses to these instruments, we abstracted the following generalizations, based on items which were marked again and again by insecure children, and we present them here because they provoked us to further thought:

Insecure children seem to have more fear of getting hurt than secure children.

Insecure children more often wish for personal property and betterment than for the betterment of others.

Insecure children mention adults more often than secure children do.

Insecure children seek the attention of adults more than secure children do.

Insecure children are more likely to identify with the "underdog," and more likely to believe that they are not liked or accepted by their group.

Now we turned to a similar analysis of our own direct observations, and abstracted these generalizations:

Insecure children show nervous symptoms such as nail biting and chronic fatigue.

Insecure children carry on more bullying, quarreling, disobedience, and destructiveness than secure children do.

Insecure children avoid social situations more frequently than secure children do.

We drew the following conclusions from our observations of secure children:

The secure child is more independent of adults than the insecure child is.

The secure child feels that he "belongs" and is accepted by his group.

The secure child will often inconvenience himself to be of assistance to other children.

In a way, we hadn't found out here any more than we already knew, or any more than many teachers who had studied individual children had already found. However, it seemed helpful to us to remember that many of these specific symptoms of security and insecurity were the same behaviors that we had in mind when we spoke of democratic and undemocratic children. We came to think of the self-centered, egotistic child as being preoccupied with things that were bothering him. With respect to social situations and social attitudes, it became much easier for us to understand the actual operating values of the insecure child when we tried to remember that he was *constantly* bothered by problems relating to his view of himself. His view of himself was influenced by the way other people viewed him, and certainly most profoundly by his relationships with his parents and others at home. We wondered, however, if there were not some things at school that could be done which would of themselves be reassuring to this insecure child, and which might ultimately result in making his behavior what we would call more "democratic."

School Activities That Promote Security

We identified twenty-six kinds of activities which in our opinion had been helpful to insecure children in the past. These were as follows:

Taking care of lunch order
    Taking the order
    Collecting the money
    Checking special lunches
Serving on student council
    Writing the report
    Giving the report
    Working on committees
Responsibility for group action in lunch room
    In charge of coming and going
    Serving as host and hostess
Responsibility for group action in the halls
    (Reminding forgetful children of group decision as to ways of coming and going)
Taking care of room materials
    Books
    Paper and pencils
    Science material
    Art and craft materials
    Playground equipment
Serving on Safety Council
    Writing reports
    Giving reports
    Serving on committees
Arranging for trips
    Making necessary calls
    Writing letters
    Transportation arrangements
    Reporting to the group
Work in arts and crafts

Parties
   Planning games
   Serving on refreshment committee
Programs for assemblies or special occasions
   Planning the program
   Taking part in the program
   Responsibility for stage properties
Making announcements in other rooms
Taking care of projects such as a paper drive, etc.
Opportunities to take part in pupil–teacher and pupil–pupil
   planning
Taking part in organized groups such as band and orchestra
Taking care of room pets such as hamsters and rabbits
Being chosen by the peer group for play on the ball team
Sharing things such as snakes, cocoons, tadpoles, etc.
Taking part in science demonstrations before a group
Being a member of organizations such as Girl Scouts, Gray Y, etc.
Answering the phone and being office messenger
Learning to play ping pong, kick ball, baseball, etc., well
Having mothers as Den Mothers, Scout Leaders, etc.
Having the teacher visit in their home
Being able to teach others to crochet or to braid gimp, etc.
Giving a birthday party for the whole group
Choosing children for games, committees, etc., so as to give every
   child a chance and to leave no one out.

These approaches to increasing security constituted, for
us, a sort of stockpile. We knew we couldn't use them all, and
we knew, too, that we could think of many others any time.
But we had never put a list of them together before.

Having found this close relationship between security and
democratic behavior, we turned now to attempting to use
our twenty-six approaches to increasing security. We wanted
to see whether we could actually help our children toward a
more secure, less self-centered set of attitudes.

Measuring Change in Security

By the time we had administered all the psychological instruments mentioned earlier, scored them, and talked them

over, we thought that we had found a way of measuring improvement in security, if improvement took place. That is, we could use these test results as "bench mark" data—beginning points. Later, if we readministered these tests, we would have evidence of any change that might have occurred. Having identified these twenty-six activities that had been helpful to children in the past, we now attempted to make some children measurably more secure. The sixth grade teacher in our staff agreed to undertake this experiment, and the rest of us watched with interest. She carried on a study of five insecure children, gathering evidence from all of the published and homemade instruments that we had developed, and carefully observing and re-observing the "democratic" behavior of these children.

First the teacher measured the security of the five children, using the instruments we had found and developed. Then she deliberately provided opportunities for each of the five children to do things that would be likely to increase his own feeling of security. Having done these things, she then retested for his feeling of security in much the same manner that had been used at the outset. This process was carried on during an entire school year. The first measures were taken in October and the last in May.

In each of the five cases, this sixth grade teacher was able to identify a definite, but small, movement toward security. We will conclude our report with the reproduction of one of these studies in its entirety—the study of an insecure sixth grade girl whom we shall call Susan.

Susan

I. Origin of Insecurity (results of October tests)
   A. *California Test of Personality* gave these data:
      Low in self-reliance.
      Low in sense of personal worth.
      Nervous symptoms.

Low in feeling of belonging.

B. *Wishing Well* indicated unfilled needs:
Need for belonging.
Need for economic security.

C. *Completed sentences* which were significant were:
I wish I didn't have to—be afraid when I'm alone.
I am afraid—of the dark.
I wish I knew—what to do to make people like me better.

D. *Completed story* of why one child helped another child
clean up spilled milk in the lunch room read:
She did that because she was polite and wanted people
to like her better.

E. *When I am alone, I think* was completed:
of getting scared and how I would like to have a pretty
formal and it is pink and with a pretty flower on it.

F. *Three Wishes* are:
1. I wished I had a whole lot of money.
2. I wished my Daddy could find a job.
3. I wished we could find us a house.

G. *My Problems in Growing Up* were checked as follows:
Personal
1. I keep forgetting things.
2. I'm afraid of making mistakes.
3. I daydream too much.
People
1. Most people don't like me.
2. I don't make friends easily.
Money
1. I want to earn my own money.
2. I have less than my friends.
3. I don't have enough for lunches.
Home
1. I'm afraid my father will lose his job.
2. I'm ashamed of the house we live in.
3. We have sickness in our family.
Social
1. I want to know how to choose my clothes well.
2. I have no place to entertain my friends.
3. I don't have anything to do in my spare time.

H. *What I Think, Feel, and Do* had these significant questions marked "Yes."

    1. Do you think that many people make quite a lot of fun of you?

    2. Do you feel you are different from other people?

I. *Sociograms* for the first four months showed that no one chose her. Classroom Social Distance Scale listed her in the group "I would rather not have these people in the group with which I work or play" more than any other child in the room. When choosing people for special activities, such as to help with math or science, to play in a game, etc., no one chose her.

J. Behavior as observed and recorded bore out the tendencies suggested above.

II. Opportunities Provided (between October and April)

Having identified the origin of Susan's insecurity to be lack of self-reliance, lack of a sense of personal worth, need for belonging, and need for economic security, these things were done that seemed to help:

A. Her mother and father were personally invited to come to Play Night and play and mingle with other parents. Susan and the other children came, too.

B. A job was provided so that Susan could work and earn her dollar to become a member of our Girl Scout troop.

C. She was given charge of stacking and making ready the plates for washing, in order that she might pay for her lunch at school.

D. A job was secured for her mother at a laundry.

E. The whole group was taught a square dance. Jackie, of his own accord, asked Susan to be his partner.

F. Susan crochets well. She was able to teach several girls to crochet hot mats.

G. Most of the children were going to the Clare Tree Major Plays. Susan dusted Venetian blinds to earn money for her ticket and her twin brother's.

H. Our room was asked to send six water color pictures for the Art Exhibit. Susan's picture was chosen as one of the six.

I. Susan wove a rug for her room.

J. We are now working on our operetta, *Cinderella*. Susan has the part she wanted in the operetta so that she can wear an evening dress. Her mother has promised to make one for her. "A pink one," I hope, "with a pretty flower on it."

III. Movement Toward Security

   A. Sociograms for January, February, March, and April have given Susan one, two, one and three choices. She now has a best friend. The best friend is, however, one of the insecure children, and almost an isolate herself.

   B. Observations have shown many evidences of positive behavior with only an occasional "backsliding" to undesirable or negative behavior.

   C. *Three Wishes* written in April were:
     1. I wish I had a new permanent.
     2. I wish I were not so tall.
     3. I wish we would have *Play Night* again.
    It would seem that her wishes were no longer so intensely concerned with *money* or *people liking her* as they were before.

   D. *What I Want to Learn to Do Better* written in April read:
     1. I would like to learn to help the Brownies.
     2. I would like to learn to be a better friend.
     3. I would like to play Miss X [teacher] in ping-pong better.

She seems to place emphasis on being a better friend now.

It will be noted that the "movement toward security" was neither dramatic nor very great. The point here is that it could be identified, and that there was some movement. Among the other four cases reported by this teacher, only one child, a boy, made a very considerable "movement toward security." In the other cases, the movement was similar to that reported in the case of Susan. This would seem to indicate that the process for these children is slow, and that such purely school-centered activities as this teacher identified as being helpful would have to be continued over a long period of time for a very substantial change in the feeling of security to be accomplished. Of course, the teacher would normally do more than she did here: she would enlist the parents' help in analyzing the problem and working toward improvement. If trained guidance workers had been available (they were not), she would have used their help. For purposes of our study, the important thing here is that *some definite progress was made,* and that it had an identifiable result stated as the democratic behavior, and thus the democratic values, of the child in question.

How to Verify These Findings

We shall not offer a step-by-step plan for verifying these findings, since the case of Susan outlines the plan in detail. The things our sixth grade teacher did to improve the security were sharply focused, we think, on the sources of Susan's insecurity as identified through the instruments she used.

PART III

WHAT WE THINK
ABOUT ACTION RESEARCH

Introduction

IN PART II, we have reported the way we worked, the data we gathered, and the conclusions and inferences we arrived at.

Part III is the report of a study of us, the cooperative action research workers. This study was not cooperative in the way the work reported earlier was. One of the Institute consultants stood at a distance, so to speak, and studied us as we carried on the action research process. He sought answers to questions raised by the fact that we classroom teachers were attempting to apply what we could of the research process to these particular classroom problems.

As we carried on our work, we knew exhilarating success and exasperating failure. Most of the time, our consultants were very helpful; sometimes they missed the mark.

In this section, our feelings about our work are reported—what we liked about it, what we didn't like. We were interested and surprised at some of the "fringe benefits" of this kind of in-service activity. Most of us grew and thrived on it, achieving greater professional self-respect. Our school staffs became more unified.

We feel strongly that other teachers should undertake such research activity as this. This being the case, we have been willing to speak frankly to the Institute consultant when he interviewed us, and to respond fully (and sometimes bluntly) to his questionnaires; we therefore offer his report of our reaction to this experience.

CHAPTER 9

We Learn to Cooperate

EFFECTIVE WAYS for involving teachers in cooperative action research should be suggested by a study of the reactions of participants to the procedures in which they were involved. The purpose of this and the following chapters is to report how the Springfield teachers felt about the ways of working employed in the action research projects they were conducting. The information in these chapters was obtained from three sources: (1) notes on meetings in which teachers and consultants discussed research procedures, (2) records of interviews with individual teachers, and (3) a questionnaire. The comments of teachers quoted throughout this study were taken from the notes and records. The action research procedures identified during these discussions formed the basis of the forty-one item questionnaire, which was administered twice—first in December and again in May—during the first school year of the project.

Teachers were asked in the questionnaire to rate each procedure's value to them on a three-point scale, and also to indicate the extent to which each procedure was used in their school. The questionnaire administered in May was identical with that given in December, except that two items were added to the list of procedures. Teachers' ratings of each item were tabulated in order to indicate (*a*) the number of times each procedure was judged of great value, of some value, or of little or no value, and (*b*) the extent to which each procedure had been used in the school. To establish a composite index of the value of these procedures to teachers, the ratings for each item were converted to an index score. A table of index scores for all procedures included in the questionnaire is presented in Appendix D, with an explanation of the manner in which the scores were determined and an interpretation of the scores on separate items.

This chapter reports the teachers' reactions to the *ways by which the action research was made a cooperative endeavor*. Ratings of procedures by teachers will be reported and discussed as a means of indicating the value assigned to action research procedures which enabled teachers to work cooperatively with others.

Procedures for Helping Each Other

Most teachers placed great emphasis on cooperative endeavor. They liked those procedures which allowed them to work out their problems and carry on their study cooperatively. Evidence of this fact can be seen in the ratings they assigned to the following procedures in the questionnaire: [1]

[1] In reading the tabular material, bear the following in mind:

There were 41 items on the questionnaire as a whole. Each teacher was asked to rate the value of each procedure on a three-point scale, from "very great value to me" to "little or no value to me." These ratings were converted into scores, and the "index-of-value" is the average score assigned by the 58 teachers who responded. The items are ranked according to their index-of-value scores; their numbers indicate their original order in the questionnaire.

Differences in index scores between consecutive single items are not significant, but the differences between the first, second, third, and fourth *quarters*, of the items, when ranked, are significant. Therefore, under "rank order," we have used a Roman numeral to indicate which quarter each item belongs to, from highest (I) to lowest (IV).

Item	Rank Order	INDEX-OF-VALUE SCORES (December)	(May)
22. Reaching an agreement by teachers prior to observation as to the meaning of categories for recording and interpreting behavior.	I	2.8	2.7
11. Having time to talk difficulties out with other members of the staff when they occur.	I	2.8	2.6
14. Discussions of terms by all teachers of a school for the purpose of being together on meanings.	I	2.8	2.8
29. Having all the teachers in a building studying the same behavior and recording it in identical categories.	I	2.8	2.8
36. Evaluating observations of behavior by having entire staff discuss anecdotes reported by individual teachers.	II	2.7	2.6
12. Meetings of the entire staff of a school to work on the project between visits of the HMLI people.	II	2.6	2.7
31. Having other teachers classify behavior anecdotes under given categories as a check on an individual's interpretation of behavior.	III	2.4	2.4
13. Meetings of small groups of teachers from a school to work on the project between visits of the HMLI people.	III	2.4	2.2
23. Arbitrary definition of terms by a school staff when it is not possible to arrive at a satisfactory definition through discussion.	III	2.3	2.3
24. Using tape recorder to record classroom work in order that a common understanding of what kind of behavior is to be observed can be gained by all teachers in a school.	III	2.3	2.3
32. Having teachers observe and record data in each other's classroom.	IV	2.0	2.1

The procedures listed above enabled teachers to work very closely together. These as well as other ways of working cooperatively are discussed in the subsequent sections of this chapter.[2]

EACH STAFF WORKS AS A WHOLE [3]

In each of the schools all teachers participating in the study were working on the same problem and were attempting to observe the same type of behavior. This served to weld groups together and to give them a basis for common understandings. Teachers liked this procedure. This was a typical report:

The fact that our entire school staff has been working together at the same time on the problem has helped us all to improve.

Some teachers, in discussing ways of working, thought that it was too hard to get the entire staff of a school together for study. They preferred small committee work, because of the difficulties involved in relieving all teachers of classroom responsibilities at one time. Most of the teachers, however, did not agree with this. This comment expressed the view of many:

I think in our particular building it would be better to work as a whole staff. We need that contact. There has been a growing feeling of team work with our teachers and I think it is important to continue to work this way so we can continue to grow in that feeling.

[2] In this and subsequent chapters, the three sources of data mentioned: i.e., the notes on meetings, transcribed interviews, and responses to the consultant's questionnaire, will be treated simultaneously. Themes that are mentioned in one source are identified, and data relating to each theme are applied. Thus, for example, the importance of the staff working as a whole and the place of sub-committees of the staff, are identified on this page. The teachers' responses to certain questionnaire items are relevant to this theme and a footnote calls attention to these items (footnote 3). The matter is mentioned repeatedly in interviews, and sections from the interviews are quoted. The consultant's notes on the meetings suggest some administrative arrangements in connection with the "whole staff" theme, and these suggestions are in the text. The purpose here is less to display the data than it is to develop the themes that emerge from the data.

[3] See items 22, 11, 14, 29, 36, 12, 13 of the responses to the questionnaire given above.

Arrangements were made during visits of Institute consultants to supply enough substitute teachers to relieve all of the members of a school staff for research activities. In some schools, however, it was difficult to arrange for all teachers to meet together for planning and study between consultants' visits. Substitute teachers were not normally supplied for all teachers each week. Nevertheless, teachers attempted to work out ways for meeting as a unit. Two of the schools arranged to share substitute teachers so that each school would have enough substitutes to relieve all teachers once every two weeks instead of half of the teachers every week. Teachers from schools where there had been no whole-staff meetings between consultants' visits felt the need for such meetings. This need was expressed thus by one teacher:

We have done less discussing and sharing of ideas than we should have. I think it would be helpful if we could do more of it. I think this would be one way of improving our study next year. That is, group meetings between visits of the Institute people would be helpful. We need to actually sit down in a series of meetings to talk about what we are doing and to discuss our problems and to pass on ideas that we have.

While most of the teachers would not have discontinued working as a total staff group in their schools, many teachers pointed out the value of working in small groups at times to accomplish certain jobs and to guarantee greater participation by some teachers. The principal and teachers of one school stressed particularly the great value to them of work in small groups. A new teacher in the school talked at some length, at one of the meetings, about her unwillingness to make contributions to the large group discussions because she felt that anything she might say would have to be worth the attention of the large group. She reported no such unwillingness to speak in small groups. Other teachers agreed with her.

"Talking out" difficulties

Responses to item eleven, above, indicate that many teachers considered it important to have time to "talk out" difficulties, as they occurred, with other staff members. By this, they meant time to discuss a problem so that all members of the staff would have an opportunity to express their ideas. In this way of working, misunderstandings are brought out and can be cleared up, and the teachers can carry out plans because they thoroughly understand the thinking which went into those plans. Talking a problem through was considered by many to be a basic procedure of cooperative research, as is illustrated by this exchange during a group interview:

Consultant: Are there other procedures which have been helpful in carrying the research forward?

First Teacher: I think talking the thing out is important.

Second Teacher: Some of the devices other schools used are good. The scale which they developed for recording anecdotes of behavior is a way to reach common understanding. That is really why they set up a scale—to know what they meant by certain behavior.

First Teacher: Was the scale developed by your entire group, or was it prepared by a small group and given to the entire group? Doesn't a scale or device for recording observations always have to be prepared by everyone in order to get it talked through and understood?

Third Teacher: It has to be talked through and planned by the entire group and then organized by a small group. We talked it through and then a committee of three worked it out. . . . Don't you think that this way of working is one of the main procedures of group research?

First Teacher: I think so. Talking it out is important.

Reaching agreements

Frequently, all members of a school staff were studying a common problem which required observing children's behavior in different classrooms. Usually the teachers developed a guide to observation for recording the behavior. They learned in the process that it was necessary for a staff to reach agreement *prior* to observation on the meaning of categories to be used for recording behavior if comparable results were to be achieved. Teachers thought that the practice of attempting to reach such agreements was a valuable study procedure. One staff reported:

We found that several people could come out of an observation with the same results if an agreement as to what we were looking for and how we were going to check for those things was reached *before* we began our observation. We thought that this was so necessary that we spent some time trying to come to agreements.

Teachers reported not only that agreement was important for getting comparable observations, but also that in the process of reaching agreement a number of misconceptions were cleared up and new insights were gained which helped in moving the research forward. They considered this so valuable that they worked out several procedures for facilitating the process of reaching agreements. Two of these will be discussed here: training (or practice) periods, and the use of tape recordings.

—training periods

Most school groups planned for training or practice periods to develop facility in making observations or using whatever other research methodology was contemplated. Sample data were collected according to the methods devised by the teachers during planning sessions. These were brought to staff meetings where they were discussed by the entire group. During these meetings misunderstandings concerning the application of the procedures were cleared up. The staff was enabled, too, to revise the procedure if they seemed not to get the information desired. Teachers felt that this way of working was valuable.

One teacher said:

. . . our sessions were more than training sessions for specific situations. We did that, but other agreements and insights which we reached as we discussed ways of observing and recording were just as important. Those discussions during the training period were important for giving us security . . .

—tape recordings

Several school staffs used tape recordings as a means for reaching agreements concerning observational technique. In one school, a tape recording was made of a planning session with children. Teachers then practiced tallying children's comments as the tape was played back during a staff meeting. In this way, they were able to compare the results of their individual tallies to check the extent of agreement on the categorizing of the comments. The tape was played several times in order to clear up disagreements and misunderstandings. In other schools, recordings were made of teacher interviews with children who responded to unfinished stories, so that teachers might work out better ways of conducting such interviews. The recordings helped to check the relationship between the kind of question the teacher asked, and the way in which it was asked, with the answers given by the children. This procedure resulted in a number of changes in the way teachers used the unfinished stories.

One teacher reported:

The tape recorder served as a means for all the teachers to have a common experience in order that we could say, "These are the things we are looking for . . ."

Another teacher said:

It [the tape recording] also served as an instrument for clarifying meaning. For instance, one teacher would interpret a child's contribution to the recorded planning session in the way she saw it and another teacher would say, "But that doesn't mean that to me at all." We would all listen to the recording again and try to clarify our ideas as to the meaning of the children's responses.

DOUBLE-CHECKING INTERPRETATIONS OF DATA

Observation was used in most schools as the basic procedure for studying children's behavior. During or immediately after an observation, each teacher recorded descriptive anecdotes which he later sorted into categories that had been developed by the whole faculty group. Teachers were sometimes uncomfortable in categorizing because they were not sure that their interpretation agreed with the staff decisions. Several schools worked out a procedure that made it possible to double-check the interpretation of an individual teacher. In these schools several teachers classified the anecdotes independently. When this had been done the classifications were compared. It was found that with practice a high degree of agreement among the separate interpretations could be achieved. Teachers found this procedure helpful, and once they had tried it, they employed it whenever possible.

One teacher said this about the experience of the staff at his school:

We recorded anecdotes of children's behavior which seemed to indicate certain things to us and we checked them as such. Then, when the substitute teachers came in and we had an opportunity to work together, we let other people check the anecdotes without knowing how we had checked them in order that we might see if they were consistently like our checks. We plan to do this more fully from now on.

Some schools used a variation of this procedure. They asked other school staffs who were not engaged in the study to classify certain anecdotes in order to test the adequacy of the categories used by the teachers involved in the research. A degree of success was achieved, but it was difficult for a staff that did not have background in the study area to interpret and classify isolated anecdotes. This procedure, however, had an important beneficial result not directly related to the study: it gave the teachers participating in the action research study an opportunity to meet and talk with teachers who, though not participating in the study, were in the same school system.

TEAM OBSERVATIONS

Having teachers observe and record in one another's classrooms was checked rather low on the questionnaire (see item 32, page 209). This procedure was used in only three of the six elementary schools. However, the practice is one which was highly valued by those teachers who used it. In these cases, two or three teachers formed a team to work together to collect certain kinds of data. In one school, one teacher conducted a planning session with the children in her classroom while another teacher observed and recorded the behavior being studied. Later the teachers reversed roles in the other classroom. In another school, one teacher interviewed individual children from her classroom about unfinished stories while a second teacher recorded the questions and answers.

Persons who employed team observations as a means of collecting data thought the practice had a number of advantages. It was very helpful for the teacher to be able to give full attention to the work with children and not have to be concerned with recording. At the same time, the recording teacher had no other task, and the records were more complete. Most helpful of all was the fact that it was possible to sit down afterwards with a person who had also been through the experience and discuss the interpretation of the data collected. The teachers felt that this led to sounder analysis of the behavior being studied. While it is true that there were many advantages inherent in the use of team observations, it was easy to understand the reasoning of some of the teachers who had not tried it:

The teacher who works with children knows the background of the situation and is better able to record fully than a person who comes into the room.

We felt in using team observation that it was easier to get everything down, but that it was not always possible to have the person observe at the time when you felt you had a situation which should be described.

Another cause for reluctance, and the way it was finally set aside, was reported thus:

One of the techniques we used near the first was that of having one teacher observe another. The observing teacher took notes and helped get down information. When we first started out we didn't know whether we wanted someone else coming into our room to watch us teach. Soon we saw that that wasn't what they were doing: they were there to help. Now, I think no one in our building has a hesitancy about going into another teacher's room or in having another come into his room. It is a very helpful technique.

Some Difficulties

The process of making the study cooperative was not without its difficulties. This has been obvious in the preceding discussions of procedures employed by the teacher researchers in helping each other. Several difficulties were identified by teachers as ones which should be given attention if cooperative action research is to be truly cooperative.

GETTING ENTIRE SCHOOL STAFF TOGETHER

If teachers are to develop plans and evaluate results cooperatively, they must have opportunities to meet together for periods of time sufficient to talk difficulties out and reach agreements. Sometimes this wasn't done. Many teachers reported that it was hard to find time to meet together when teachers could bring their undivided attention to the job.

Many of the participants felt that the administrative arrangements were an important factor in getting together for cooperative endeavor. Constantly adding to the teacher's load of activities without ever subtracting has resulted in teacher loads which prevent giving adequate thought to the job of teaching. Participants in this study believed that teachers who are to undertake special work must be relieved of some of their extraclassroom activities.

One teacher said:

I think teachers should have some time set aside . . . for this sort of work. Some of us have had to make this of secondary importance because of the other things we have to do.

Other teachers thought that the administrative policy of relieving half a school staff at a time for planning needed to be revised in order to provide for whole-staff cooperation.

One teacher discussed the difficulty as follows:

. . . if the mechanics of our planning group could be so arranged that we didn't have to have half of our group together at one time and half together at another time it would be very helpful. As it is we have only enough substitute teachers for half of our group, so we meet together the first part of the morning and go over our plans and talk about our problem; then during the last half of the morning the other group of teachers comes in and we have to rehash the plans. We spend twice as much time as we might if we were in one group and yet we don't get twice as many ideas.

COMMUNICATING IDEAS

A number of communication difficulties were mentioned. Teachers frequently mentioned the fact that it was difficult to get together on the meanings of terms when they planned for study and observation. Understanding the ideas others were trying to convey and reaching agreements as to what should be studied and observed were difficulties of considerable importance.

A teacher confirmed this point in this comment:

Terms do not always mean the same thing to everyone. One person has his own interpretation of a term and another an entirely different concept. . . . I think it is hard to find common ground for making recordings and for analyzing your findings.

Some of the researchers felt that their efforts to reach agreement on certain aspects of the study had resulted in "hairsplitting." They believed that the attempts to develop a precise way of expressing ideas had been unprofitable and a waste of time.

One teacher expressed this point of view:

. . . to me, one of the most difficult things in this whole study has been the pinpoint fineness we were held to so many times on words. Now, that has been bad for me and very hard but there seems to have to be one word to say just one thing and that is all.

Participants in the study realized that they had not worked out a satisfactory way to carry the entire school staff along with the process of thinking which took place in a small group. Due to the difficulties involved in getting the school group together for frequent meetings much work had to be delegated to small committees of teachers. When these committees attempted to report to the staff they found it difficult to interpret their ideas to persons who had not participated in each step of the committee work. This made cooperation difficult. A teacher described the problems his group encountered in trying to share techniques for interviewing children:

We have the same problem of communication that we have had all along. When we interviewed a child with a group of teachers present it helped those who were there, but we found it impossible to share what had gone on with those teachers who were not able to be there. In order to get the benefit from the trial run we had to have everyone there. This was difficult and we could not manage it with our set-up.

Another communication difficulty which teachers identify is that of securing adequate follow-through on plans. It was difficult to make plans clear enough so that everyone could carry them out. A great amount of time was needed for talking plans over if this difficulty was to be overcome. But time was not always available. As a consequence, some teachers misinterpreted plans, and others found they could not carry through the plans they had set up because they were more complicated than they had realized.

Varying degrees of interest

Some participants identified problems that resulted because of varying degrees of interest on the part of teachers involved in the action research project. Teachers who lacked interest were not willing to spend the time necessary for planning and making decisions cooperatively. They did not follow through on plans wholeheartedly, occasionally causing a step in the study to break down because of insufficient data. Those who identified this problem felt that it was not the most serious difficulty encountered, but said that it did exist and should be recognized.

Summary

Teachers placed great emphasis on the cooperative aspect of action research. They identified a number of obstacles to cooperative endeavor. These included the difficulty of finding time for an entire school staff to get together for planning and discussion frequently enough to carry the study forward cooperatively; the difficulty of carrying a large group along with the process of thinking which took place in a small working group; the difficulty of achieving common understanding sufficient to enable teachers to follow through on plans; and the problem of varying degrees of interest in the study on the part of teachers.

Teachers felt that they were able to develop a number of effective procedures for dealing with the difficult problem of making their action research truly cooperative. They liked the procedure of having an entire school staff work on the same research problem. They found the practice of talking out difficulties whenever they arose very helpful. They found several techniques useful in reaching agreements. These included: training periods preceding each new stage of study, using tape recordings in giving teachers a common experience, and using teams of teachers for observation and for double-checking interpretations of data.

CHAPTER 10

How We Like
the Research Procedures

WHILE the project was under way, it was necessary to adapt some well-known research procedures for use. Some were planned for in advance; others were devised on the spot. In this chapter are reported the feelings of the staff about four types of procedures: those used in studying children; those used to help the participants maintain their own perspective; those used to share ideas (interim reporting); those involving consultant help.

Procedures for Studying Children

Three basic methods for studying children were used in the action research project in Springfield. These consisted of observation of behavior, children's responses to projective devices, and children's answers to tests and direct questions. In the questionnaire which was administered by the Institute Consultant in December and May, teachers were asked to rate specific procedures for applying the basic methods. The value scores of each of these procedures are given on page 223.[1]

Item	Rank Order	INDEX-OF-VALUE (December)	(May)
27. Considering the total situation in which behavior occurred when making an evaluation or interpretation of that behavior.	I	2.9	2.8
26. Including a description of the situation in which certain behavior occurred when writing behavior anecdotes.	I	2.9	2.8
28. Determining children's ideas of the behavior studied.	II	2.7	2.6
34. Observing and recording behavior of a certain kind wherever it occurs in the group.	II	2.7	2.5
19. Using observations of behavior to check results of devices such as sociograms, California Test of Personality, and others.	III	2.5	2.5
37. Testing findings obtained from observation of a few children by looking for same things in the entire group.	III	2.5	2.6
18. Using devices such as sociograms, social distance scales, etc. to identify children to be observed for certain kinds of behavior.	III	2.4	2.5
35. Observing and recording the behavior of a few children as a basis for generalizing about the behavior of the group.	III	2.3	2.1
20. Use of published tests to check teacher's evaluation of children's behavior.	IV	2.2	2.3
40. Using projective devices such as unfinished stories or unfinished sentences as means of determining values youngsters hold.	Not given in December	Not given in December	2.3

[1] To interpret the summary offered here, notice whether the index of value changed much between December and May, and notice its rank. Item 27, for example, ranked high (second of 41 items), and its index-of-value did not change appreciably. Generally speaking, the authors do not consider a change of less than .2 to have any meaning. Changes of .3 and more are considered appreciable. The rank order as given is based on the index-of-value scores, calculated to two decimal places. Differences in rank of less than .4 are not appreciable.

LOOKING AT THE WHOLE SITUATION

Items 27 and 26, having to do with consideration of the total situation in evaluating behavior, received the highest scores in this group and stood second and third from the top in the entire group of procedures. They imply a fundamental insight which teachers felt they achieved during this study. Very early in their efforts to evaluate the behavior they had observed, they found that an interpretation of behavior apart from the total situation in which it developed had little if any meaning. This accounts for the high value teachers place on "looking at the total situation."

OBSERVATIONS

Items 34, 35, and 37 were included to get the teachers' reactions to the methods of observation used for studying children's behavior. The results shown here are in accord with the comments teachers frequently made concerning these methods. Many teachers felt that limiting observation to a few children (as was done in several schools) was not the best way to get at the things they wanted from the study. They recognized that observing a few children makes observation easier, but they felt that such a procedure did not move them as rapidly toward their goals as observing specific types of behavior wherever it occurred. When the goal is to determine the situational causes for certain behavior and ways to change it, emphasis should be on observing the behavior wherever it occurs, they thought, rather than on observing the behavior of a few children. Teachers were consistent in the value they ascribed to the various methods. Item 34, "Observing specific behavior wherever it occurs," received the highest rating of the three; item 37, "Testing findings obtained from observation of a few by looking for the same thing in the entire group," received next highest rating; and item 35, "Observing and recording the behavior of a few children as a basis for generalizing about the behavior of the group," received the lowest rating. Actually, none of the ratings is extremely low. This probably means that the teachers would reject none of them as a way of working.

It is significant to note the relative positions of item 19, "Using observations of behavior to check results of certain devices," and item 20, "Using published tests to check teacher's evaluation of children's behavior." This seems to indicate that for their purposes teachers who checked the questionnaire felt that firsthand observation resulted in better understanding of behavior than did the use of published tests. Again, however, the score of item 20 is not extremely low. The teachers did not wholly reject the procedure.

PROJECTIVE DEVICES

The ratings given those procedures dealing with ways to determine the children's ideas about the behavior being studied (items 28 and 40) indicate the high value teachers placed on projectives and similar devices. Several types of projective materials were used in Springfield.

—unfinished stories and sentences

Some schools used unfinished stories and one school used unfinished sentences. In both, a situation or problem was presented which had no solution stated. Children were asked to tell what they would do in the particular situation and from their answers were inferred the values the children held in terms of the situation presented. Teachers were aware of certain limitations inherent in the answers they received from the children. Some teachers felt children's responses to the stories and their behavior in similar situations were inconsistent. In a recorded interview, one teacher said:

I think we all agree that a great deal of what the youngster says is what he thinks we want him to say. That is, he says what he thinks is socially acceptable. There may be a great gap between his behavior and what he says he should do.

On the other hand, one teacher thought that anything the children might say about the story would reveal their values.

Another point that will bear consideration is the fact that, if the child seems to get off the point, you let him talk himself out. After all, it is not straight answers to your questions you want. It is anything he might say to reveal how he feels about the situation.

The stories and sentences used were based on the anecdotal records of children's behavior which had been collected in each school. Teachers attempted to write stories that would involve the values they were studying. (See Chapters 4, 6, and 7 for examples.)

Several methods of obtaining children's responses to the stories were used. Most teachers interviewed each child individually. A few teachers of upper elementary school youngsters had children write the answers to the stories. In most cases a few children were chosen rather than administering the test to an entire group. Children who demonstrated extreme forms of the behaviors being studied (for example, extremely high and extremely low follow-through) were chosen in some cases. Choice of children was based on observations of the teachers or on certain devices such as the Classroom Social Distance Scale or sociograms.

As a result of their efforts to develop satisfactory stories, teachers set forth a number of criteria for desirable stories. One group lists these four criteria:

Stories should:
1. contain a clear, single issue.
2. embody a variety of content according to some scheme for variety—that is, situations, types of follow-through, etc.

3. be meaningful to all age groups.
4. call for more than yes or no answers.

Another group listed other criteria:

Stories should:
  1. be within the realm of the experiences of the youngsters.
  2. be brief and clear.
  3. have several possible answers.
  4. not include too many problems.

—reactions to pictures

Teachers liked other projective devices which were used. Some teachers sought children's reactions to pictures as a means of understanding children's feelings.[2] In this procedure (used at Weaver School) a child was asked to describe a picture which the teacher had presented to him and to tell what it meant to him.

One teacher said:

I like the Picture Test. It was a good way of working with first grade youngsters. They entered into the spirit of the Picture Test and enjoyed describing and telling what they thought about the picture.

—three wishes

Some teachers liked the "three wishes" device. In using this device the children were asked to list the things they would want if they could have three wishes granted. The results were found to be revealing of certain values children hold, especially in the category of possessions.

These were two teachers' comments:

I found the *Three Wishes* good for third grade youngsters. They enter into the spirit of the game of three wishes. I think it is very important that we know what youngsters think and want in order to be able to help them. The *Three Wishes* seemed to reveal that.

[2] For an illustration and description of this and other devices for studying children see Ruth Cunningham and Associates, *Understanding Group Behavior of Boys and Girls* (New York: Bureau of Publications, Teachers College, Columbia University, 1951), pp. 340-440.

. . . the *Three Wishes* was a good thing to use with first grade youngsters too. They liked that and I think I got information that was helpful from it.

SOCIOGRAMS

The sociogram was very popular with teachers. It proved to be an effective way to learn about the social groupings of children within a classroom and to study the acceptance and rejection of certain youngsters by their classmates. The device was easy to use and teachers found the information it yielded helpful in their study.

One teacher said:

I found the sociogram the most valuable device we used. It was an excellent way to get to understand the youngster in relationship to all the other children in the group.

RATING FORMS AND SCALES

A procedure which teachers found valuable in helping them to handle anecdotal records of children was that of developing appropriate scales or categories into which the anecdotes were fitted. This gave teachers a basis for interpreting their written accounts of behavior as well as for giving direction to their observations. The scale developed in one school—for rating and recording behavior which demonstrated the extent to which children assumed responsibility for the welfare of the group—is illustrative of the rating forms used in the action research projects. (See Chapter 8.) A three-point scale was used with these categories: (1) an act initiated by the child, (2) an act readily performed but suggested by the teacher or someone else, and (3) an act required by the teacher and reluctantly performed. As teachers observed behavior of children they wrote a brief description of the behavior and rated in on the scale.

In some schools rating forms and scales were made to help teachers record ratings of behavior without writing long anecdotes. The categories for checking behavior on the scales were based on records teachers had made during preliminary observations of the behavior being studied. Teachers found that the use of rating scales gave them an adequate record of behavior only when all teachers understood the meaning of the scales used.

Teachers discussed this problem in a recorded group interview:

First teacher: I wonder whether the use of a scale would result in an accurate recording of behavior. You could rate things on a scale quickly and I just wonder how they compare in accuracy with anecdotal records.

Second teacher: We believe they compare fairly well in accuracy. We tried to check accuracy when we were studying participation as an element in follow-through. We used anecdotal records and it did take a great deal of the teachers' time. Then we made our scales based on this record. We felt that they saved the teachers a great deal of time and the results we obtained compared favorably with those obtained through recording behavior anecdotes.

PROBLEMS FACED

Teachers pointed out a number of difficulties which they faced in using the procedures for studying children. Their problems fell into two categories—lack of time to do an adequate job and difficulty in using the child study techniques.

—lack of time

Teachers frequently mentioned the problem of finding time to carry on the research activities as well as their many other professional duties. Although an effort was made to keep the procedures employed in studying children and collecting data about their behavior closely related to the classroom activities of teachers, it took additional time to use them.

One teacher discussed this difficulty thus:

I believe the biggest difficulty is the lack of time. We have so much to do in our own classrooms. Many times you see something that, if you just had time to stop and put it down, would really make a fine observation. But maybe you can't, and time elapses. When you are able to make a record, it is cold and isn't as good as it would have been.

There were participants in the study who felt that this time element alone was not the most serious problem involved in cooperative action research. They felt that as teachers gained experience in using research techniques they would be able to carry on the study without greatly interfering with other activities. To these people it was lack of experience, not lack of time, that was the real difficulty.

—using child study techniques

Many of the difficulties teachers encountered in their research activities had to do with the use of certain methods and procedures of getting evidence. Projective devices, observations, anecdotal records, and questionnaires all presented difficulties to the teachers. Most of the teachers were of the opinion that these difficulties arose because of lack of experience with the research procedures, and looked upon such difficulties as things to be overcome by further preparation and experience. They identified many areas where they need more experience.

The use of the sociometric techniques employed in the study was a problem identified by some teachers.

I think it is lack of background as far as the teacher is concerned that holds up this sort of study. . . . There are several ways of working with which we had never come in contact. One of them was sociometric techniques. I think there was only a third of the faculty that had ever seen a sociogram, let alone ever having made one.

Problems connected with observing and making anecdotal records were mentioned frequently by the teachers.

One teacher said his inability to write good anecdotes was a serious problem with him. Another teacher said this:

One thing that seemed to me to be confusing was knowing how to record, what to record, and what to leave out that wouldn't be of value to the other fellow if he were reading it. We need to know how to make our anecdotes meaningful to someone else and to ourselves as well.

And some teachers found it extremely difficult to observe and record data while teaching, as this teacher's comment shows:

At first we had a great deal of difficulty in developing the skill of taking down anecdotes. We would get interested in what we were doing and forget to write the anecdotes. I think at the beginning one of the hardest things we had to do was getting acclimated to the study—remembering that while you were doing everything else in the classroom you were supposed to be observing children and recording certain behavior.

Many teachers found it difficult to make anecdotal records without putting in a personal interpretation. They considered it important to have anecdotes of behavior free from any explanation; only in this way could the behavior be analyzed without the bias of the recorder influencing the analysis. Teachers said that unconsciously they wrote interpretations of children's behavior into many anecdotes by stating why they thought the children behaved as they did or by using certain adjectives to describe the behavior.

Those teachers who used projective devices in attempting to determine children's interpretation of behavior encountered a number of difficulties. It was difficult, for instance, to write unfinished sentences or stories which would cause children to reveal the values they held in regard to certain situations. It was difficult also to conduct the interviews so that youngsters responded by expressing what they really believed, as this teacher said:

I am thinking back now to the first tape recording we made with the children and I remember how we put words in their mouths. I feel guilty about that when I think of it. I really think our problem is to know how to ask these questions and find out what they are thinking without putting words into their mouths.

Another teacher wondered about asking leading questions:

One of the problems in using the unfinished stories is the problem of how much pressure to apply to children as you question them. By pressure, I mean whether to push the child further when he answers your question. For instance, in response to your question, "Why do you think he walked on the terrace?" the child says, "It may have been that Mr. Randolph was mad at him and he was getting even with Mr. Randolph." The question with me is whether or not you ask the child why he thought Mr. Randolph was mad with him or why he thought he wanted to get even.

A serious problem with many teachers was that of organizing and categorizing the data which they had collected. Several of the school staffs had trouble in getting their data to fit into categories which they had set up. This was a typical complaint:

We ran into trouble in assigning behaviors to categories according to our plan. It was hard to be sure that you had the right number attached to the behavior.

Teachers also said that they felt inadequate when it came to analyzing and interpreting the data they had collected. Many teachers felt that the difficulty they had in drawing valid inferences from their material kept them from receiving maximum benefits from their data. One teacher said:

We need very much help in analyzing data. We would have liked to have Horace Mann–Lincoln Institute people with us long enough to help us go through some of the anecdotes we had and analyze them. We feel very inadequate in that phase of our study.

Procedures for Helping Teachers Maintain Perspective

The practice of leaving purposes and methods of study open to continuous re-examination and redefinition caused many teachers to lose perspective at times. Teachers who had never conducted action research before felt that purposes and procedures should be clearly set out and held until the study was completed. This made it necessary for the working groups to point out repeatedly the relation of what they were doing at the moment to the broad purposes of their study. The value teachers placed on procedures which they thought helped to maintain perspective is reported below:

Item	Rank Order	INDEX-OF-VALUE (December)	(May)
8. Summarizing at the beginning of a school staff meeting with HMLI people in order that all persons present will know what has been done previously, i.e. "bringing people up to date."	I	2.8	2.8
10. Discussions from time to time of what we are trying to accomplish in the study.	I	2.8	2.9
7. Summaries of meetings sent back by HMLI people.	I	2.8	2.9
5. Written accounts of the entire Springfield project, e.g., the report, An approach to Evaluating the Social Learnings, sent to you in September.	II	2.7	2.5
6. Summaries of work done in each school written at intervals by members of the staff of the school.	III	2.3	2.4

Three of the five items in this category fall in the upper third of the responses to the questionnaire as a whole, and the fourth item (item 5) is well above the middle of the responses. While the fifth item (item 6) ranks in the lower half of the responses, it must be remembered that even the lowest scores did not indicate extremely negative evaluations. The relatively low score given this last item is consistent with the feeling many teachers expressed elsewhere about dull moments or uncomfortable times during the study. The questionnaire revealed that some teachers were most uncomfortable or experienced dull moments when it was necessary for them to write summaries and reports of their research.

SUMMARIES AT THE BEGINNING OF EACH MEETING

The procedures having to do with summarizing previous work and discussing purposes of the study from time to time (items 8 and 10 above) were essential to the success of the study. Summaries of preceding work were consistently given at the beginning of meetings. The practice of devoting time at regular intervals to a discussion of the broad purposes of the study and the relation of current activities to those purposes was adopted when the need for it became apparent. The following excerpts from notes made by one of the consultants on two meetings at one school illustrate this point. At an early meeting of the staff of this school the teachers had a great deal of difficulty in moving ahead on plans:

Mrs. —— and Miss —— both expressed dissatisfaction with the general vagueness of the study as they saw it now. The matter of vagueness that had been brought up, however, led the group as a whole to a reconsideration of the fundamental purpose of the study. It looked at this point as if every member of the staff had lost sight of the purpose for which they had embarked on the study. An interpretation of this low point in the meeting occurred to —— and me. We think that the staff, having lost sight of what it was trying to do, in effect, recapitulated its thinking for the entire six-month period beginning in January.

Having analyzed the difficulty as one of lost perspective, the consultants adopted the practice of reviewing purposes at regular intervals to prevent a recurrence of the trouble.

Notes on meetings at all of the Springfield schools reveal that at least once during most meetings an attempt was made to relate the current plans for study to original purposes. The following report shows how this was accomplished in the school mentioned above:

Following the discussion of the questions and answers by children, the staff then looked back over the purposes of the things they were doing. Miss ―――― summarized by saying that the purpose was to try to see if there was a discrepancy between what the teachers thought and the children thought was considerate behavior. She said, "We then set out to study the values children hold. We thought that by trying to determine the values that children hold, we would improve our judgment of whether the children were behaving considerately or not. We would know what they believed considerate behavior to be and that would aid us in helping children to achieve greater acceptance by their peers."

SUMMARIES SENT BACK BY CONSULTANTS

Throughout the study, consultants made it a regular practice to send to each school a summary of each meeting. This was done following the consultants' return to New York after each trip. Separate summaries were written for each school and contained the consultant's notes on the meetings and his interpretation of the way the plans developed helped to achieve original purposes. Teachers said they found the summaries very helpful.

NEWS SHEETS

A procedure closely related to the meeting summary was the practice of sending a news sheet to all schools at least once between visits from the consultants. These news sheets contained news from all the schools and discussed in detail certain aspects of the study. One teacher said this about a report in the form of a dittoed copy of an article on the Springfield study written by one of the consultants.

I thought that last one sort of tied the whole study up and gave it direction. . . . It gave me a feeling that we were all doing the same thing and that it fit right into a pattern. . . . I appreciated that last news letter.

Summaries Written by Teachers

In some of the participating schools teachers wrote summaries and reports of their study. Although some of the teachers found this practice annoying, others considered it a valuable experience. One teacher commented:

I have helped write many of the reports in our building. This bit of concreteness has helped me to keep my direction.

A teacher who had participated previously in a similar study had this to say about the practice of writing summaries at regular intervals:

One thing I wish we had done was to make a summary at the end of each year. We didn't. We haven't written it yet. That is the reason I was interested in the folks who were ready to write something. I believe that is one way to get around this confusion you are talking about.

Detailed Plans for Each Stage of the Study

It was the practice at every new stage in the study to plan very specifically and to outline every step in the process so that all teachers would know what was to be done. Teachers liked this procedure. They wanted the plans to be flexible, as has been pointed out earlier, but they liked to have specific plans to follow. One teacher expressed the views of his group in this way:

This thing was so new to us that we had to have help in setting up the plans we were to follow. It seems to me our plans have always been very definite. We have known for what we were looking and we have known where to go next. That is the thing that counts. This wandering around aimlessly is a waste of time.

LISTS OF FINDINGS

Another procedure which was used to help teachers keep perspective in the study was the practice of listing findings which had grown out of preceding steps in the study. This was done in December of 1949 in all schools, and some schools repeated the practice in the spring of 1950. Some persons thought this was a good procedure:

Looking at findings is stimulating in terms of looking at what has been accomplished. When you look ahead all of the time you tend to lose perspective. Checking on findings helps to look back and keep perspective.

Procedures for Sharing Ideas Among Schools

The problem of finding effective ways of sharing ideas among schools was serious. Teachers frequently identified sharing as a difficulty and they felt that little had been done to make it easier. Most procedures in this category were ranked lower than procedures in other categories, as is indicated below:

Item	*Rank Order*	INDEX-OF-VALUE *(December)*	*(May)*
5. Written accounts of the entire Springfield project, e.g., the report, An Approach to Evaluating the Social Learnings, sent to you in September.	II	2.7	2.5
3. Having staff of two schools meet together to share ways of working.	IV	2.2	2.0
4. Sharing tape recordings of staff discussions in one school with another school staff.	IV	2.2	2.0
2. Meetings of representatives from participating schools in which a general summary of the study is made.	IV	2.2	2.2
1. Hearing detailed reports from participating schools as to how study is being made in each school.	IV	1.8	2.0

The procedures listed here have not been tested in practice very extensively, which may account for their relatively lower ratings. Most teachers felt that they had not developed many satisfactory ways of sharing and communicating ideas.

News sheets

The preparation of news sheets of the activities of all schools (item 5), also listed under procedures for keeping perspective, were also found helpful by teachers as a means of letting them know what other schools were doing.

"Sharing" meetings

On a number of occasions meetings of representatives of participating schools and other schools in the system were held to hear reports on the action research activities. During these meetings each participating school reported the results attained thus far in their study and the research procedures used in attaining these results. Teachers saw greater value in these meetings after they had participated in them.

This teacher reported favorably on such meetings:

The meeting was one of the most specific sharing meetings we have had in Springfield. Two principals of participating schools said that it helped them to see their part in the whole study. A principal of a nonparticipating school said that it had helped her to see what her school staff could do in a less intensive way . . .

There were other teachers, however, who felt that the meetings were not particularly effective. They believed that other means of communication between school staffs should be developed.

Proposals for improving sharing

Teachers had a number of proposals for improving the procedures for exchanging ideas among schools. They felt that it was important to understand the thinking that had taken place during the process of developing the ideas reported by other schools. They were not satisfied to hear reports of results alone, because their primary interest was in achieving better ways of working. They thought they could have received more help with developing better procedures had they known how other schools were working. One group of teachers proposed that a representative of one school visit a planning session of the staff of another school.

Another group believed that it would be more satisfactory if the entire staff of one school could visit with the entire staff of another school in order to discuss ways of working.

Some teachers felt that the key to the improvement of communication between schools lay in the quality of preparations for the sharing meetings. They felt that it was necessary to have information circulated on the work in a school prior to a reporting meeting.

One group who had used tape recordings as a very satisfactory means of exchanging ideas with the consultants proposed this as a way of communicating between buildings also. A member of the group reported rather fully and very enthusiastically on this:

We found it [tape recorder] very valuable, too. First of all, we used it in recording [children's] replies to the unfinished stories. After the children were gone we played the tape back to the faculty group in a meeting. Then we recorded the reactions of the teachers to the replies on the tapes and we sent those tapes, the stories of the children and the faculty reactions to New York. Then [the people in New York] listened to them and recorded their reactions to both tapes and sent them all back to us. When those tapes were returned we had another faculty meeting and listened to the whole thing again. I think they are a remarkable device for giving you the feeling that you are getting your suggestions and your reactions and your ideas first hand. You feel that the people are in the room with you and that you have had another visit from the people.

Procedures Involving Help from Consultants

The five procedures having to do with work with consultants are reproduced below, with their value scores.

Item	Rank Order	INDEX-OF-VALUE (December)	(May)
16. Visits from HMLI people more frequently than at present.	II	2.6	2.3
15. Time to discuss problems and procedures with people from the central office.	II	2.6	2.5
17. Correspondence by individual teachers with HMLI people.	IV	2.0	1.9
33. Participation by HMLI people in classrooms for the purpose of assisting in observing and recording behavior being studied.	IV	2.0	2.1
41. Conference of individual teachers with HMLI people on problems concerning the study.			2.5

The noticeable difference between the December and May scores of the item having to do with frequency of visits from consultants (item 16) is due to the fact that the intervals between visits of the Horace Mann–Lincoln Institute consultants had been reduced after the teachers indicated in December that they needed more frequent help. It is also true that busy teachers often found it difficult to complete their share of the research in the five or six weeks between visits, after December. Teachers felt that a six-week interval between visits was best. Most teachers thought that being able to get help at the time when it was needed was more important than frequency of consultant visits. Correspondence with consultants between visits was suggested as a means of meeting this problem; but teachers did not use this means to a great extent because of very full schedules.

In light of the reluctance some teachers felt about having other teachers observe and record behavior in their classrooms, it is not surprising that the practice of having Horace Mann–Lincoln Institute consultants observe and record behavior anecdotes in classrooms (item 33) was rated relatively low in the scale. The procedure was used only a few times. On the other hand, individual conferences with consultants (item 41) were very valuable to those teachers who participated in them.

Many teachers felt a great need for procedures whereby they could receive help with the analysis of the data they had gathered. Teachers looked upon the consultants as the persons who could give this help, but they were not able to get as much as they thought they needed.

We needed very much help in analyzing data. We would have liked to have had the people from the Institute here long enough to help us go through some of the anecdotes we had and analyze them. We felt very inadequate in that phase of our study.

Teachers asked for help with analysis frequently, as appears in notes on meetings at which teachers addressed consultants:

[There is] another thing we have wondered about. We have really wondered how to analyze. In what ways would we go about analyzing the results of these stories? Do you have some ways to suggest to us?

I hope we will receive some help with drawing the implications from what we have done. We haven't been able to do that yet.

We left one of our observations to be categorized with you present. It would help us all for you to go through the categorization with us.

Summary

Teachers found that the action research procedures for studying children helped them to attain a better understanding of children's behavior. They rated projective techniques more highly than observation or published tests as means of studying children. They felt that projective devices gave them a better understanding of the values children hold.

A number of difficulties were encountered by teachers in studying children. The most serious were lack of time and lack of experience in using the procedures especially in categorizing and interpreting data. Teachers were busy, and it was difficult to find time to carry on the study. On the other hand, they thought that increased skill in using research procedures increased their efficiency and thus enabled them to save time.

Loss of perspective was a problem encountered by research groups. A number of procedures were employed to help teachers maintain perspective. Teachers found summaries at the beginning of each planning meeting helpful in this respect. Summaries of work by consultants and news sheets reporting on the research were valuable procedures to teachers. The practice of making detailed written plans at the beginning of each stage of the study and of listing findings made in preceding stages helped the researchers see the relationship of their research activities to their original purposes.

A number of procedures were employed for sharing ideas among schools participating in the research and for receiving help from consultants. However, teachers felt that these were two areas where much improvement was needed.

CHAPTER 11

Our Gains As We Saw Them

THE GAINS that the Springfield teachers see coming to them from their cooperative action research study and the factors which they identify as having influenced these results should provide important cues for the effective planning and conducting of similar research. This chapter reports these results and the factors affecting them, as identified by the Springfield teachers.

The Results

Most of the teachers participating in the cooperative action research felt that they had gained many new insights and understandings which would help them teach better. In reply to an open question concerning outcomes of the study, in the December questionnaire, teachers reported that the study had given them (1) better understanding of children's behavior, (2) new insights into ways to influence values and behavior, and (3) new skills in working and studying. Statements teachers made during the interviews near the end of the study, concerning results, can be placed in these same categories. In their responses to the questionnaire, outcomes were mentioned which pertained to the specific area studied in each school. These responses were classified, however, under the three kinds of outcomes mentioned above in order to determine the comparative frequency with which they were mentioned. We summarized the questionnaire responses of the fifty-four teachers from the six elementary schools. Twenty-six teachers mentioned better understanding of children and of causes for their behavior; nineteen mentioned new insights into ways to change values and behavior; and nine mentioned new skills in working and studying. (This summary does not include responses from central office participants.)

BETTER UNDERSTANDING OF CHILDREN

Teachers mentioned most frequently that participation in the project had caused them to do more serious thinking about children as individual members of groups than they had done before.

—awareness of children as individuals

Teachers frequently pointed out that their study had caused them to be more aware of children as individuals, and consequently more alert to their needs. This is the way one teacher expressed this:

I think the thing this study has done for me is to further sensitize me to the individual. It has helped me to look at a child apart from a group and it has helped me to plan group activities that will take care of the individual.

When teachers were urged to be specific and say what they meant by increased awareness they readily cited cases. One teacher told of a child who had been considered a very generous child by all of her teachers but who had a problem no one had recognized.

When we began to study sharing, I selected her as a high sharer. . . . in my first study I found that she was a low sharer in one area which was an important area in the classroom. . . . with scissors or books or anything she was to share in the room she was a low sharer but she would bring things from home for the children to use for a day or two. I noticed too that she could not give up anything she owned. . . . I don't believe I would have ever noticed that difference had we not been studying this sort of behavior.

Another teacher cited two other examples to demonstrate what she meant by increased awareness of the needs of youngsters. She showed how the school had been able to help these children because of an awareness of their need to be accepted members of a group.

For example, ———, the insecure boy in our room, has learned to play a French horn recently. The orchestra director and the music supervisor both have told him that a French horn is a very wonderful instrument and not many people play them. That made him feel very good. He is a member of the orchestra now and he has moved up in his relationship with others. We have helped another child become a member of the Girl Scouts. We learned that she wanted to be a member very badly and we helped her to do that. I think she has been helped to move toward more security.

—understanding of causes and significance of behavior

Teachers said that their research did more than increase their awareness of children's needs. They feel that they have acquired, as well, deepened understandings of causes and characteristics of children's behavior. As one teacher insisted, "You can't study children the way we have studied them and not really get to know your children better." Another pointed out that his group had learned many things they had not anticipated. Another said:

I think that, even though we feel we are unable to say definitely that we have found this or that to be true, what we have been doing and the insights we have gained from this study are very important now in our everyday teaching.

Teachers were able to be specific about their learning when they were asked to cite examples. Their examples usually pertained to the study carried on in their own school, but the insights they imply are fundamental anywhere. One group pointed out that they learned that the child's behavior is caused to a great extent by the nature of the situation in which the child finds himself. This helped them to understand that improving the child's behavior might involve changing the situation.

We are beginning to see that you can't just educate one part of a child at a time. You have to know all about him to educate him. . . . As each thing comes up we see more and more that you can't isolate his learning from the whole situation. You have to consider the child in the total situation.

Several specific insights concerning considerate behavior were mentioned by another group. This group, like the group quoted above, believed that behavior is conditioned by the situation in which the child works. They found that they could not say that a child was consistently considerate or inconsiderate. They found other factors influencing considerate behavior:

I think our study showed that there is inconsistency in considerate behavior. We found some children who are considerate at times but who can be inconsiderate at other times. The same thing with children who are generally inconsiderate. We found at times they are considerate toward others. We found that other factors entered into considerateness more than consistency. Another of our findings was that home and community conflicts influence consideration.

One teacher told of new insights regarding the value of teacher–pupil planning which she gained as her group studied ways to help children develop initiative. She felt that planning with children helps the teacher understand children as well as helping children to develop responsibility and initiative.

When you take time to plan with children they bring up needs in the planning that you don't know about. You are not able to foresee a lot of misunderstandings they might have. For instance, I found that when I tried to tell children what to do I used certain words that had no meaning and caused children to be confused. Even though planning [with children] takes longer it is worth the time because children make their own plans and clear up misunderstandings which you are not always able to see.

—changes in teachers' attitudes

Many teachers said that they experienced changes in their attitudes toward children's behavior as a result of the study. Some of their concepts of desirable behavior became less absolute. Many were beginning to concede that behavior other than the kinds they would like to see might be acceptable; that they had often made snap judgments about children's behavior without attempting to understand what might be causing it; that invalid conclusions about children were frequently drawn from one or two isolated incidents. One teacher expressed the view that teachers' opinions of children were often not based on adequate evidence:

The thing this study has proved to me is that there has been little relation between observation and judgment—that is teacher observation and teacher judgment of students. I wonder what really lies behind the judgments we make. We have had the youngsters only a few days this semester, yet we have already made judgments about their qualities. I wonder how we made them.

One teacher felt that the attitudes of the teacher actually determine the way he interprets children's behavior.

Don't you think the teachers' attitudes play a major part in the judgments that are made? I would feel quite honored to have a youngster greet me as informally as the child did who ran down the hall and skidded to a stop in order to say good morning. [Another teacher had said that the child was being disrespectful.]

One teacher remembered that soon after his group began their study they had to consider the difference in what teachers and children consider acceptable behavior.

. . . we very early had to face up to the difference in the pupils' sense of values and the teachers' sense of values. I'm not saying that it was the first time, but I am saying that probably more dramatically than ever before in our school we found that we could capitalize on a pupil's sense of values and that we could make some educational use of it instead of just complaining that so and so doesn't know how to take care of his books or he doesn't know how to be honest.

A member of the supervisory staff believed that teachers had also changed their ideas concerning the causes of behavior.

One change has been a departure from the concept that all of children's behavior is predetermined by home environment. Now, they [teachers] are willing to look at behavior objectively and to look for all possible explanations.

New insights into ways to influence value development

Many of the participating teachers felt that they had gained new insights into ways to influence the development of values and thus to change the behavior of children. They pointed out that they were better able to see how their ways of working with children could be changed to improve value development. One teacher discussing such learnings identified this one, for example:

This study has helped me to know when to stop telling children what to do. I have just quit saying, "You do this. You do that." They know what to do. Of course, you have to watch to see how they do things and help them. It seems to me that I have been freer with the handling of my children and they have been freer in their activities around the room because I have been helped to find the place where I can stop and turn things over to them.

—planning for value development

Another teacher told how he and his colleagues had learned to check their planning in order that children have adequate opportunities for learning better values. They had come to realize that if children are to develop desirable behavior they must have freedom to practice the behavior.

It is a matter of being conscious of these things and planning for them and of checking yourself to see that you are giving children an opportunity to develop the ability to make wise choices. We try to check back to see that we have a balance of situations where we help the child to make decisions and of situations where we exercise direct control.

—changing school situations

Teachers often mentioned a growing realization that many desirable behavior patterns were not being developed in children mainly because the situation in their school did not allow for their development. This represents an insight that is fundamental to sound change. When teachers realize that they are not providing for the development of good behavior, they are more likely to try to change their ways of teaching. A member of the supervisory staff reminded the group that they had expressed this feeling about their school situations.

I recall that in a number of meetings in individual schools the point has been made repeatedly that maybe we didn't find this particular kind of behavior on the part of children because that behavior might not or could not take place in our school. Not that such behavior would not seem important to children but that it could not go on in our situation.

Different groups of teachers found various ways of changing classroom or school situations to bring about better learning and desirable behavior:

Our experience has told us that we study problems and that we change our procedures in the classrooms in the light of the answers we get to our problems instead of building our procedures entirely on a course of study. We have to look at the problems we as individual teachers are facing with our youngsters and we have to know our groups of youngsters. Then, we change our procedures in the classroom in order to solve these problems . . .

We are studying belongingness as it affects follow-through on plans. We have found that children feel that they belong more to a specific situation than they do to the general situation. It seems to me we can do something about that. We can add variety to our program so the children can find an opportunity to belong, and to develop that feeling of belongingness which is so important to learning.

We would need to provide a curriculum where children did more—where they had more opportunity to make choices. We have been trying to do that since we have been studying this problem.

A practical way would be to study the isolates in a sociogram and then let them work in a room with people they choose and help them develop friendships. The next time we made a sociogram they probably would not be isolates.

—behavior had been changed

Teachers valued their new insights into ways to change behavior because they had seen them work. They cited many cases of changed behavior to prove their point.

I have no doubt that we have learned many ways to make children better and happier individuals. We have seen it happen. . . . We have tested children and found them to be insecure and then we have tried out procedures that we think will help those youngsters to become more secure, and then we have tested again to find whether they were secure. We have had enough children change from insecure to secure behavior to indicate that we know some ways to help bring about this change.

NEW SKILLS IN WORKING AND STUDYING

Teachers reported that they were pleased with the success they had had in developing the action research project in their schools. They realized that there had been growth on the part of many persons in the skill of working together; otherwise they would not have been able to carry on this study. One teacher remembered how difficult it was to get the large staff of his school to pull together before they launched the action research project. Another said this:

The most outstanding thing to me is the fact that an entire faculty can come together on a common ground and analyze situations and procedures in such a way that thinking is stimulating and we are left wanting to get busy and *do something about problems.*

Some teachers felt that if nothing except new insights into ways of working together to solve problems had resulted from the study it would have been very much worth while. They liked the methods for gathering evidence which they had learned to use, because these methods would enable them to solve problems which would arise in the future.

. . . the how of things—how we have done things—seems to me to be more important in many cases than what we have found out. This idea of research—how you go about it—is more important than the results you get. Sometimes the how is the thing people need to know.

Another thing is to realize the difference in the purpose of this study and the value of it. Maybe the purpose will not be completely realized, but the value will be very great if it helps teachers to learn to observe and to learn to see various meanings in what they observe rather than just reading their own meaning into behavior.

Teachers were naturally pleased to find that it was possible for observations of behavior to be conducted by different teachers in such a way that the results could be compared.

They also felt that they had learned how to improve the records they keep on children, and that they better understood the importance of records in teaching.

Other teachers thought that the study had resulted in better relations among teachers—which would be of benefit later, when they needed to solve other common problems.

And the teachers feel differently toward each other because we share thoughts and ideas. We can talk about common problems because we have been working together on them.

Factors That Affected Teacher Participation

Teachers from time to time identified factors which they believed had affected their participation in the cooperative action research project. These factors will be discussed in this section. It is not to be inferred that they were the only ones operating; their significance lies in the fact that they are the factors which the participating teachers have recognized as important to them.

THE STUDY WAS TRULY COOPERATIVE

When teachers were asked to mention factors which had affected their participation in the study, the one mentioned most frequently was the cooperative nature of the undertaking. Teachers report that this cooperation greatly increased their interest and facilitated their work.

These were typical comments:

I would say the fact that we are all in on it is good. We know —all of us—every step. We participated in the planning and we feel so much a part of it. It all goes back to this belongingness, I suppose. It is our study. We feel that way about it.

I think the procedures we have used of having each teacher in her own room to make a study of certain problems and collect data and then having a small committee to get that data together and formulate some ideas and present it to the entire group has been good. After this it was good to get down to business and discuss the ideas. It is good to work on each other's ideas. To me, this has been one of the biggest things in pulling our group together and in achieving the results we have achieved.

Problems teachers considered important
were studied

Teachers felt that their participation in the study enabled them to work together on problems which they were facing every day in the classroom. This idea was expressed by one person as follows:

It seems to me that we picked a subject which turned out to be so very interesting and vital to all of us that we were more than willing to work on it. . . . it was just a part of our regular work. It wasn't something detached from our classrooms. It was just the kind of thing that goes on in our classrooms day in and out that we need to know about.

Another aspect of working on their own problems had to do with the relationships teachers see between what they are doing and the general purposes of the study. That this characterized, particularly, the study in the elementary schools is shown by a comparison of the purposes teachers list for the study with the results they see coming from it. In the preceding section of this chapter it was shown that teachers felt they had achieved better understanding of children, new insights into ways to influence value development, and an understanding of better ways to work on their own problems. When the specific learnings reported under each of these headings are compared with the purposes mentioned by the teachers in December (the purposes most frequently mentioned by 56 teachers are summarized below), it seems safe to conclude that the study in the elementary schools was built on the purposes which teachers felt important.

Size of staff makes a difference

Teachers frequently mentioned size of staff as an important factor in their participation in the study. Those teachers who worked in small schools felt that they had an advantage over those working in larger schools. While no minimum or

Purposes	*Frequency of Mention*
To gain a better understanding of children's behavior in various situations.	18
To find ways of changing school situations to bring about the development of certain values.	16
To find ways to improve behavior.	15
To better understand the child and ways to help him.	13
To find techniques for measuring the extent to which certain values were held.	12
To contribute to our knowledge of values that are important for children to develop. (To understand better what is meant by social learnings.)	9
To study the formation of social values in our children and to help children develop desirable values.	7
To find measures for making each child secure and free to participate in democratic living.	6
To help school staffs develop skill in carrying out classroom research.	3

maximum staff for effective participation in cooperative action research is suggested, the implication is that when a staff exceeds eight or nine teachers, carrying everyone along is difficult and attention must be given to the special problems of large-group involvement.

LEADERSHIP

Teachers reported that the leadership they had received from principals, consultants, and members of the central administrative and supervisory staffs had facilitated their research greatly.

—the principal

Most teachers identified the principal as an important factor in the success of their study and placed great emphasis on his attitude toward what they were doing. They felt that it was important for the principal to establish a favorable atmosphere for research. These were two teachers' comments:

Our principal builds a very permissive atmosphere. We never feel that she is imposing a job on us.

I think the attitude our principal has had toward the study and toward us has helped . . . she has considered the study something very worth while.

—the consultants

The visiting consultants were frequently mentioned as having been important factors in the success of the study. Teachers found that they received much help from consultants in planning and devising ways to achieve their purposes. This resulted in increased ability to conduct action research and, hence, in greater security.

As one of the teachers said:

This thing was so new to us that we had to have help from the people from the Institute in setting up the plans we were to follow. It seems to me that our plans have been definite always. We have known what we were looking for and we have known where to go next.

—supervisory staff

The kind and amount of support which the teachers felt they received from the central administrative and supervisory staff was also an important factor in their success. Teachers often commented on their freedom to try out any way of teaching which promised to help boys and girls. They said that the administration of the school system not only gave them this freedom but encouraged them in their efforts to improve teaching.

I think one thing that has been very helpful here is the fact that we get a great deal of help and support from the administrative department. . . . Really, I think it boils down to the fact that we feel all people concerned are really interested and willing to cooperate with us in carrying on this kind of study. I think that is the thing that has helped us more than anything else.

I think it is because here the administration has such a broad view of a child's social and emotional life and they are trying to do something to help that, along with the emphasis on subject matter.

Summary

Teachers who participated in the cooperative action research felt that they gained many new insights and new understandings which will help them to do a better job of teaching. They identified these three major areas of growth: (1) increased understanding of children's behavior and its causes, (2) new insights into ways to influence the development of children's values, and (3) development of new skills in working and studying.

When the teachers were asked to identify factors which affected the success of their study they pointed out several which they considered important. The fact that the study was a truly cooperative endeavor was important to them. They emphasized the fact that they studied problems which they considered important. They also mentioned other factors such as the size of the school staff and the leadership provided by school principals, supervisory staff, and visiting consultants.

CHAPTER 12

What We Learned to Watch Out For

TEACHERS REPORTING on their participation in the cooperative action research projects did not give the impression that there had been no problems. They encountered many difficulties in conducting their research, and they believed that other teachers attempting similar studies would have similar experiences. Most of the teachers felt that the satisfaction achieved far outweighed the difficulties involved. Some even believed that the pitfalls or barriers encountered had contributed significantly to their understanding of curriculum problems.

We think this teacher had a very good point:

These blind alleys that you talk about are very important. I think it is important that they be included in a report of this study because there is nothing more discouraging to me than to read an account of a perfect research project in a magazine and attempt to carry out a similar one or to apply it and find that it doesn't go as smoothly as it has been pictured in the article. I think that it is important for people to see that we had some trouble.

Teachers, administrators, and consultants must understand the difficulties teachers face in conducting cooperative action research if this method of improving instruction is to be widely exploited. This chapter summarizes the difficulties encountered by teachers in the Springfield projects as well as what was learned about ways and means of facilitating cooperative action research.

Difficulties Encountered

Teachers reported a number of difficulties. The questionnaire to which teachers replied in December of 1949 contained three questions having to do with difficulties or trouble spots in the study.

In your opinion what have been the major barriers to our study?
Research always has its dull moments. What were some dull moments in our study?
Most people have unhappy or uncomfortable times when engaged in research. When were you most uncomfortable or unhappy?

Replies to the question regarding barriers to the study fit into four categories as indicated below, and frequency of mention by 56 teachers is given for each category.

Categories	*Frequency of Mention*
Replies having to do with the difficulty of finding time to conduct study and carry on other activities.	49
Replies having to do with difficulties arising from lack of skill in conducting research.	40
Replies having to do with communication difficulties.	9
Miscellaneous.	9

Responses to the questions referring to dull moments and uncomfortable times fell into similar categories, although not in the same order of frequency. The most frequent response to the question regarding dull moments was that there were none! A number of teachers, however, experienced dull moments or were unhappy or uncomfortable when they felt they lacked the skill to do what was expected of them, when they felt they did not have time to do justice to the study and to their other professional duties, and when they had to write summaries of their studies and the results of their observations. Some teachers reported they were most uncomfortable during exceedingly long meetings concerning the study. This was especially true if the meetings were held *after* a school day. Many teachers were unhappy when they were unable to see that they were making progress toward the goals which they had set.

There were difficulties all the way along. The sections of this report dealing with the method of cooperative action research indicate or imply some of them. Making the studies truly cooperative posed problems, as did getting the entire school staffs together long enough to talk difficulties out and reach agreements. Individuals and groups found it hard to communicate with one another. It was difficult to understand the ideas others were trying to express and to reach agreements as to what should be studied and observed. Most teachers felt a lack of satisfactory ways to carry an entire staff along with the thinking which took place in a small group when it was necessary to delegate responsibility to committees.

The research procedures employed for studying children gave rise to two problems. It was difficult (a) to find time to observe and record behavior adequately and (b) to use the procedures: devising and using questionnaires, informal projective devices, and guides to observation; making, categorizing, and recording observations; and analyzing the data collected. Increased facility in these would alleviate the time problem.

Other difficulties were identified by teachers from time to time. The practice of leaving purposes and methods of study open to continuous re-examination and redefinition caused many teachers to become confused and even discouraged. It was also difficult to obtain help from consultants as frequently as teachers would have liked. This problem and the one of sharing ideas and ways of working among schools participating in the study were two areas where teachers thought much improvement was needed.

Administrative Arrangements for Facilitating Research

It is important to realize the great importance to teachers of help and support from administrators and consultants. The teachers who participated in these research projects felt that one of the major factors in the success of their cooperative action research was the supportive attitude of the administrative staff of the school system toward research and experimentation by teachers. Administrators who desire a sound program of curriculum improvement through cooperative action research in the schools must make administrative arrangements which serve to facilitate such a program, for teachers interpret such action as reflecting the administrative support which is so crucially important to them.

TIME FOR TEACHERS TO PARTICIPATE

The practice in most school systems of continually adding to teachers' loads and never subtracting from them has been mentioned as a factor which operates against effective curriculum study. Many teachers reported that finding time to carry on the activities involved in cooperative action research was the greatest difficulty they encountered. Most of these teachers had heavy teaching loads. Class sizes in the participating schools ranged from thirty to forty-four children. In addition to teaching large classes and carrying on the research activities, most of the teachers also assumed a number of extraclass responsibilities in their schools and served on time-consuming system-wide committees.

Certain administrative arrangements were made to provide time for study and research. To avoid the necessity of long meetings after school hours, when teachers were fatigued, provision was made for meetings during the school day. The school system maintained a staff of full-time substitute teachers who moved from school to school relieving teachers from classroom responsibilities. Under normal conditions, enough substitute teachers went to a building once a week to relieve half of the regular teachers for half of one day. In some schools half of the staff was relieved for the first part of the morning and the other half for the last part of the morning. In other schools half of the staff was relieved for a full half-day every other week. The plan used was determined by the nature of the work in which the teachers were engaged during the time they were relieved from classroom responsibility. When Horace Mann–Lincoln Institute staff members were working in the schools, substitute teachers relieved the entire staff for meetings.

Administrators will need to study other ways of providing adequate time for teachers participating in research. Attention should be given to the reduction of classroom and extraclassroom duties. Teachers actively engaged in curriculum research should, whenever possible, be relieved of participation on committees or in activities of a purely administrative nature. In many school systems additional clerical help could relieve teachers of much of the routine work involved in reports and records and of the responsibility involved in collecting fees and purchasing supplies.

CONSULTANT HELP FOR TEACHERS

Teachers who engage in cooperative action research need guidance and help from persons who have had experience with the techniques and ways of working involved in this method of curriculum study. The teachers in the Springfield projects valued highly the consultative help they received.

They wanted and needed more help than they were able to get. The two supervisors employed by the school system worked with a large number of schools and were not able to devote as much time as necessary to each of the action research projects. The consultants from the Horace Mann–Lincoln Institute were able to work with the teachers only for a short time every six weeks. This arrangement resulted in periods when teachers were not able to move ahead as rapidly as they might have because of the necessity of waiting for needed help. The stimulation resulting from bringing in consultants from outside the school system at intervals is beneficial, but it cannot outweigh the value of a consultative staff that would be available for help whenever needed. The additional staff necessary to provide for consistent available help requires additional funds, but expenditure for services such as these should result in significant curriculum improvements.

MATERIAL AIDS

Provision should be made for certain material aid to teachers engaged in cooperative action research. The budget set up for curriculum research will need to provide for an adequate professional library, mimeographing services, recording devices, published tests and evaluation instruments, new instructional materials, and occasional clerical assistance. The provision of such aids as these is essential to effective teacher participation.

PROVISION FOR EXCHANGE OF IDEAS

Communication among teachers and schools participating in the research was a problem teachers frequently mentioned. They considered it very important to be able to know what other school staffs were doing to carry their research forward. They wanted to know what techniques and ways of doing things other teachers found successful. During the progress of the study several attempts were made to provide opportunities for the sharing of ideas among schools. Meetings were held at which teachers reported on the research under way in their schools and discussed ways of working. Some of the meetings were held during school hours and were attended by one or two representatives from each participating school. On these occasions substitute teachers relieved those persons attending the meeting. On other occasions meetings were held after school hours, and each school in the system, whether participating in the action research projects or not, was asked to send at least two representatives. Because teachers were very interested in learning about ways of working in action research, more than the minimum representation attended these meetings. At one time all teachers in all schools were invited to an afternoon meeting to hear a systematic report from each participating school.

These meetings were valuable means of sharing ideas, but teachers were not satisfied with them. They found that they were not able to probe deeply enough into ways of working to get real help with their problems. They were not satisfied with the system of having representatives attend and report to them on the "sharing" meetings. They felt that the reports did nothing but let them know *what* other schools were doing and they preferred to know *how* they were working.

Teachers, near the end of this study, made a number of suggestions for improving communications among schools participating in similar projects. They suggested that arrangements should be made for the staffs of two schools working on related problems to get together from time to time to share ideas and help with plans. As an alternative procedure they proposed that arrangements be made for representatives of a school staff to attend a planning session of another school staff and report in detail how the school attacked its problems. This same group of teachers could see value in making recordings of staff meetings in individual schools, and playing these recordings back to other school staffs in order to communicate ways of working.

DEVELOPING A DESIRABLE PROFESSIONAL CLIMATE

The professional climate of the schools is a significant factor in the successful development of cooperative action research. This approach to curriculum improvement requires a climate in which teachers feel free to talk about problems which exist in their schools, to devise ways to study those problems, and to try out new ways of working which give promise of improving their teaching. Whether this climate exists in a given school system depends to a large extent on the attitude of the administration toward experimentation and on the efforts of the administrators to give teachers security in working to improve school conditions. Such security is not a result of verbal assurance by the administration that teachers are free to devise and suggest improvements. It comes as a result of putting into practice over a period of time a policy that calls for active participation by teachers in all matters pertaining to the operation of the schools. This is illustrated in the experience of school systems whose attempts to involve teachers in curriculum study have met with opposition or failure because teachers had never been given an opportunity to do more than accept administrative decisions about other school matters and were not prepared to assume responsibility for curriculum improvement.

Teachers who undertook the cooperative action research in Springfield had had long experience with teacher participation in all aspects of the administration and operation of the schools. They had participated for many years in the selection of teaching personnel, in developing salary schedules, and in planning curriculum study, to mention only a few areas of participation. They saw the action research as one other way in which they could contribute to the improvement of the schools. They attributed much of the success of their work to their feeling that the administration valued their efforts and would support their attempts to develop better ways of teaching.

People on the administrative staff were very careful lest anything impair the integrity of groups or individual members of the teaching corps. At all stages in the development of the cooperative research project they kept the channels of communication open so that all teachers involved in the study could be informed of each new development. It was members of the supervisory staff who insisted on reporting, at regular intervals, the progress of the study in participating schools to all other schools in the system. They felt that such communication was necessary since all schools had participated in the planning stages and so had a stake in the entire enterprise.

It was apparent to those who worked with the teachers in the development of the action research projects that the high morale was not due to the actual amount of material aid the administration was able to provide. Springfield is a low-cost system and was not always able to provide funds for all the help necessary. The high morale was primarily a result of the teachers' feeling that the administration was concerned with their welfare and supporting their efforts to improve the schools. The supply of substitute teachers who relieved classroom teachers for research activities was tangible evidence of administrative support.

The Role of the Consultant in Facilitating Action Research

Teachers look to consultants for a kind of support somewhat different from that which they seek from administrators. Because consultants presumably have had more experience with action research procedures teachers look to them for a considerable amount of direction in planning and conducting research. Consultants are expected to propose best ways of working and to appraise proposals made by teachers. Teachers who participated in the Springfield action research projects sometimes spoke of insecure moments when they were unable to get consultants to express their appraisal or when they felt consultants were not saying what they really believed about certain ideas.

Consultants who worked with the research projects did not consider that their function was to tell teachers how to conduct research. They considered themselves, as well as the teachers, to be learners from the research undertaken. Because action research procedures were devised for particular situations and tested in action to determine their effectiveness, the skill of both consultants and teachers was required. Consultants from their experience with action research in other situations suggested techniques and procedures; but teachers were in a better position to judge the feasibility of the procedures in their classrooms. There were, however, certain areas where teachers who participated in the research needed help and leadership from persons with more experience in conducting action research. They reported that they valued the work of the consultants in making the research cooperative, in expediting the research activities, in helping them gain research skills, and in helping them maintain perspective in regard to the study. Let us consider these kinds of help.

MAKING THE RESEARCH COOPERATIVE

One of the most difficult tasks faced by consultants and teachers engaged in cooperative action research is keeping the undertaking truly cooperative. From the outset all who participate must share the responsibility for decisions on plans, procedures, and interpretations as they arise. At no point in the undertaking can any one person assume a dominant role and give precedence to his notion of the way the research should be developed. All persons involved, no matter how inexperienced in the techniques of action research, must have a voice in the planning and development of their activities. Herein lies the difficulty. The consultant must give specific help to participants, still encouraging them to keep most of the responsibility for planning and developing the research.

The cooperative aspect of action research begins with the selection of a problem to be studied—a problem which has meaning to all persons involved. Consequently in Springfield much time was spent in selecting and defining a problem for study before work was begun. When the school systems proposed to the Horace Mann–Lincoln Institute that they work together on a study of the measurement of attitudes and values held by boys and girls the Institute could have defined a specific problem in this broad area and proceeded from there. Instead, consultants from the Institute and personnel from the schools met together to discuss the meaning which the problem held for them. After a series of meetings the problem was stated as, "What can teachers do that will make a difference in the attitudes and values that govern children's social behavior?" This "action definition" as worked out cooperatively involved not only the problem of measuring attitudes and values but also the curricular problem of what could be done to improve attitudes and values. Even though the teachers participated in defining the problem they had an opportunity later to decide freely whether or not the problem as stated was of sufficient significance to them to warrant their participation in research on it. Some school groups decided not to participate. This freedom to choose was very important, because those who finally affiliated themselves had seen an identity of purpose from the beginning and they were ready to work with enthusiasm.

As each new stage in the action research evolved, an attempt was made to keep the research closely related to the problems which teachers saw as real problems. This involved devoting much time and effort to defining problems and planning procedures for studying them. This was not always easy. The teachers often felt frustrated because of their inexperience in planning research procedures, and wanted the consultants to tell them what to do. Sometimes the consultants did succumb to these requests, proposing detailed plans for study. The result of this procedure on most occasions was a breakdown of the plans when teachers attempted to put them into practice. Additional time had to be spent in working through the plans in order that the teachers might understand what was to be accomplished.

Providing group support for ideas was an aspect of making the action research cooperative—a task which consultants and teachers considered very important. Teachers were willing to study many teaching problems that might have seemed threatening to individuals had not all of the teachers been concerned about them. For example, the extent of teacher domination of the classroom situation and the influence on the security of youngsters of certain procedures used by teachers were considered without seriously threatening any individual. It was felt that the success of the action research projects was largely due to the efforts made to provide the support which comes from group effort to study and improve a situation. These efforts required considerable attention because of the need for developing many of the special skills necessary for effective group work. At the beginning of the study, after the planning with the consultants had been completed, teachers in many schools carried on their study as individuals because little or no group work was done between consultant visits. It was necessary to encourage group effort and to develop skills of cooperative endeavor as rapidly as possible. This was done in a number of ways. Schedules of activity were set up which called for group meetings between visits of consultants; meetings other than planning meetings were arranged at which teachers and consultants analyzed data; and committees of teachers were named from time to time to undertake certain jobs.

EXPEDITING THE RESEARCH ACTIVITIES

There were times when it was necessary for the consultants to provide direct help for teachers with certain aspects of the action research. Teachers who were busy with all of their many classroom and extraclassroom duties often found it difficult to compile and summarize research data adequately after they had collected them. On many occasions consultants took the data collected by individual teachers, compiled the material, and presented the summaries to the research groups for cooperative analysis and interpretation. This greatly helped matters; it enabled teachers to use the results of their research activities to move the study ahead more rapidly. There were times, however, when this procedure was not followed. As the research progressed and teachers gained more skill in handling data, there were occasions when they preferred to prepare their own summaries. There is a warning to be given here: The distinction between compiling or summarizing data and analyzing or interpreting data must be observed. The latter is best done cooperatively. There is a real danger that those who work with teachers will, in their attempts to save teachers' time, take over data analysis and interpretation. What should be *cooperative* action research then becomes a matter of teachers collecting data for consultants to analyze and interpret. This must be avoided.

There were other ways in which the consultants sought to expedite the research activities of teachers. An effort was made to relate the research activities very closely to the regular classroom activities of the teachers. It would not have been possible to gather the great amount of data collected by teachers participating in the study had not ways of working been developed whereby the collection of data was made an integral part of teaching. Such ways of working are illustrated in the case of the teachers who studied the values children held regarding cooperative planning while they were planning classroom activities with children.

The feeling of satisfaction often expressed by teachers regarding the way in which the research was related to their classroom activities is an important cue. Teachers' interest increased noticeably when an effort was made to relate the research activities closely to the classroom program. This was demonstrated by teachers in one school who began their study by observing inconsiderate behavior in children. This part of the study moved along satisfactorily enough, but interest increased markedly when the teachers decided not only to observe inconsiderate behavior but to test various teaching procedures for increasing considerate behavior.

Mechanical means for reducing the amount of time involved in conducting the cooperative action research and for making participation easier for teachers were developed by consultants and teachers. Charts and guides for recording behavior were devised to eliminate the necessity of teachers' writing lengthy anecdotes. Checklists were developed to reduce the amount of time involved in using materials such as unfinished sentences or unfinished stories. Recording devices were used to record children's oral responses to unfinished stories. Team observations were initiated so that teachers could get important data without neglecting their teaching.

HELPING TEACHERS GAIN RESEARCH SKILLS

The difficulties which teachers met in conducting cooperative action research suggest the responsibility of consultants in helping teachers develop research skills. Even the time element which teachers stressed so frequently seemed to be related to skill in carrying on research. It was the conviction of many teachers that if they could be helped to work more skillfully in observing and in recording data much of the feeling of time pressure would be relieved, because they would be able to accomplish more in a given amount of time. Consequently an effort was made to help teachers become more proficient in gathering data. As has been mentioned in a preceding chapter time was given to training sessions in which teachers learned the best ways of doing certain jobs.

The attitude of the teachers and consultants regarding the need for developing skill in conducting cooperative action research was an important factor in the success of the research projects. The teachers who participated in these studies were inexperienced in the use of many of the study techniques involved. The work was looked upon as a learning period in research procedures as well as a study of children's values. Attention was therefore given to introducing new ways of working in such a way that teachers were not made to feel inadequate in this respect.

Teachers naturally prefer to use those procedures of research with which they have had experience and which they feel secure in using. In Springfield, there was a tendency to use repeatedly those research procedures which were learned early in the study. Many teachers reported that when new aspects of the research called for new techniques they were reluctant to use them. It was necessary to do several things designed to give teachers security with new procedures. When a new way of study was to be undertaken, very detailed plans for its use were developed. The plans usually included provision for a "trial run" with an opportunity to check results before launching into the real study. On certain occasions it was necessary for the consultants to demonstrate the use of the procedure. This was done at times through role-playing, with consultants assuming the role of teacher or child to illustrate the way in which the procedure might be used with children. On other occasions consultants participated with teachers in the actual use of the procedures. It was necessary, however, for consultants to use caution in order to avoid becoming a threat to the security of teachers. Teachers were sometimes hesitant to have consultants observe and record data in their classrooms.

Teachers wanted much help in developing skill in analyzing data and in seeing implications of their study for improved teaching practices. They relied very heavily on consultants for this help. The consultants realized that not as much attention was given to this aspect of the research project as should have been given. Teachers felt that the analysis of their data was very inadequate and that there was much more they could have learned from the data. The tendency was to push on to a new phase of study frequently when data already collected could have been used more effectively.

HELPING TEACHERS MAINTAIN PERSPECTIVE

The problem of keeping perspective with regard to the study was one which required the constant attention of teachers and consultants. Teachers who had never conducted action research felt that purposes and procedures should be clearly set out and held to until the study was completed. The practice of developing objectives and appropriate methods of study for each new aspect of the research caused teachers to lose sight of the big purpose at times. In the early stages of the study they frequently mentioned their confusion. They felt they did not know where they were going in the study or how their activities fit into the original purposes of the research. This confusion was a frequent topic of conversation at meetings of teachers who were participating in the study. As the study progressed this reaction decreased, and near the end of the school year it was unusual to hear anyone mention such confusion. Instead, most teachers were discussing the purpose and need for continuing the action research another year.

Those who worked with the teachers attribute this change to a number of factors. First, throughout the study an effort was made to take sufficient time in planning with teachers that each step in the process could be adequately discussed. Second, an attempt was made at each new step to examine with teachers the purpose of the step and its relation to preceding steps. A third factor, mentioned in an earlier chapter, was the written reports of individual school projects and of the total project which helped teachers see the place of their work in the total picture. A fourth factor was the series of general meetings in which teachers reported their research activities. However, communication among schools was a problem which teachers felt was never adequately solved, and the "sharing" meetings were not entirely satisfactory, though they helped somewhat.

Summary

The difficulties which the Springfield teachers encountered in conducting cooperative action research point to the need for careful consideration of ways in which the effective participation of teachers in classroom research can be facilitated. Help and support from the administrative staff of a school or school system are important facilitating factors in teacher participation. Such help and support are made apparent to teachers through administrative arrangements which help them to have time to participate in needed action research, which provide a consultative staff with sufficient time and numbers to work consistently with participating teachers, which make it possible for teachers to meet and exchange ideas with other teachers engaged in related research projects, and which build a feeling among teachers that their efforts to develop better ways of teaching are appreciated and supported.

Consultants working directly with teachers in planning and conducting action research play an important role in facilitating such research. Their most difficult job is that of keeping cooperative action research truly cooperative. Consultants are faced with the dual role of giving guidance and direction to research while helping and encouraging teachers to take an active part in planning and directing their own study. It is necessary to help teachers get the job done without usurping their prerogatives. Teachers were enabled to participate more effectively by the practices consultants employed in helping them gain needed research skills and by the practices employed in keeping teachers aware of the relation of their activities to original purposes as the study developed.

CHAPTER **13**

Action Research
and Curriculum Change

$\mathbf{T}$HOSE PERSONS who see in cooperative action research a desirable way to reduce the gap between theory and practice in our schools do so because fundamentally they think of curriculum development and improvement as a process that involves changing and extending the teacher's understanding of the curriculum. This study of children's social values was based on such a conception [1] of curriculum

[1] In this discussion, the terms *conception* and *perception* will be used frequently. The meanings of these terms are sometimes confused by non-psychologists. Let us attend to them.

A *conception* is simply an idea, or notion. One's conception of the curriculum is one's notion of what the curriculum is—a list of school subjects, or a plan for the day, or (as the authors state) the experiences the children have under the guidance of the school.

A *perception* is what one perceives; it is what one sees in a given situation. One's actions are largely determined by what one perceives consciously or unconsciously in a situation.

The point that is elaborated in the discussion is that what one perceives in any given situation is largely determined by one's conception of the perceived situation—by what one *expects* to see, or considers *significant* to see.

Thus, action depends on perception, and perception depends on conception. For a teacher to change his way of teaching (his action) he must first have developed a new *conception* of the curriculum; having done this, the way is open for him to *perceive* the teaching–learning situation differently (to see things in it that he previously overlooked, or thought unimportant). His perception having changed, his action will change, too.

275

development. At the outset of the study a number of basic assumptions concerning curriculum development and change were accepted. It was recognized that the quality of experience provided for learners is dependent to a large degree on the teacher's conception of the curriculum. This proposition having been accepted, the recognition of curriculum change as a consequence of change in the teacher's conception of the curriculum naturally followed. The way in which the teacher's conception of the curriculum is changed was described as a process of re-education which consists of actual testing of educational theory in practice.

It was one of the purposes of this study to test the effectiveness of cooperative action research as a means of involving teachers in this process of re-education. The favorable reaction of participating teachers to the way in which action research methods enabled them to improve teaching and learning makes it possible to say that cooperative action research is an excellent way to involve the teacher in the process of re-education.

The three premises accepted at the outset of the study, together with this conviction concerning action research which came as a result of the study, may be stated as a series of propositions which states the attitude of the participants toward cooperative action research as a means of curriculum change:

1. The quality of experience for learners, that is, the curriculum for learners, is dependent to a large degree on the teacher's conception (understanding) of the curriculum.

2. Curriculum change is therefore a consequence of change in the teacher's conception of the curriculum.

3. Changes in the teacher's conception of the curriculum result from involvement of the teacher in a process of re-education which consists of actual testing of educational theory in practice.

4. Cooperative action research is an excellent way to involve the teacher in this process of re-education.

Each of the above propositions will be discussed in some detail in the following sections of this chapter.

The Teacher's Conception of Curriculum Is Basic to Curriculum Development

The teacher occupies a key place in the development of the curriculum. Our definition of the curriculum as all of the experiences which learners have under the direction of the school serves to emphasize the influence of the teacher in curriculum building. It is the teacher who participates directly with children in choosing and developing learning experiences. It is he who sets the emotional tone of the environment in which these experiences of children take place. "The learner's real curriculum emerges through the teaching-learning process, as teachers and learners work together on the problems which have meaning to them." [2] Many believe that because the teacher carries major responsibility for pupil learning experiences and because of his close relationship with the learner, he is probably the most important influence in shaping the curriculum. [3]

If the teacher is the strategic figure in curriculum development, it is pertinent for those interested in programs of curriculum improvement to inquire as to what factors will determine the way in which the teacher builds a curriculum with learners. The work of social psychologists on the importance of conceptual development in determining behavior

---

[2] Florence B. Stratemeyer, Hamden L. Forkner, and Margaret G. McKim, *Developing a Curriculum for Modern Living* (New York: Bureau of Publications, Teachers College, Columbia University, 1947), p. 72.

[3] Department of Curriculum and Teaching, Teachers College, Columbia University, *Toward Curriculum Improvement* (New York: Bureau of Publications, Teachers College, Columbia University, 1949), p. 36. Reprint of *Teachers College Record,* Vol. 50, No. 5, February, 1949.

supplies an answer to this inquiry.[4] Members of this group have shown that an individual's behavior is determined by his perception of the total situation in which he is acting and that this perception is based on the understandings and values which he brings to the situation. These understandings and values condition his interpretation of the forces in operation within a given situation. In the case of a teacher, his understanding of the purposes and organization of education, and the values which color this understanding, will determine the way in which he approaches his job with learners. That is to say, the way in which a teacher perceives a teaching–learning situation is conditioned by his belief as to what should go on in such situations and by his security in the adequacy of such a belief. Both the belief and the security are aspects of the individual's basic concept of teaching, which has been developed and modified through successive experiences in teaching–learning situations.

Hence, it can be said that the teacher's conception of the curriculum is the key to the quality of learning experience which will be provided for learners. If the teacher conceives of the curriculum as a series of subjects to be taught, he will proceed to develop those experiences which he believes will bring about the acquisition of such knowledge. If, on the other hand, his conception of education is that of improving the present adjustment of individuals, he will proceed to develop those experiences which grow out of the immediate concerns and interests of the learner.

In schools, as elsewhere, the situation may be said to consist largely of the beliefs and perceptions of the people in it. If the school is considered to be primarily devoted to preparing individuals for life, it is likely that hypotheses having to do with the

[4] Kurt Lewin, "Frontiers in Group Dynamics," *Human Relations*, I (1947), pp. 5-41; also Kurt Lewin and Paul Grabbe, "Conduct, Knowledge, and Acceptance of New Values," *Journal of Social Issues*, I (1945), pp. 53-64.

success of the school as a preparatory institution will be formulated. If the school is conceived of as dealing largely with the present needs and interests of the students, it is likely that hypotheses having to do with present needs and interests will be formulated.[5]

Changing the Curriculum Involves Changing the Teacher's Conception

If the teacher's basic understandings and attitudes determine the manner in which he develops the curriculum with learners, it follows that in order to change the curriculum the teacher's attitudes and understandings must be changed. Efforts to change the curriculum solely by means of revised courses of study, lists of educational objectives, and even the production of new learning materials have been relatively ineffective because they did not change the conception of curriculum in the minds of the people who were to use these aids. Therefore, the introduction of such materials often did not result in changing the teacher's perceptions of the teaching–learning situation and the curriculum remained basically unimproved.

Those who have worked in curriculum development programs are familiar with the way many teachers interpret and use the most flexible courses of study. The frequent comment, "You have to do that because the course of study requires it," is an outgrowth of a conception of the curriculum as certain specified subjects or units which *must* be taught. The fate of other well-stated learning materials prepared to aid teachers to put into practice newer theories of education is well known. They collect dust on library shelves because there is little inherent in the printed materials to change the basic conceptions of the people who use them. Mackenzie

[5] A. Wellesley Foshay and James A. Hall, "Experimentation Moves into the Classroom," *Teachers College Record*, 51 (1950), p. 355.

and Lawler, in a recent survey of educational research, found a rather general recognition of the fact that curriculum change involves more than the preparation of new materials. They found that those who define the curriculum as the experiences which learners have under the direction of the school agree that changing the curriculum involves changing the factors which shape or influence the learners' experiences. The factors were believed to be many and varied. Some are within the school and some are outside, but there was a general recognition that any change in the curriculum involves changes in teachers. Only as teachers' values, understandings, and skills are changed will the curriculum be modified. The reviewers concluded that "even changes in materials in the school necessitated changes in people." [6]

The Teacher's Conception Is Changed
By a Process of Re-education

The process of changing the teacher's conception of the curriculum will of necessity be a process of re-education in which the teacher will be involved in the kind of study that relates educational theory directly to his classroom problems. Participation by the teacher in the process of testing, revising, and retesting theory in practice is an excellent way of bringing about the change in basic understandings and attitudes so essential for improved curriculum.

This process of re-education is not simple. It amounts to changing well-established attitudes and habits which have been in the process of developing during the entire lifetime of the teacher. A teacher's concept of education embodies many beliefs and understandings developed during his own period of schooling. Few teachers have experienced any form of modern education. Many of them have been educated in

---

[6] Gordon N. Mackenzie and Marcella R. Lawler, "Curriculum: Change and Improvement," *Review of Educational Research*, 18 (1948), p. 274.

traditional practices and values in teacher-preparing institutions. Because of this, the possession of correct knowledge regarding teaching is often not sufficient to change inadequate concepts. The difficulty involved in changing wrong concepts and incorrect stereotypes is emphasized by Lewin and Grabbe in their presentation of a set of basic principles underlying social change.

When we consider resistances to re-education, we usually think in terms of emotional obstacles. It is important, however, not to underestimate the difficulties inherent in changing cognition. If we keep in mind that even extensive experience with physical facts does not necessarily lead to correct physical perception, we will be less surprised at the resistances encountered when we attempt to modify inadequate social stereotypes.

Incorrect stereotypes (prejudices) are functionally equivalent to wrong concepts (theories).[7]

Sharp points out the difficulties involved in changing basic understandings and characterizes the re-educative process as a "working through." He asserts that the changing of the understandings which influence the way an individual perceives a situation is a long and complex process and is never a mere sudden insight. It may *start* with such an insight, brought on, perhaps, by unknown factors; but this is rarely sufficient actually to change behavior. Change of a concept usually calls for a testing of the insight in all relevant phases of living until its meaning and implications become a part of perception, and thus of behavior.[8]

If re-education is the means to changing the teacher's conceptions, it becomes important to ask just what is involved in the process. It has been implied that it will be more than the preparation of new curriculum materials and the imparting of correct knowledge regarding teaching. It has been

---

[7] Lewin and Grabbe, *op. cit.*, pp. 57-58.

[8] George Sharp, *Curriculum Development As Re-education of the Teacher* (New York: Bureau of Publications, Teachers College, Columbia University, 1951), pp. 4-5.

said that it will be necessary to help the teacher "work through" to new insights and conceptions of the curriculum. This process involves a number of factors which must be considered prerequisites to successful change. Consideration should be given to readiness for change, encouragement to seek better ways of working, group support for individuals, degree of involvement in the problem, and the wholeness of the process.

READINESS FOR CHANGE

Change seldom takes place in individuals who are completely satisfied with their present conditions. Re-education must be built on a readiness for change which grows out of the individual's recognition of the unsatisfactoriness of his present adjustment and his desire to effect a change. Mere dissatisfaction is not, of course, the only factor in readiness for change. Strother says that re-education is rarely successful with an individual "who, although not so satisfied, is unwilling to relinquish the more or less tolerable disadvantages of his habitual behavior for the unknown and perhaps intolerable difficulties of a new adjustment." [9] This is to say that the readiness of an individual to change will depend on the way he sees his personal security affected. In capitalizing on dissatisfactions as motivating factors in teacher re-education, care must be exercised to avoid threatening the personal security of those persons involved, insofar as possible.

Miel, in discussing the utilization of dissatisfactions in motivating change, points out the difficulties involved. She emphasizes the fact that the strength of the dissatisfactions will differ greatly from person to person and group to group.

At various times and in relation to various problems different individuals and groups may be arranged on a scale stretching all the way from a tendency to be controlled by tradition, habit,

[9] Charles R. Strother, "Methods of Modifying Behavior," *Journal of Social Issues*, I (1945), p. 50.

inertia, social pressure, fear of and hostility to innovation to a tendency to become bored and discontented with the old and curious about innovation.[10]

It is important for those concerned with change to study the groups involved in order to determine the state of readiness of individual members. The classification of individuals set up by Miel is helpful in understanding the various stages of readiness for change. She has identified three groups, namely: persons dissatisfied and willing to work to bring about change; persons dissatisfied but, because of previous experiences, skeptical of the productiveness of energy expended on change; and persons satisfied with conditions as they stand.[11] Approaches to curriculum change will be different with each of these groups. Teachers who are dissatisfied must be given ample opportunity to register their dissatisfactions and those who are satisfied must be helped to see the need for changes in the schools. This is imperative if re-education is to take place, because change in teachers will be achieved only as they have a readiness for it.

ENCOURAGEMENT TO SEE BETTER WAYS OF WORKING

No matter how strong the dissatisfaction with present conditions may be, re-education cannot be effective unless teachers are encouraged to seek and discover for themselves better ways of satisfying their needs. It is important that the climate in which change is to take place be as free as possible of threat and be permeated by a respect for the ability and integrity of the individuals in the situation. Teachers must feel free to admit difficulties they are having, and to seek help, without feeling that such admissions will be used against them at some future time. The process of re-education will be seriously impeded if this freedom is not present.

School administrators and supervisors have important roles

[10] Alice Miel, *Changing the Curriculum* (New York: Appleton-Century-Crofts, Inc., 1946), p. 40.
[11] *Ibid.*, pp. 42-43.

to play in the development of the atmosphere in which teachers will feel free to seek and try out better ways of working. Corey, in discussing conditions conducive to curriculum experimentation, says that there is little likelihood that teachers will be willing to admit inadequacies in situations where status leaders are unwilling to discuss their own problems. He believes that if status people are able to discuss their problems and inadequacies teachers will find it easier to do so. However, Corey believes that the conventional concept of the successful administrator results in a relatively small number of school superintendents, principals, or supervisors who feel that it is wise to admit that there are aspects of their own jobs which they are unable to handle adequately.

In their relations with teachers, many status leaders imply, first, that they themselves have few serious limitations, and, second, that they stand ready and willing to help teachers with their many difficulties. This attitude almost forces teachers to assume the same attitude, although they rarely add that they are ready and willing to help administrators.[12]

GROUP SUPPORT FOR INDIVIDUALS

It is felt by many that the purposes of re-education for curriculum change are best served when the process of re-education becomes a cooperative endeavor. Such an emphasis on cooperative efforts in curriculum development and change stems from the understanding that it is easier for individuals to change as members of a group than it is for them to change in relative isolation from others. Lewin reported studies which compared individual and group procedures in securing change.[13] He showed that in individual instruction the dependence of the individual on a valued standard acts as an obstacle to change. When, on the other hand, group

[12] Stephen M. Corey, *Action Research to Improve School Practices* (New York: Bureau of Publications, Teachers College, Columbia University, 1953), p. 88.
[13] Lewin, *loc. cit.*

standards change, the same dependence will facilitate change in the individual, and the individual's behavior tends to remain at the new group level.

Other writers [14] believe that it is impossible to treat the curriculum as a thing apart from the social context in which it is developed. They point out that the modern school is composed of a number of working groups and that between these groups and members of these groups there exist patterns of relationships expressing social status, expectations, and sentiments. The work of the school and the curriculum provided for learners are inextricably woven into these relationships. Teachers who have become accustomed to the relationships by which their expectations and status are defined will resist change which seems contrary to their expectations or which would upset their status. Any successful attempt to change the curriculum, then, must involve an attempt to change group expectations and sentiments in order to support changes in individuals.

Newcomb stresses the motivational factor of cooperative endeavor as a strong force in the process of re-education.

When many or most of the members of a group have strong attitudes of belongingness, they tend to serve as sources of increased motivation for one another. A kind of circular reaction is set up. The more frequently and obviously members demonstrate to one another that they are already motivated to take their roles in "proper ways," the more they intensify one another's motivation to do so—this increase in motivation by mutual interstimulation is what we have already referred to as group reinforcement.[15]

DEGREE OF INVOLVEMENT IN THE PROBLEM

It would appear that one of the main factors facilitating re-education is the degree to which individuals become ac-

[14] B. Othanel Smith, William O. Stanley, J. Harlan Shores, *Fundamentals of Curriculum Development* (New York: World Book Company, 1950), pp. 634-636.

[15] Theodore M. Newcomb, *Social Psychology* (New York: The Dryden Press, 1950), p. 633.

tively involved in the process. Involvement begins with the selection of problems for study and consideration. This stage is of vital importance if teachers are to become deeply involved in the process leading to change. The problems selected must have meaning for those who will work on them. They must be the ones which are of *real* concern to the teachers involved. This means that those who work with teachers must be willing to begin with felt problems no matter what they are. Foshay and Hall [16] warn that many of these may be such "problems" as gum chewing and tardiness, but that it is necessary to begin with them if they are the ones that have meaning for all the teachers.

While the selection of the problem is an important step toward involving teachers in the process of re-education, it is not possible to stop here. The involvement must be extended if the behavior of teachers is to be influenced. The possession of correct knowledge is not sufficient to change behavior. Merely collecting theory developed by someone else and urging teachers to apply it to their problems accomplishes little. Likewise, techniques of telling, advising, and persuading will have limited usefulness in changing conduct. The process must be one in which the teacher is involved at every step in testing the appropriate theory in action in the problem situation, collecting evidence as to its effectiveness, modifying it in the light of the evidence, and testing it again in the situation under study. This is the process which Caswell has described as the interaction of theory and practice.

If satisfactory results are to be achieved, theory and practice must interact constantly, each influencing the other. What is needed is the constant, rigorous testing of theory in practice, the collection of evidence from practice upon which to modify theory, the revision of the theory, and the continual retesting in practice. Only through this process can either sound theory or

[16] Foshay and Hall, *op. cit.*, p. 359.

sound practice be developed. In fact, it is only in this way that soundness can be determined.[17]

It would appear that only as teachers are helped to engage actively in programs of testing theory in practice can the involvement necessary to change conduct be brought about. Teachers must accept new facts and values as an action-ideology rather than a verbal-ideology [18] if change in attitude and behavior are to be accomplished.

THE WHOLENESS OF THE PROCESS

Studies in social change have emphasized the fact that change is not an adding-on process, that new conceptions are not built item by item. It has been shown that no change of conviction on any specific point can be established in more than an ephemeral way so long as the individual has not accepted the new value or belief and integrated it into a *new* understanding. Social psychologists [19] consider this principle fundamental to all attempts to bring about basic changes in belief and conduct. Conceptions do not change; one conception is substituted for another.

This idea has far-reaching implications for the re-education of teachers. Our efforts to study segments of teaching in isolation from the total process has resulted in distortion and confusion. An example of this confusion is the conviction of teachers that a curriculum built on the concerns of children is desirable and the fear of these same teachers that *all* the conventional subject matter will not be covered during the year. The result is that most teachers act in terms of their original conception of education and in most cases the conventional subject matter gets covered and the concerns of children are neglected. This happens when too little has been

[17] Hollis L. Caswell, Chapter XI, "Sources of Confusion in Curriculum Theory," in *Toward Improved Curriculum Theory* (Chicago: University of Chicago Press, 1950), p. 115.
[18] Lewin and Grabbe, *op. cit.*, p. 59.
[19] *Ibid.*, pp. 61-62.

done to help these persons integrate the new learning into their total conception of the curriculum so that they are able to act in terms of new beliefs and values. Only as teachers are helped to study their problems in terms of the total teaching process can a desirable integration of the new learning into a *new* understanding be achieved. This is best done when the teacher has an opportunity to try out various solutions to problems and is given help in interpreting their effect on the on-going, complex teaching–learning process. In order to be effective, re-education will have to achieve an integration of new beliefs and values into a new conception of education at each stage of the teacher's learning.

Cooperative Action Research Is a Means of Re-education for Teachers

A look at factors in the re-education of teachers such as those discussed in the preceding section serves to emphasize the need for a process adequate to control these factors in such a way that change will be facilitated. Cooperative action research such as that conducted in Springfield, Missouri, holds promise of being one effective methodology for bringing about fundamental change in teachers' conceptions of the curriculum. Teachers who participated in this study have repeatedly said that their use of action research methods helped them gain many new insights and understandings which enabled them to do a better job of teaching. An indication of the way teachers feel about cooperative action research is the enthusiastic way in which the participants urge other teachers to undertake research studies of their own teaching problems.

It has been evident in this report of teacher participation in cooperative action research that such research offers one means by which the factors involved in change through re-education can be controlled. Re-education begins only when readiness for change exists and when that readiness is a consequence of dissatisfaction with present conditions. In the third chapter it was shown that cooperative research makes use of readiness by starting with the concerns of participants in the research and by seeking to define the problem as it exists in the situation where the research is to be conducted. This is precisely what happened in the schools where this study was conducted. Teachers initiated the study when they set out to learn about the development of social attitudes. The problem studied by each school staff was defined by members of that staff in terms of the way they perceived the needs in their own school. This identification and study of their own teaching problems is considered by participating teachers to be an aspect of cooperative action research which makes it a valuable means of improving teaching. There was the teaching situation. Such imposition would have caused no imposition of problems or purposes from persons outside the research to become less than cooperative and would have violated the principle of readiness for change. Elliff and Foshay emphasize the importance of beginning with problems which have meaning to the teachers involved. They point out that the cooperative research pattern "differs radically from that in which a carefully predesigned experiment is brought into a school or community and worked out with or without the aid of local personnel." [20]

Following the defining of problem areas the method of cooperative action research is to develop hunches as to possible solutions of the problems. These are stated in the form of hypotheses which predict specific results if certain procedures are used in the situation. The fact that the hypotheses are stated as programs for the solution of the actual prob-

[20] Jessie Elliff and A. Wellesley Foshay, "Action Research Means Cooperation—From the Viewpoint of Consultant and Principal," *Educational Leadership*, 7 (1949), pp. 168-169.

lems [21] means that inherent in action research is the encouragement to seek better ways of working. Teachers who participated in this study frequently pointed out that they were able to see implications for change in their teaching at every step in the action research process because the emphasis was always on better ways of working at specific problems. They credit the methods of study used for many of the changes they made in their teaching procedures.

There can be no question that cooperative action research utilizes the factor of involvement in facilitating the re-education of teachers. The description of the action research process in Chapter 3 emphasized the active participation of teachers at every step in the process. Teachers who participated in this study of children's social attitudes gathered data describing the status of the situation before any new procedures were tried; they formulated action hypotheses concerning the use of certain procedures; they tried out the procedures; and they collected data to measure the results of the procedures used. Based on the data collected, the teachers drew conclusions, made certain generalizations as to the effect of the procedures used, and then looked at next steps in the process of solving their problems. These teachers said that an important factor in the success of their study was the fact that action research enabled them to study their problems in the process of solution. They pointed out that this way of working was more satisfactory to them than merely attempting to apply to their own problems the results of research done by someone else. They were better able to put into action their new understandings of teaching because of their involvement in the total action process.

Because cooperative action research is research undertaken to guide action, teachers are involved in a *whole* process

[21] Ruth Cunningham and Alice Miel, "Frontiers in Educational Research in Elementary School Curriculum Development," *Journal of Educational Research*, 40 (1947), p. 370.

which enables them to reconstruct their conceptions of education in terms of the way in which they perceive the effect of changed practices on the job they are doing. The "opportunity to test hunches immediately in the situation from which the hunches grew, and from which the data were collected, gives an important advantage to the classroom research." [22] One of the points frequently made by teachers who participated in the study was that the way in which the research was related to their classroom procedures and problems had made it possible for them to carry on the study without jeopardizing the quality of their teaching.

In cooperative action research, the support individuals get from the group at all stages is an important factor in change. Teachers in Springfield often said that the fact that all persons were working on problems erased the stigma that is sometimes attached to "having problems." The support teachers got from other members of the group in planning and in interpreting data was valuable. These teachers gave very high ratings to those procedures which allowed them to work out their problems and carry on their study cooperatively. Rucker and Pittman in a report on the study in Springfield indicate the dynamic effect of group action as resulting in one of the most powerful challenges to teachers who participate in cooperative action research.[23]

Summary

People who have had experience with cooperative action research believe that it is an effective means of bringing about desirable curriculum change and of adding to the existing body of tested educational knowledge. Participants

---

[22] Horace Mann–Lincoln Study Group, "Recommended: Group Research for Teachers," *Teachers College Record*, 50 (1948), p. 110.

[23] D. C. Rucker and Alice Pittman, "Action Research Means Cooperation —From the Viewpoint of the School Supervisors," *Educational Leadership*, 7 (1949), p. 165.

in this study of children's social values recommend cooperative action research to other teachers as a means of gaining valuable help with teaching problems. It is hoped that the descriptions of methods of involving teachers in cooperative action research presented in the preceding chapters will be of help to those interested in the process.

EXAMPLES OF INITIATIVE CATEGORIZED AT TEFFT SCHOOL

Initiative: TYPE OF CONSEQUENCE

SELF	GROUP
Grade One (Age 6 years)	
Children dismissed by groups to play. Theo's group being last, he went to first boy out, told him to get ball before all balls gone.	Voluntarily helped one child with reading and returned to own work.
Grade Two (Age 7 years)	
Had shoe off working with it, left room, came back. Showed teacher. Had gone to custodian to get tack removed.	Many classmates needed paint cloths for afternoon lesson. Child came with bundle of cloths for all who did not go home for lunch. Was not asked to do so.
Grade Three (Age 8 years)	
"I just have one more thing left to do and it won't take long. May I paint at the easel when I'm through?"	Couldn't find spelling book on shelf (disorderly). Straightened it. "Now, I can find my book and so can everyone else."
Grade Four (Age 9 years)	
"I had money laid out for stamps, forgot it. May I order $2 and get money at noon?" Teacher: "Hadn't you better talk to stamp people?" Made arrangements and brought money at noon.	Group making wall picture, map of pioneer settlement. Child made several trees for group on map. Spent considerable time straightening under map.
Grade Five (Age 10 years)	
Children listed names for oral reports. Number two dropped out, Ross slipped name ahead of others.	Eight dictionaries had been put on ledge for use. Norris went to closet, brought five more to ledge; took one for himself.
Grade Six (Age 11 years)	
Late for school in A.M. because of dental appointment. Child asked if could make up assignment.	Leora went to music teacher to see what books were needed so she could have them ready.

Initiative: NUMBER OF PEOPLE INVOLVED

SMALL NUMBER	LARGE NUMBER

Grade One (Age 6 years)

Had been pasting. Cleaned hands before reading book. (1 child)	Group planned to make an Easter picture. Bill brought six pictures from home to give ideas to group. (30 persons)

Grade Two (Age 7 years)

Hid checkers in closet so he would be the one to use them at the play period. (1 child)	Responsibility for buying cookies at noon hour for Valentine party. Rain. Brought cookies to school directly before going home for lunch, "Was afraid they would get wet." (30 persons)

Grade Three (Age 8 years)

Copied names from lunch list to add to Valentine list. (1 child)	Overflow from lunchroom required a number of children to eat in classroom. Teacher, after dismissal: "I forgot to tell children our room would be used for lunchroom." Phillip without further suggestion cleared all desks. (35 persons)

Grade Four (Age 9 years)

Went after Kleenex. Used it and returned to place. (1 child)	Children listening to recording of "Pied Piper." Shirley left group, went to bookcase, found poem "Pied Piper." Brought it to group. (35 persons)

Grade Five (Age 10 years)

Uncomfortable in chair because glider was loose. Got up, turned chair upside down, secured glider, resumed work. (1 child)	Robert suggested a showing of their pets for entire school. Pet show planned and held. (288 persons)

Grade Six (Age 11 years)

Perry was not working. Loretta tapped him on the shoulder, pointed to his work. Nothing was said. (2 children)	Charles phoned post office and gave school saving stamp order. (60 persons)

Initiative: DEFERMENT OF GOAL

IMMEDIATE   DEFERRED

Grade One (Age 6 years)

Coy could not see work on board. Walked over and sat on floor near the work.

Cafeteria committee came for flowers for lunch table. Group had none for them. Three days later Glenda brought artificial flowers for group so they "always have some." (3 days)

Grade Two (Age 7 years)

Had no apron to use during painting lesson. Made arrangements with another boy to exchange scrub cloths for use of apron.

Sally found song in book about Brownies. Mother sponsors group. She asked to take book home so she and Mother could learn song to teach to Brownies. (6 days)

Grade Three (Age 8 years)

Napkins needed for upstairs lunchroom. Luella went to bathroom, returned, held out freshly washed hands to teacher, "See, may I bring the napkins?"

Boy responsible for passing number books absent. "I'll pass number books and if Paul doesn't come back I'll collect them." (6 hours)

Grade Four (Age 9 years)

Told teacher she was going to leave a few minutes before noon to wash hands and put straws in milk bottles.

Returned stamp box and stamps. Also too much money. Marjorie checked her list of orders, stood up, said, "Next time please don't put money in box until I get your name on list." (7 days)

Grade Five (Age 10 years)

"I strained my back and can't play ball. May I umpire so I won't have to stand around?"

Worked out plan for papers she wanted to keep for future use. Wrote "save these" on them. She always knew where to find what she needed. (30 days)

Grade Six (Age 11 years)

Jeanette was going to Kansas City. She had not returned her report card. Asked Saundra to return it for her.

Ronald came up with original jokes for school paper. He had written these during preceding month. (30 days)

Initiative: COMPLEXITY (NUMBER OF STEPS)

SIMPLE   COMPLEX

Grade One (Age 6 years)

Charles saw need for lights to be turned on and *turned* them on. (1)

Teacher intentionally left up lunch order of preceding day. Child *asked* if it should be changed. Was told teacher had not time to make changes. *Asked* permission to make change. *Did* so. *Added* teacher's name. *Checked* report. (5)

Grade Two (Age 7 years)

Was to share book with another child, *stayed* at beginning of recess to move desk so she would be ready after play time. (1)

Boy came to announce assembly program for following day; as he left Linda *asked* if program were to be at same time as Council meeting. *Volunteered* to check with Council president. *Went* alone to right person, *checked* information, *brought* back report for other Council members. (5)

Grade Three (Age 8 years)

Fixing date on work sheet, noticed month on calendar had run out. *Tore* off old sheet so new one would show.

On own *decided* to clean and arrange locker and table. *Went* to supply closet, *got* cloth, *cleaned*, *washed* and *rearranged*. *Went* back to own work. (7)

Grade Four (Age 9 years)

Brought cricket in glass jar for science table. (1)

Virginia *brought* letter had from Germany. *Talked* with group about why she got letter. Teacher suggested custodian might translate. Virginia *took* letter to custodian and *made* arrangements. *Brought* translation next day. *Read* it. (6)

Grade Five (Age 10 years)

Returned Girl Scout paper and *placed* it on bulletin board with others. No comment from anyone. (2)

Sheila *collected* plates at lunch table. Found way to kitchen blocked by stools in aisle. *Studied* situation, *set down* plates, *moved* stools under table, *picked up* plates, went on her way. (5)

Grade Six (Age 11 years)

Gail writing article for newspaper, *went* to calendar and *counted* back to date of event. (2)

Sue in charge of checking books in library *noticed* that a girl who had withdrawn from school had a book checked out. *Checked* to see if book was in library. Found it wasn't. *Reported* to teacher and *brought* question of how book could be obtained. (4)

Initiative: CONTENT

CONCRETE ABSTRACT

Grade One (Age 6 years)

Teacher had placed puzzles on hall table. Child recognized them as belonging in her room. Carried them back to own room.

During a planning period teacher called to phone. Child told original story. Explained to teacher group wanted to wait for her before continuing. Child said story would keep group quiet.

Grade Two (Age 7 years)

Reading group did not have enough books for all. Had borrowed from another room on other occasions. Child left room and returned with enough books for all.

Teacher asked Betty to help Ruth with her work. Betty had not finished own tasks. Betty went to Mary and asked her to give Ruth needed help.

Grade Three (Age 8 years)

Reading table had to serve as serving table for Valentine party. Bernadine put books away, got cloth, washed table without suggestion.

Grade Four (Age 9 years)

Mona took down library books displayed on top shelf. Chose different books, arranged shelf.

Telephone rang. Jack answered. Wrote message and number. Took it to another room. Asked at recess if remembered to make phone call.

Grade Five (Age 10 years)

Paste jars empty. Terry went to basement, brought paste bucket,

James, looking up meaning of words, found another word in the defini-

filled jars, returned jars to shelf and bucket to storeroom.

tion which he did not understand. "What does this mean?" he said. "Oh, I guess I'll have to look up that word first."

Grade Six (Age 11 years)

Joyce brought a lizard to school. Joyce and Marilyn asked to look up lizards in the World Book and report to class. Fixed display because bottle crowded. Brought in leaves and rocks, two wormy apples and a can of water.

Jean (takes building lunch order) explained she would be absent next day but that Ann understood about it, and would care for building count.

Initiative: TIME INVOLVED

SHORT   LONGER PERIOD

Grade One (Age 6 years)

After lunch in classroom. Charles got brush and pan and cleaned up crumbs. (2 minutes)

A week before group had discussed games appropriate for indoor play. At home Phyllis cut out animals for game, presented game to group, explained game to group and showed where game to be kept. Invited all to use it. (7 days)

Grade Two (Age 7 years)

Stayed in at recess, by choice, to copy names from the board for Valentines. "I think this is an important thing to do." (10 minutes)

Teacher using razor blades to clean fish bowl. Mentioned she needed more blades. Three days later Don brought a handful of blades wrapped in paper. (3 days)

Grade Three (Age 8 years)

Volunteered and made Valentines for patterns. (30 minutes)

Class to make stencils for art, only two stencil knives, ——— came with jar of razor blades. Supplied each person. (1 day)

Grade Four (Age 9 years)

Sun shone on desk, ——— adjusted shade, returned to work. (5 seconds)

Assumed responsibility on her own for helping first graders who stay for lunch. Planned Valentine games and brought penny suckers for them. (7 days)

Grade Five (Age 10 years)

"Today is Mother's day off and I'm afraid she won't remember we go to Sunbeams and will worry about us. I think I should phone her." (Sheila) (5 minutes)

Jeanette brought pictures, nut cups, and magazine ideas to be used by cafeteria table decoration committee for a whole month. (30 days)

Grade Six (Age 11 years)

Loretta, while working on news for paper, made trip to bulletin board in hall to get information on where CARE packages were sent. (2 minutes)

Filibustering was discussed in class. Charles brought newspaper article and placed on bulletin board. It was about present use of filibustering. (1 day)

CHECK SHEET USED TO STUDY CONSIDERATENESS AND POPULARITY

The reasons below for the popularity of certain people were given by students on the reaction sheet for "You and Your Friends." Please check in the space provided whether you believe considerate behavior is important to the reason given.

Reasons for Popularity	*Yes*	*No*	*Undecided*
Personality	___	___	___
Friendly with everyone (makes friends)	___	___	___
Athlete	___	___	___
Nice looking (pretty, handsome)	___	___	___
Has talent (music, artistic ability, dramatics)	___	___	___
President of some organization	___	___	___
Nice and fun	___	___	___
Intelligent (smart, studious)	___	___	___
Cute	___	___	___
A good comedian (school clown)	___	___	___
Considerate	___	___	___
Sense of humor	___	___	___
On pep squad	___	___	___
Sweet	___	___	___
Courteous	___	___	___
Good sport	___	___	___
Voice (southern drawl)	___	___	___
Liked by everyone	___	___	___
Drum majorette	___	___	___
Fiesta queen	___	___	___
Just wonderful	___	___	___
Nice smile	___	___	___
Public speaking	___	___	___
Good character	___	___	___
Takes part in many activities	___	___	___
Home-coming queen	___	___	___
Good nature	___	___	___
Thinks of others before self	___	___	___
Friend of very popular student	___	___	___
Best friend	___	___	___
Cooperative	___	___	___
Not conceited	___	___	___
Has model-A Ford	___	___	___
Efficient	___	___	___
Her dancing	___	___	___
Small	___	___	___
Very active	___	___	___
Loyalty	___	___	___
Kindness	___	___	___

Reasons for Popularity	Yes	No	Undecided
Money	___	___	___
New in school	___	___	___
Love for teachers	___	___	___
Thoughtfulness	___	___	___
Likes sports	___	___	___
Willing	___	___	___
Interesting	___	___	___
Trustworthy	___	___	___
Clothes	___	___	___
Tough	___	___	___
Ability without sophistication	___	___	___
He's himself	___	___	___
Tall	___	___	___
Calm	___	___	___
Good leader	___	___	___
Seems gentleman	___	___	___
Big-hearted	___	___	___
Helpful	___	___	___
Casual	___	___	___
Red hair	___	___	___
Enters into class discussion	___	___	___
A big talker	___	___	___

INSTRUMENTS USED AT WEAVER SCHOOL TO STUDY SECURITY

THINGS ABOUT ME *

Name _____

Date _____

1. What I like best about school _____
2. What I like least about school _____
3. I would like to take part in these things this year:
   _____ a. Sports
   _____ b. Dramatics
   _____ c. Singing
   _____ d. Orchestra
   _____ e. Crafts
4. This year I would like to learn more about:
   _____ a. An interesting hobby
   _____ b. How to express myself clearly without being afraid
   _____ c. How to make friends more easily
   _____ d. What kind of person I want to be
   _____ e. Reading easily for pleasure
   _____ f. Science
   _____ g. Arithmetic
   _____ h. Spelling
   _____ i. What my country was like a long time ago
5. My favorite comic story is _____
6. The best motion picture I have seen lately is _____
7. My favorite sports are _____
8. The things I like to do better than anything else are _____
   _____
9. The most fun I ever had at school was when _____
10. The best time I ever had in my life was when _____
11. How many close friends have you? _____
12. Have you a best friend who likes you best, too? _____
13. If you could sit at a table with three people, whom would you choose?
    _____

WHO WOULD IT BE? †

Name _____

Date _____

1. If your mother said you could invite a friend for dinner and the movies on Saturday, who would it be? _____

* Developed by the staff at Weaver School.
† Adapted from *Guidebook* for *The Girl Next Door*, by Shacter and Bauer. Copyright, 1948, by Scott, Foresman and Company, and reproduced with their permission.

2. If this child couldn't come, whom would you ask? _____
3. Suppose this second person couldn't come either, whom would you ask then? _____
4. Suppose you needed help with your arithmetic and your teacher told you to ask a friend for help, whom would you ask to help you? _____

5. If you were working on a science exhibit, whom would you want to help you? _____
6. Write here the name of the boy who you think gets along best with his classmates. _____
7. Write here the name of the girl in the class who you think gets along best with her classmates. _____
8. If you were choosing sides for a baseball game, which boy in the class would you choose first? _____
9. Which girl would you choose first to be on a ball team? _____
10. What have you done this year here at school that you have enjoyed more than anything else? _____

MY PROBLEMS IN GROWING UP †

Name _____

Date _____

Health Problems

_____ 1. I often have colds and sore throat.
_____ 2. I am often sick.
_____ 3. I often have headaches.
_____ 4. I don't hear very well.
_____ 5. I have trouble with my eyes.
_____ 6. I get tired easily.
_____ 7. I am (too tall, too short).
_____ 8. I am (too thin, too fat).
_____ 9. I don't have any appetite.
_____10. I don't get enough sleep.
_____11. I need to play more.

Personal Problems

_____ 1. I lost my temper easily.
_____ 2. I am stubborn.
_____ 3. I am jealous.
_____ 4. I am self-conscious.
_____ 5. I am bashful.

_____ 6. I keep forgetting things.
_____ 7. I don't like to work.
_____ 8. My feelings are easily hurt.
_____ 9. I am easily discouraged.
_____10. I'm afraid of making mistakes.
_____11. I'm unhappy much of the time.
_____12. I day-dream too much.

People Problems

_____ 1. I don't like most people.
_____ 2. Most people don't like me.
_____ 3. I don't make friends easily.
_____ 4. I'm left out of most things.
_____ 5. People often make fun of me.
_____ 6. I often hurt other people.
_____ 7. I argue with other people.

† This and "Things I Wish" were adapted from various tests on personality.

Money Problems

_____ 1. I want to earn my own money.
_____ 2. I don't have enough money.
_____ 3. I have less than my friends.
_____ 4. I don't have enough for lunches.
_____ 5. I want to learn how to spend money.
_____ 6. I want to learn how to save money.

School Problems

_____ 1. I'm behind a grade at school.
_____ 2. I have trouble with _____.
_____ 3. I don't use good English.
_____ 4. I'm afraid to speak out in class.
_____ 5. I don't finish work on time.
_____ 6. I'm afraid of getting low grades.
_____ 7. I don't like school.

Home Problems

_____ 1. I talk back to my parents.
_____ 2. I quarrel with my brother and sister.
_____ 3. My parents expect too much of me.
_____ 4. I get punished for things I don't do.

_____ 5. We have sickness in our family.
_____ 6. (My mother, my father) isn't living now.
_____ 7. My mother and father don't live together.
_____ 8. I'm afraid my father will lose his job.
_____ 9. I'm ashamed of the house we live in.

Social Problems

_____ 1. I want to learn to meet people.
_____ 2. I have trouble with people.
_____ 3. I want to learn how to take care of guests.
_____ 4. I want to have better manners.
_____ 5. I want to know how to act at a party.
_____ 6. I want to learn how to dance.
_____ 7. I want to know how to choose my clothes well.
_____ 8. I have no place to entertain my friends.
_____ 9. I don't have a chance to get into sports.
_____10. I don't have anything to do in my spare time.
_____11. I want to know how to treat people of the opposite sex.

THINGS I WISH

Name _____

Date _____

About School—

_____ 1. I wish I could help to make the rules.
_____ 2. I wish my teacher liked me.
_____ 3. I wish she would praise me when I work hard and do my work well.
_____ 4. I wish I were chosen to do things more often.
_____ 5. I wish my classmates liked me.
_____ 6. I wish I were not afraid to speak up in class.
_____ 7. I wish I knew how to study.
_____ 8. I wish I did not have trouble with _____.

About Myself—

_____ 1. I wish I could have nicer clothes.
_____ 2. I wish I could do more things without having people tell me what to do.
_____ 3. I wish I did not worry about things like _____.
_____ 4. I wish I did not have bad dreams.
_____ 5. I wish I were not afraid of making mistakes.
_____ 6. I wish I were not afraid of being criticized.

About Playing—

_____ 1. I wish I had someone to play with after school.
_____ 2. I wish my playmates would choose me as "leader" more often.
_____ 3. I wish I played games so well that children would want me on their side.
_____ 4. I wish my friends wanted to play the games I want to play.

About People—

_____ 1. I wish I had a best friend who liked me best, too.
_____ 2. I wish people did not "pick" on me.
_____ 3. I wish people did not say things that hurt my feelings.
_____ 4. I wish people did not tease me.
_____ 5. I wish I belonged to a club or some organization.
_____ 6. I wish people liked me.

About Home—

_____ 1. I wish my family knew I was growing up and treated me that way.
_____ 2. I wish my family noticed when I did things right and praised me.
_____ 3. I wish I could help plan more things at home.
_____ 4. I wish we did more things together.
_____ 5. I wish I were not punished unfairly.
_____ 6. I wish I could stay up later.
_____ 7. I wish I did not have to get up so early.
_____ 8. I wish my parents lived together.
_____ 9. I wish I had more time to play.
_____10. I wish I didn't have so much work to do at home.
_____11. I wish I didn't have to take so many lessons.
_____12. I wish we did not move so often.

TEACHERS' RATINGS OF THE ACTION RESEARCH
PROCEDURES

WHILE THE STUDY WAS IN PROGRESS, teachers and consultants frequently discussed the procedures which they were using. The ways of working identified during these discussions formed the basis of the questionnaire which was administered in December of 1949 and in May of 1950. Teachers were asked to rate each procedure's value to them on a three point scale and to indicate as well the extent to which each procedure was used in their school. The questionnaire administered in May was like the first, except that two items were added to the list of procedures. Teachers' ratings of each item were tabulated so as to indicate (a) the number of times each procedure was judged of great value, of some value, or of little or no value, and (b) the extent to which each procedure had been used in the school. To establish a composite index of the value of these procedures to teachers, the ratings for each item were converted to an index score. This was done by assigning a weight of 3 to the top category in the value scale, "great value"; two to the middle category, "some value"; and one to the lowest category, "little or no value." The summation of tallies in the respective categories was then multiplied by three, two, or one, as the case might be, totaled, and divided by the number of teachers responding to an item. The same procedure was followed in obtaining an index score for the extent of use of each item. The maximum index score for an item under this system would be 3.00. If all teachers responding to a procedure, for example, had rated it as having great value, this item would have an "index-of-value" score of 3.

The accompanying table is a summary of the index-of-value scores and the index-of-use scores. The items are ranked on the basis of their index-of-value scores as obtained in December. It is significant to note, however, that when the scores obtained in December and in May are compared, the differences for separate items are not striking. Column four shows differences ranging from .0 to .3 points. Only five of these are above .2.

Many of the differences in index-of-value scores can be accounted for by a difference in emphasis in the study at the times when the questionnaires were checked. For example, item 1, which has a difference of .2, is the item in which teachers were asked to check the value of hearing detailed reports from participating schools regarding the study in each school. Prior to the use of the questionnaire in December, there had been one meeting in which reports were given of the work in individual schools. Before the questionnaire was used again in May, there had been at least three such meetings. This is indicated by the difference in the December and May index-of-use scores for item 1—also .2. Having participated in these meetings, teachers saw value in them and rated them more highly the second time. Item 16, which shows a difference of .3 in value scores, is the one in which teachers were asked to check the value of more frequent visits from Horace Mann–Lincoln Institute consultants. When the questionnaire was used in December, a period of nine weeks had elapsed between visits of consultants, and teachers felt there were advantages in more frequent visits. In May, when the second questionnaire was checked, only four weeks had elapsed since the previous visit, and other visits following December had been made at intervals of six weeks. Those teachers who did not check this item high the second time probably felt that there was no need for visits more frequently than every four weeks. Items 3, 4, and 5, which show relatively high differences, are items having to do with the sharing of information among schools. It is possible that the increased interest in reporting meetings as a means of sharing could account for the slight drop in value in these items. Item 34, which shows a drop of .2, is one that has to do with observing and recording behavior of children. In May, many teachers were experimenting with projective devices as a means of understanding the behavior of children. Those who used the projective techniques felt that they were getting satisfactory results from them. This fact could account for the reduced interest in the procedure outlined in item 34.

Teachers tended to assign high value to those procedures which they had tried. In other words, there is a high positive relationship between index-of-value scores and index-of-use scores. If the value score is high, the use score is usually high, and vice versa. Evidence of the relationship of the use of a procedure to the value teachers see in it can be found in items 32 and 1 in the index-of-value column for December. These items changed positions in May, and an examination of the index-of-use columns shows a similar change. There are other cases which could be cited as evidence of this relationship. There are exceptions, of course. Teachers saw value in procedures which they had not used if those procedures promised to help them achieve their purposes. In only two cases, however, items 30 and 35, did the index-of-use scores exceed the index-of-value scores, and in these cases the differences were not great. In other words, 95 per cent of the procedures represent cases in which the frequency of use did not exceed the value teachers felt the procedures held for them.

The fact that all of the value scores except one in December and one in May fell in the upper half of the scale used in computing the scores, and the fact that twenty-seven scores in December and twenty-six in May fell in the upper third of the scale suggest clearly that teachers thought most of the procedures used were effective. The top score of 2.9 is very high and the low score of 1.8 is not extremely low in terms of the scale used.

The relatively wide range in the index-of-use scores indicates that each school worked differently. Most procedures had not been used by all teachers to the same extent. It appears that the teachers recognized this, and felt that the policy of adapting the procedures used to the needs of the individual school groups made for success in the study. The items in the questionnaire relating to flexibility in planning received high value scores, and this is an indication of the emphasis the teachers placed on being able to work out procedures to suit the specific purposes of each group. Item 9, which was among the most used in December and in May, has to do with the practice of planning each new step in the study in terms of new insights gained in the preceding step. Item 25, which received high scores, has to do with changing a plan of study when it seems difficult to apply. Item 21, which was rated favorably, has to do with the practice of developing forms and scales for studying behavior which fit the needs of individual schools.

SUMMARY OF INDEX SCORES FOR "WAYS OF WORKING" QUESTIONNAIRE ITEMS

	Rank Order[1]	Index-of-Value Scores December	May	Differences in Value Scores	Index-of-Use Scores December	May
9. Developing general pans for the study as each new phase is reached.	I	2.9	2.9	.0	2.8	2.9
27. Considering the total situation in which behavior occurred when making an evaluation or interpretation of that behavior.	I	2.9	2.8	.1	2.8	2.4
26. Including a description of the situation in which certain behavior occurred when writing behavior anecdotes.	I	2.9	2.8	.1	2.6	2.4
8. Summarizing at the beginning of a school staff meeting with HMLI people in order that all persons present will know what has been done previously, i.e., bringing people up to date.	I	2.8	2.8	.0	2.8	2.7
22. Reaching an agreement by teachers prior to observation as to the meaning of categories for recording and interpreting behavior.	I	2.8	2.7	.1	2.5	2.5
10. Discussions from time to time of what we are trying to accomplish in the study.	I	2.8	2.9	.1	2.6	2.6
7. Summaries of meetings sent back by HMLI people.	I	2.8	2.9	.1	2.7	2.7
11. Having time to talk difficulties out with other members of the staff when they occur.	I	2.8	2.6	.2	2.2	2.2
14. Discussions of terms by all teachers of a school for the purpose of being together on meanings.	I	2.8	2.8	.0	2.4	2.6
38. Making changes in classroom procedures for the purpose of correcting difficulties discovered by observation and tests.	I	2.8	2.8	.0	2.3	2.4
29. Having all the teachers in a building studying the same behavior and recording it in identical categories.	I	2.8	2.8	.0	2.6	2.8
28. Determining children's ideas of the behavior being studied.	II	2.7	2.6	.1	2.2	2.2
34. Observing and recording the behavior of a certain kind wherever it occurs in the group.	II	2.7	2.5	.2	2.4	2.2
5. Written accounts of the entire Springfield project, e.g., the report, An Approach to Evaluating the Social Learnings, sent to you in September.	II	2.7	2.5	.2	2.3	2.2

[1] Items ranked according to Value Scores; ranks stated as quarters: I (highest quarter) to IV (lowest).

SUMMARY OF INDEX SCORES FOR "WAYS OF WORKING" QUESTIONNAIRE ITEMS—*Continued*

	Rank Order	Index-of-Value Scores December	May	Differences in Value Scores	Index-of-Use Scores December	May
36. Evaluating observations of behavior by having entire staff discuss anecdotes reported by individual teachers.	II	2.7	2.6	.1	2.5	2.2
25. Changing a plan of observation and recording behavior when the plan seems difficult to apply.	II	2.6	2.8	.2	2.2	2.3
12. Meetings of the entire staff on a school to work on the proejct between visits of the HMLI people.	II	2.6	2.7	.1	2.3	2.5
16. Visits from HMLI people more frequently than at present.	II	2.6	2.3	.3	2.2	2.2
15. Time to discuss problems and procedures with people from the central office.	II	2.6	2.5	.1	2.0	1.8
39. Checking the effect of certain procedures teachers use to modify the values held by children by observing behavior before and after using them.	II	2.6	2.7	.1	2.0	2.0
19. Using observation of behavior to check results of devices such as sociograms, California Test of Personality, and others.	III	2.5	2.5	.0	1.9	1.8
21. Having groups of teachers develop scales and forms for recording and interpreting behavior to fit the needs of particular situations.	III	2.5	2.6	.1	2.1	2.2
37. Testing findings obtained from observation of a few children by looking for same things in the entire group.	III	2.5	2.6	.1	2.0	2.3
31. Having other teachers classify behavior anecdotes under given categories as a check on an individual's interpretation of behavior.	III	2.4	2.4	.0	1.8	1.8
13. Meetings of small groups of teachers from a school to work on the project between visits of the HMLI people.	III	2.4	2.2	.2	2.2	2.0
18. Using devices such as sociograms, social distance scales, etc., to identify children to be observed for certain behavior.	III	2.4	2.5	.1	2.1	2.2
23. Arbitrary definition of terms by a school staff when it is not possible to arrive at a satisfactory definition through discussion.	III	2.3	2.3	.0	1.8	1.9

SUMMARY OF INDEX SCORES FOR "WAYS OF WORKING" QUESTIONNAIRE ITEMS—*Continued*

	Rank Order	Index-of-Value Scores December	May	Differences in Value Scores	Index-of-Use Scores December	May
6. Summaries of work done in each school written at intervals by members of the staff of the school.	III	2.3	2.4	.1	2.0	2.0
24. Using tape recorder to record classroom work in order that a common understanding of what kind of behavior is to be observed can be gained by all teachers in a school.	III	2.3	2.3	.0	1.5	1.5
35. Observing and recording the behavior of a few children as a basis for generalizing about the behavior of the group.	III	2.3	2.1	.2	2.3	2.4
20. Use of published tests to check teacher's evaluation of children's behavior.	IV	2.2	2.3	.1	1.5	1.5
3. Having staffs of two schools meet together to share ways of working.	IV	2.2	2.0	.2	1.3	1.2
4. Sharing tape recordings of staff discussions in one school with another school staff.	IV	2.2	2.0	.2	1.2	1.2
2. Meetings of representatives from participating schools in which a general summary of the study is made.	IV	2.2	2.2	.0	1.9	1.7
30. Using the individual teacher's judgment as the basis for interpretation of behavior anecdote.	IV	2.2	2.1	.1	2.2	2.2
17. Correspondence by individual teachers with HMLI people.	IV	2.0	1.9	.1	1.3	1.4
33. Participation by HMLI people in classrooms for the purpose of assisting in observing and recording behavior being studied.	IV	2.0	2.1	.1	1.3	1.2
32. Having teachers observe and record data in each other's classrooms.	IV	2.0	2.1	.1	1.6	1.6
1. Hearing detailed reports from participating schools as to how study is being made in each school.	IV	1.8	2.0	.2	1.2	1.5
40. Using projective devices such as unfinished stories or unfinished sentences as means of determining the values youngsters hold.	IV		2.3			2.2
41. Conferences of individual teachers with HMLI people on problems concerning the study.	IV		2.5			1.5

INDEX

Index

Academic achievement, prestige and, 148
Acceptance
  compliance and, 39
  considerateness as basis for, 142
  follow-through and, 83-102
Action research
  administrative arrangements for facilitating, 260-265, 273
  beliefs basic to, 14-15
  categorizing in, 110 *n*
  consultants in, 261-262, 265-273
  cooperation in, 266-269
  cooperative aspects of, teachers' reactions to, 207-221
  curriculum development and, 275-292
  data collection methods, 59-62
  defined, 55
  difficulties encountered in, 257-274
  gains resulting from, 243-256
  leadership and, 5-6
  location of, 11-14
  as means of teacher re-education, 288-291
  methods, classroom use of, 4-5
  participation time for teachers and, 260-261
  pattern of, 56-62
  plan formulation in, 58-59
  practicality of, 68-72
  problem identification in, 56-57
  questions underlying, 19-23
  school selection for, 14
  skills of teachers in, 270-272
  staff size and, 253-254
  study methods, 65-68
  teacher participation, factors influencing, 252
  teachers' ratings of procedures, 306-311
  teachers' reactions to, 65-72
    agreement reaching, 213-215
    data interpretation, 215-216
    difficulties in, 217-220
    procedures for helping each other, 208-210
    staff's working as whole, 210-211
    "talking-out" difficulties, 212
    team observations, 217-220
  teaching direction and, 4
  validity of findings in, 63-65
  see also Research procedures; and under specific attitude, e.g., Follow-through
Action Research to Improve School Practices (Corey), 64 *n*, 284 *n*
Actions, *see* Behavior
Age level, initiative and, 127
Agreement reaching, teachers' reaction to, 213-215

315